DATE DUE

MY 2 3 00			
JY 2 4 00			
NO 1 4 00			

DEMCO 38-296

The Future of State Taxation

THE URBAN INSTITUTE PRESS
Washington, D.C.

Library of Congress Cataloging-in-Publication Data

The Future of State Taxation/David Brunoir, editor.

Includes index.

1. Taxation—United States—States. 2. Local taxation—United States. I. Brunori, David.

HJ2053.A1F88   1998   98-16507
336.2′00973—dc21   CIP

ISBN 0-87766-680-6 (cloth, alk. paper)
ISBN 0-87766-681-4 (paper, alk. paper)

Printed in the United States of America.

Distributed in North America by:
University Press of America
4720 Boston Way
Lanham, MD 20706

The Future of State Taxation

DAVID BRUNORI
Editor

THE URBAN INSTITUTE is a nonprofit policy research and educational organization established in Washington, D.C., in 1968. Its staff investigates the social and economic problems confronting the nation and public and private means to alleviate them. The Institute disseminates significant findings of its research through the publications program of its Press. The goals of the Institute are to sharpen thinking about societal problems and efforts to solve them, improve government decisions and performance, and increase citizen awareness of important policy choices.

Through work that ranges from broad conceptual studies to administrative and technical assistance, Institute researchers contribute to the stock of knowledge available to guide decision-making in the public interest.

Conclusions or opinions expressed in Institute publications are those of the authors and do not necessarily reflect the views of staff members, officers or trustees of the Institute, advisory groups, or any organizations that provide financial support to the Institute.

ACKNOWLEDGMENTS

This book would not have been possible without the assistance of many people. I am indebted to the authors who have taken the time and effort to provide their opinions on the future of state taxation. I was fortunate to have the best and brightest scholars—all profoundly committed to the field—contribute to this work. They have shaped past debates on state taxation and will greatly influence its future. It was an honor, indeed a privilege, to work with them. Richard Pomp contributed not only provocative essays but much-needed encouragement as well. Tom Field of Tax Analysts unknowingly provided the inspiration for this work. My goal was to foster public debate on state tax issues; no one is more committed to that idea than Tom Field. Oswald Graham of *State Tax Notes* provided advice and counsel. Felicity Skidmore of the Urban Institute Press shepherded me through the process; she is the consummate professional. Finally, this book would not have been possible without Elisse Brunori, my wife and best friend. She had faith in me.

CONTENTS

FOREWORD

Since tax revenues finance what government spends to meet society's needs, the tax policy debate will be with us as long as we have government. The Institute has had a strong presence in helping inform this debate for almost two decades, including Joseph J. Minarik's *Making Tax Choices* (1985), Rudolph Penner's and Alan Abramson's *Broken Purse Strings: Congressional Budgeting* (1988), and C. Eugene Steuerle's *The Tax Decade: How Taxes Came to Dominate the Public Agenda* (1992). Until now, except for a detailed study of the tax system in Nevada, our focus has been primarily on federal taxation. This new book addresses state taxation and its future.

The potential impacts of the recent devolution of social policy responsibility from Washington, D.C., to state capitals combine with the anti-tax dynamics of much state and local politics to make a review of the present and future of state taxation extremely timely. That neither the structure of state tax systems nor the relative importance of their component taxes has changed much in 50 years—even though the economic and policy environment in which they operate has been transformed—adds to the importance of the effort.

The discussion of the future of the sales tax is a particularly important contribution. The sales tax is still the single largest source of state revenue, and the unspoken presumption among most observers seems to be that it will remain so. However, as political considerations lead to more and more exemptions from this tax, its tax base is shrinking. The future of the sales tax is additionally threatened because services have been traditionally exempt, but changing consumption patterns are leading to ever higher proportions of consumer spending going for services. More and more goods and services are also being purchased from outside the state. This complicates administration of the tax because states are limited in their ability to impose collection responsibility on out-of-state vendors.

The combined effect of changing consumption patterns and rising compliance costs has lost the sales tax one-quarter of its tax base in the past 17 years, until it now accounts for less than 35 percent of total tax revenues collected by state governments. Even if political decisions do not further reduce the sales tax base, the tax rates necessary to maintain this share of total state revenue collections may become politically unsustainable, particularly because the overall impact of the sales tax falls disproportionately on lower income groups. Despite all this, the future of the sales tax and the actions states may need to take, as a consequence, to shore up their revenue base are hardly visible in the current tax debate.

The whole problem is vastly complicated by the advent of electronic commerce—selling through the Internet, Intranet, or on-line services. As one of the contributing authors puts it, "Jurisdiction to impose state taxes on electronic commerce has been defined by the traditional concepts of territoriality and physical presence. Basing jurisdictional decisions on such criteria makes little sense in cyberspace."

It is my hope that this book helps inject a sense of urgency among tax practitioners, business, community leaders, and researchers, all of whom will need to be involved in the effort to reform state tax systems for the next century.

William Gorham
President

Chapter One

INTRODUCTION

David Brunori

State and local taxation has generally not changed much in the last half-century. To be sure, there have been innovations with respect to collection, periodic Supreme Court pronouncements on state taxing power, and the trauma of the property tax revolt movement. But the structure of state and local tax systems has remained the same. States are still levying sales, income, and corporate taxes in much the same way. Nor has the relative importance of those taxes changed dramatically. The sales tax remains the single most important source of tax revenue for state governments, with the individual income tax a close second. The state corporate income tax is a smaller but still substantial source of revenue for state governments. The property tax remains the most significant source of local government revenue—as it has been for most of the nation's history—accounting for 95 percent of local revenue.

History will note, indeed perhaps marvel at, the endurance of these tax structures. For they have remained in place for decades despite being designed in a different era and for a vastly different economy. The modern sales tax began in the throes of the Great Depression; the modern income tax was put in place slightly earlier. Both systems were developed in and for an economy dominated by the manufacturing sector. People bought food (from family farms) and manufactured goods. And they bought them from American businesses.

Yet the sales, income, and property tax systems in the nation have endured, despite the tremendous political and economic changes experienced in the last half-century. The economy has moved from a manufacturing base to one dominated by the service sector. Business began to evolve, even while these tax systems were in their infancy, into multi-state, indeed multinational, enterprises. What Americans buy and from whom and from where they buy products, is far different today than in the 1930s or even the 1970s. The political climate, too, has changed dramatically. The burdens of taxation, real or perceived, and the weariness of governments have changed the dynamics of state and local politics. The "anti-tax" rhetoric that dominates all levels of politics has incited nationwide tax revolts, shortened political careers, and resulted in tighter state budgets. Paradoxically, the federal government, itself the target of downsizing pressures, has shifted many of its responsibilities to the states. This "devolution" has resulted in more and more governmental functions being transferred from Washington to state capitals.

The political and economic changes experienced in the last decades have accelerated in recent years. European and Asian countries have emerged as economic giants, challenging and in many cases surpassing American productivity. Today much of what is sold in America is produced overseas. Emerging democracies and expanding markets, spurred by the end of the Cold War, have changed the political and economic landscape in which we live. The world has never known greater political freedom or economic opportunity than it does today. Unprecedented technological advances—computers, satellite communications, and the ubiquitous Internet—are influencing all aspects of society.

The political, economic, and technological changes that the world is experiencing are affecting how the world works, plays, shops, and communicates. These changes, one would think, are bound to affect the traditional methods of how states levy and collect taxes. After all, state and local governments collect taxes from people and businesses; if the ways in which people behave and businesses operate change, it stands to reason that state tax collection structures will also change.

But as we stand on the threshold of a new century, it does not appear likely that state tax systems are in fact going to change very drastically. Whatever the problems, and there are many, with existing state tax collection procedures, there is no public outcry for reform of existing tax systems. State legislatures are not busily preparing elaborate contingency plans to cope with current and future societal and economic changes. Nor is there a groundswell of citizen dissatisfaction, similar to California's Proposition 13, that might produce dramatic changes in state and local tax systems.

With no wholesale reform on the horizon, however, what will be the result when the political, economic, and technological changes occurring throughout the world eventually collide with enduring but often archaic state revenue systems? What will the states do when their pre–depression era income tax systems are forced to operate in a world of unprecedented global trade and often unimaginable technological developments? Assembled in the pages that follow are the thoughts of the nation's leading academics on the future of state taxation as we enter the new millennium. The contributors have vast academic and practical experience in the political, legal, and economic aspects of how states raise revenue. They are the preeminent scholars in the field.

The purpose of this book is to foster public debate on the future of state and local government finance and taxation. The contributors were asked to provide their opinions on the future of various aspects of state taxation. They were given wide latitude in determining what topics to address. Some present new research to support their views on what lies ahead, while others offer novel arguments and fresh approaches to age-old problems. They all offer provocative essays on the future of state taxation.

While the contributors have noted what they think works—and what doesn't—the goal was not to provide solutions to all of the potential challenges to the ways state and local governments collect revenue. Rather, the book is designed to highlight issues for consideration by policymakers, practitioners, and community leaders. The hope is that the essays contained herein will provide the basis for future discussions on the serious challenges facing state and local governments.

The work begins with two essays on the future of the sales tax, the single most important source of state government revenue. Forty-five states and the District of Columbia impose a tax on sales, and it accounts for about 34 percent of total tax revenue collected by state governments. (That percentage is even greater in states such as Texas and Florida that do not impose personal income taxes.) In most state revenue systems the tax is levied on the sale of tangible personal property; sales of services are usually exempt from the tax. The sales tax has been accepted by the public—at least to the extent that any tax is or can be "acceptable" to the public. The relatively low rates and ease of compliance generally reduce the sales tax to an afterthought for consumers. And because sales tax is collected by the vendor, states are generally not burdened by it. Administrative and enforcement costs are relatively low compared with those for other taxes. The drawback, from a political and policy perspective, is that the sales tax is regressive.

In chapter 2, then, University of Indiana professor John Mikesell highlights the critical challenges to the sales tax as we reach the end of the century. The sales tax taxes consumption, and Mikesell believes that the assignment of government costs according to how much a person chooses to spend coincides with fundamental notions of consumer sovereignty and private markets. Mikesell maintains that the logic of the sales tax is rooted in its special advantages in terms of economic efficiency (the tax is levied independent of timing) and transparency (the consumer witnesses the imposition of the tax at the time of sale and is aware of the costs of government). That logic helps explain why the tax has endured for more than half a century.

But, as Mikesell points out, several trends are converging to challenge the logic, and hence the efficiency and efficacy, of the sales tax. As those who have studied this subject are well aware, the problem of subjecting production inputs to a tax has been a problem since the inception of the sales tax. According to Mikesell, that problem has become acute. He notes that 41 percent of the sales tax now falls on business purchases. The results, he warns, are increasingly greater costs of business expansion and a system that creates barriers to growth. The other trend threatening the logic of the tax is the unprecedented movement toward exempting household goods. There are strong political and policy reasons for exempting from the sales tax household goods such as food, clothing, and medicine. But, notes Mikesell, despite the good intentions behind such exemptions, they have the undesirable effects of making the sales tax more regressive, while at the same time costing states millions of dollars.

Mikesell cites the continued exclusion of *services* from the sales tax as the last, converging threat to the logic of the tax. For largely political reasons, states have been reluctant to expand the sales tax base to include services. Besides costing states enormous amounts of potential revenue, however, the exclusion of services from the tax base greatly complicates both taxpayer compliance and state administration of the tax. Mikesell says that these trends defeat the logic of the tax, reducing the economic efficiencies of the tax and placing future acceptance of the tax in jeopardy. In order for the sales tax to survive, he argues, it is critical for states to stem these converging trends. Because it is unclear whether states will take the necessary steps, Mikesell concludes that the continued survival of the sales tax as the dominant source of state revenue is uncertain.

University of Tennessee economist William Fox takes an even more pessimistic view of the future of the sales tax in chapter 3. He cites two trends that severely threaten the entire sales tax regime. First, Fox cites the continuing change in consumption patterns: Purchases of durable and nondurable goods are declining, while purchases of services are increasing. Moreover, Fox notes, there is a greater propensity to purchase both goods and services from outside the state. The former threatens the sales tax because the tax is still aimed primarily at tangible personal property. The latter complicates administration of the tax because of now well-established constitutional limitations on the states' ability to impose collection responsibility on out-of-state vendors. If vendors have no collection responsibility, the sales and use tax regime, at least as we know it, collapses.

Second, policy decisions have continually narrowed the sales tax base, as politicians manage to grant exemptions to more and more types of goods and services. From a tax policy standpoint, Fox argues that the shifting tax base dangerously increases compliance and administration costs and distorts consumption decisions. These trends, asserts Fox, have resulted in a stunning loss of one-fourth of the tax base as a share of personal income in the last seventeen years. Even assuming that states refrain from further depleting the sales tax base, Fox predicts that states may have to increase tax rates beyond acceptable levels for the tax to remain the dominant source of state revenue. At a minimum, predicts Fox, the sales tax will be replaced as the largest source of state tax revenue in the near future. Unless states take a more aggressive approach to the taxation of services, obtain jurisdiction over out-of-state vendors, or exhibit some political fortitude to stem the exemption bonanza, the demise of the sales tax occur even more quickly.

While the taxation of business inputs reduces the efficiency and efficacy of the sales tax, state taxation of business *income* faces many more profound challenges in the years ahead. Taxation of corporate income comprises only 7 percent of total state revenue, yet accounts for over $28 billion dollars of tax revenue. Over the years, corporate taxation has been the subject of much debate and litigation as taxpayers and state governments have contended with the seemingly nonstop growth in multi-state business.

In chapter 4, University of Connecticut law professor Richard Pomp provides a critical examination of the problems inherent in levying a state tax on corporate income. In a spirited essay, Pomp explains that the weaknesses of the corporate tax system are well known and exploited by tax practitioners. He argues that the intellectual firepower that the private sector brings to bear on the corporate income tax results in legal yet undesirable avoidance of the tax. Practitioners, says Pomp, are continually developing new ways to shift income away from corporate tax liability. Essentially, state revenue departments, understaffed and underfunded, are losing the battle over state corporate taxation. Next, Pomp argues that the obsession with tax incentives has cost the states dearly—nearly a half a billion dollars in New York alone. Incentives cause other states to adopt retaliatory incentive measures, further shrinking the aggregate tax base. And, says Pomp, incentives don't work.

The corporate tax is threatened by its very structure. The traditional apportionment formulas do not work well in our modern economy. But the alternatives adopted by the states, particularly the use of double-weighted and single-factor sales formulas, have magnified the structural deficiencies of the tax. Other serious problems with the structure and administration of the tax include the failure of most states to require combined reporting and the relative ease with which corporations can convert business income into nonbusiness income. These problems, says Pomp, leave states vulnerable to aggressive planning, transfer pricing, and the use of holding companies to shift income. Pomp does not argue that the corporate tax should expire. But he warns that the tax requires constant vigilance. The problems are predictable, and fixable. States can adopt combined reporting rules, curtail the use of incentives, and broaden the definition of business income. He predicts, however, that given the political climate, the necessary reforms are unlikely of enactment. In the future, he notes, the corporate tax will be a minor player that consumes a disproportionate amount of intellectual capital.

Pomp's criticism of incentives is, of course, consistent with most scholars' views on the subject. Commentators generally agree that incentives violate the most basic principles of sound tax policy. Incentives result in tax systems that are less accountable, less efficient, and less fair. Moreover, there is more than ample evidence that incentives do not work. Still, the use of tax incentives has increased primarily because political leaders lack the will to reject them. The political benefits of new jobs and increased economic activity are attractive inducements for offering incentives. Northeastern University Law professor Peter Enrich asserts in chapter 5 that in light of the political realities there is only one way to stop the proliferation—legal challenges to tax incentive programs under the commerce clause. In an innovative argument, Enrich asserts that for political reasons it is virtually impossible to end the practice of granting generous tax incentives to entice a business to relocate to or remain in a jurisdiction. Moreover, while states have instituted safeguards to ensure that companies receiving incentives produce the requisite measures of jobs and economic development, these safeguards actually increase the likelihood of continued incentives. It is not illogical to think that with such safeguards in place, the granting of incentives then appears much less risky politically.

Given the politics of tax incentives, Enrich asserts that the only plausible means of halting the spread of incentives is through judicial challenges under the Commerce Clause. He argues that the Commerce Clause's anti-discrimination principle is "straightforwardly" applicable. Enrich explains that established judicial precedent provides that a tax measure discriminates against interstate commerce if it provides an advantage to local commerce over out-of-state competitors. And measures that forestall tax-neutral decisions about where to do business while favoring local commerce are discriminatory. Tax incentives offered by state governments, particularly investment tax credits and targeted jobs credits, would often meet the criteria of being unconstitutional under the tests enunciated by the Supreme Court, argues Enrich. He asserts that the likely plaintiffs in such constitutional challenges are in-state businesses placed at a competitive disadvantage by incentives, public employee unions, and maybe even state governments themselves. Because there are no reasonable alternatives, Enrich predicts that legal challenges—perhaps successful legal challenges—will inevitably arise in the coming years.

In chapter 6, Thomas Pogue, professor of economics at the University of Iowa, offers his insights into the future of state taxation of business. While Pogue recognizes that taxes on business are indirect taxes on consumers—i.e., they are ultimately passed on in the form of higher prices—he puts forth a compelling argument for the continued taxation of business entities. He says that business should be charged for the costs they generate, but would otherwise ignore, when determining when, where, and how to produce products. Indeed, Pogue asserts that business taxes reflect nonmarket costs of production and are necessary in a market economy to ensure the efficient allocation of resources. Such taxes, he argues, equitably distribute the external costs—which would otherwise be borne by the public—of production. Pogue calls this the "social cost rationale" for business taxation. But, Pogue contends, current revenue systems, with their widespread use of business exemptions and tax incentives, fail to distribute nonmarket costs fairly. Pogue recognizes that political pressures lead to tax competition among states and that competition inevitably leads to more exemptions and incentives. But, he argues, the social cost rationale for taxing business must be widely understood and accepted by the public. Without such understanding and acceptance, the states will continue to reduce overall taxation of business and thus further distort the external costs of production.

While concerns about how and why states tax, or in the case of incentives don't tax, business will be an important topic of discussion in the coming years, the question of the future of the property tax has immediate ramifications that directly affect nearly all Americans. The property tax, of course, is an old tax. Its longevity can be attributed to the fact that it is easy to administer (you cannot hide land) and generally results in growing revenue because of appreciation. It has endured despite being regularly identified as the most disliked of all taxes. While transparent, the tax results in severe "sticker shock" as property owners receive their bills during the year. Moreover, the property tax has an adverse effect on those with fixed incomes, since their property usually appreciates at a rate faster than the rate of growth of their income. These problems gave rise to California's Proposition 13 in 1978 and the many similar, albeit quieter, revolts in other states.

In chapter 7, Lincoln Land Institute Fellow Joan Youngman provides a fresh perspective on the problems faced by this age-old source of income. She recounts the profound paradoxes of the tax. It has a long history yet has been under incessant attack; it commands approval from economists (as efficient) and political theorists (as transparent) but remains vilified by the public. Within those paradoxes, Youngman identifies several challenges to the continued survival of the tax as the dominant source of local revenue. She explains that the problems associated with the tax include long-time, but still fundamental, questions of value and valuation. The assignment of value, she points out, touches on deeper social questions that themselves involve value judgments. Those value judgments are at the heart of the political debate about the property tax; they affect everything from determining what should be included in the tax base to the relative value of diverse property such as farmland, forests, historic sites, family residences, nd commercial buildings. Youngman pays particular attention to the issues of which property should be exempt from tax and to the tension between valuing appreciating, but undeveloped, land and the costly preferences provided to farmland and open space. She claims that it is easy to predict that the ambiguity concerning valuation, and thus the political debate about the tax, will continue. She concludes, however, that despite the often heated debate, the property tax will survive. Experience has shown that there are no viable alternatives to it.

University of California professor Steve Sheffrin predicts in chapter 8 that the property tax will remain the primary source of revenue for local governments. It will not, however, be the same system long idealized by economists and political theorists. Sheffrin predicts four trends that will fundamentally change the property tax in the next several decades; these trends will inevitably reduce the significance of the tax as a source of local government revenue. First, he contends that the ongoing, and successful, legal challenges to the use of the property tax to finance public schools severely undercut the political rationale for the tax—for no other local government expenditure has the appeal of education. A second, but related, trend is the unrelenting political pressure to limit overall property taxation. Many such limitations, spurred by Proposition 13, are already in place, and only six states are free of limitations on imposition of the tax. The public, predicts Sheffrin, will keep sharp limits on the tax in effect. Third, local governments have begun to adopt alternatives to *ad valorem* taxation that sharply reduce reliance on the traditional property tax. Fees, charges, exactions, and special assessment districts have sharply increased as a result of property tax limitations. Finally, Sheffrin predicts increased "direct democracy" in local government, by which voters and property owners will have a greater voice in public finance policy decisions. Correspondingly, he believes there will be a decrease in the discretion of elected officials to set fiscal policy.

According to Sheffrin, these trends will reduce the significance of the property tax considerably but will not signal the complete demise of the tax. The property tax will remain an important source of revenue as we enter the next century. Because it is a proven revenue raiser, easily administered and without viable alternatives, the tax will continue to provide local governments with funding well into the future. The real change, says Sheffrin, will be property tax systems capped at lower rates and under little practical local autonomy.

As both Youngman and Sheffrin note in their essays, much of the debate surrounding the property tax arises in the context of school finance. Public school systems have traditionally relied on the property tax for the bulk of their revenue. In chapter 9, Georgia State University professor William Waugh provides an insightful look at our changing approaches to funding public education as we reach the end of the century. Waugh describes the many legal and fiscal challenges that have forced an examination of public school financing and predicts that the way schools finance their operations in the future will be far different than today. He predicts that school districts will continue their efforts to reduce their reliance on the property tax, partly as a result of legal challenges to such financing and partly owing to the general public dislike of the tax. He predicts an increase in the use of local option and special-purpose sales taxes dedicated to particular education-related programs, such as school construction. He also notes that states are now granting more direct aid to local school districts. State funding was originally intended to equalize spending among school districts but more often is used to alleviate the financial burdens on local systems. And it will, Waugh predicts, increasingly be tied to state-mandated performance standards.

State aid was traditionally allocated from state general funds, but states are also experimenting with using revenue from their lotteries as a dedicated source of state education funding. In turn, predicts Waugh, the school districts will also experiment with imposing student participation fees, obtaining contributions from the public and private sectors, and even entering into profit-making joint venture agreements with business. All of these new modes of revenue raising will reduce reliance on the property tax and lead to a more eclectic system of education financing.

The essays set forth in chapters 10 and 11 explore the difficult question of how equitable tax systems of the future will be. This is, of course, no minor matter, for public attitudes about taxes are directly related to whether taxes are perceived to be fair. Andrew Reschovsky, professor of economics at the University of Wisconsin, examines the distribution of state and local tax burdens. He notes initially that most states have attempted to achieve some measure of progressivity with respect to their income and sales taxes. But he offers a critical examination of the published research, explaining the flaws inherent in some of the methods used to determine the progressivity of tax systems. He estimates that for a majority of states the incidence of the three main sources of tax revenue (sales, income, property) is clearly regressive.

When discussing the future of relative tax burdens, Reschovsky points out two trends that will affect the progressivity of state systems. First, states will be under extraordinary pressures to raise revenue as a result of federal budget cuts and the simultaneous increase in service demands on state governments; the latter will be fueled by the continuing devolution of fiscal responsibilities from the federal government to state and local governments. Second, Reschovsky argues that despite the looming budget crises, the continued intense competition among the states for economic development will affect how states distribute their tax burdens. If the competition for capital (or the appearance of it) remains fierce, states will continue to lower their tax rates and reduce their tax base. This will lead inevitably to more regressive state revenue systems.

In chapter 11, I offer my own thoughts on the future of the personal income tax, long a dominant source of revenue for state governments. (Only the sales tax rivals it in importance.) The success of the personal income tax is attributable in part to its adherence to widely accepted principles of sound tax policy. That is, the personal income tax is effective, efficient, and most importantly, fair. Its effectiveness as a revenue source is unquestionable: Nearly a third of all state tax revenue is collected from the taxation of personal income. In 1996, states collected over $130 billion dollars of personal income taxes. Conformity with the federal tax system has resulted in a method of collecting revenue that is efficient for both taxpayers and the government. Taxpayers incur few administrative burdens beyond those experienced as part of the federal income tax system. State governments, for their part, have found the personal income tax to be a cost-effective method of collecting revenue. The state personal income tax has long been thought of as the most fair of all forms of taxation. Its perceived fairness is due in part to its status as the least regressive of all forms of taxation.

My conclusion is simply that, barring a radical change in the federal income tax system, the state income tax will remain a dominant source of revenue in the future. Neither technological nor economic developments will change the structure of the tax. The advent of electronic commerce will not have the detrimental effects on the personal income tax that it is likely to have on corporate or sales taxes. The ever-growing dependence on international trade also has little effect on personal income taxation. For nearly half a century the public has considered the state personal income tax to be an acceptable means of raising revenue. That public acceptance has led in turn to continuous growth of the tax. There is nothing in the future that will likely change that trend.

The book concludes with a discussion of what may have the most widespread effect on state taxation in the future: In chapter 12, University of Georgia law professor Walter Hellerstein discusses the challenges state revenue systems face in the age of electronic commerce. The nation, indeed the world, has already experienced the dramatic changes brought on by new technology. Today over a third of American families own a personal computer. Millions of people access the Internet on a regular basis. People are using the Internet to communicate, to retrieve information, and, with increasing regularity, to purchase products and services. By all accounts, electronic commerce— the selling of goods and services through the Internet, intranets, or on-line services, will dramatically increase in the coming years. Conservative estimates of total Internet sales of goods and services range from $7 to $150 billion by the year 2000.

Electronic commerce poses profound, and by now well-documented, challenges to the way states have traditionally raised revenue.

That is not surprising considering that state revenue systems were developed in an era when it was impossible to imagine a world in which goods and services would be sold via computers.

Hellerstein steps back from present-day discussions and considers the challenges that electronic commerce brings to our conventional modes of thinking about state taxation. He maintains that before policy-makers can discuss the effects of electronic commerce on state taxation, several fundamental questions need to be addressed. First, is the current constitutional and statutory framework adequate to deal with electronic commerce? If the answer is no, and Hellerstein certainly implies as much, how might the framework be altered to provide a sound tax policy in the electronic age? For example, jurisdiction to impose state taxes on electronic commerce has been defined by traditional nexus criteria. Yet nexus is rooted in the concepts of territoriality and physical presence. Basing jurisdictional decisions on such concepts makes little sense in cyberspace. Hellerstein says that a fresh approach that "reverse engineers" the nexus issue is needed. Rather than asking how electronic commerce should be treated under traditional nexus criteria, we should be asking what kind of taxing regime will allow consumers and businesses engaged in electronic commerce to pay taxes in an efficient manner to states with legitimate claims to revenue and collect taxes therein.

According to Hellerstein, states will have to take a fresh approach to many traditional areas of taxation. He cites, as an example, definitional issues surrounding the administration of sales and use taxes. Because much of electronic commerce involves the sale of services, transactions are likely to be characterized as nontaxable unless those services are deemed to fall into the category of taxable services. The problem, maintains Hellerstein, is that the definitions we are using were not designed with electronic commerce in mind. Similarly, the concept of sale for resale and the determination of where a sale takes place (a particularly acute problem in the age of electronic commerce) should not be addressed in terms of traditional thinking.

Hellerstein points out that our approach to imposing income taxes must undergo similar revisions in order to cope with the structure of electronic transactions. In particular, he notes that the delineation of the sales or receipts factor in traditional apportionment formulas raises difficult issues. Whether electronic commercial transactions should be treated as sales of property or of services—and if the latter, where those services are deemed to have been performed—are daunting questions, without clear answers under current thinking.

The problems posed by state taxation of electronic commerce are significant. Hellerstein's warning for the future is that efforts to resolve those problems within traditional state tax structures are unlikely to succeed.

The coming century will require policy-makers to focus on political, economic, and technological changes occurring throughout the world. These changes will inevitably influence state tax systems that were designed long ago. State lawmakers will need to examine not only the mechanics of how their revenue systems work, but also the underlying rationales for those systems. In the end, reform of state tax systems is likely. Whether such reforms are relatively mild or dramatic, they will certainly be marked by heated debate and controversy. Adopting state tax systems for the next century will require input from tax practitioners, business, community leaders, and academia. Hopefully, this work will lead to more discussion on the pressing challenges facing state and local governments in the years ahead.

Chapter Two

THE FUTURE OF AMERICAN SALES AND USE TAXATION

John L. Mikesell

Sales and use taxes have been a reliable source of state tax revenue since the Great Depression. Mississippi originated the tax in 1932 by converting its general business tax into a 2 percent tax on retail sales. By 1938, twenty-six states (plus Hawaii) had adopted the tax, thus replacing revenue lost with the collapse of the property tax. The tax replaced motor fuel taxes as the most productive state tax in 1944 and supported the considerable expansion of state expenditures in the post–World War II years: Retail sales tax revenue was vital for the expansion of state (and local) government activities in the last half of the twentieth century. The tax proved robust in hard times—a few pennies per transaction provided a relatively painless and simple-to-collect tax that brought considerable revenue to the state—and productive when the economy grew. New challenges in the American economy and in American governmental organization, however, raise important questions about the continued vitality of the tax. The sections that follow will explore the nature of this important tax and will highlight several critical challenges to its future fiscal contribution.

RETAIL SALES TAXES IN THE REVENUE SYSTEM

States collected $135.3 billion from their retail sales and use taxes in fiscal 1995, more money than from any other state tax. The next-largest producer, the individual income tax, generated $125.6 billion in the same period.[1] The yield margin between these two fiscal giants remains considerable but is not as great as it has been. The sales tax also plays an important, although smaller, role in local government finance: In the aggregate, localities raise slightly more than 10 percent of their tax revenue from their sales taxes, a low percentage because of the property tax domination of school district finances. Thirty-three states include localities levying sales taxes. Of the 200 cities with populations above 100,000, 116 levy retail sales taxes; 37 more are in counties of special districts with such taxes, including several instances in which the city receives a portion of revenue from that overlapping tax (Due and Mikesell 1994). Cities and counties raise more revenue from these taxes than from any tax except that from property; special districts, especially transit districts, levy such sales and use taxes as well. States do dominate overall, however, collecting more than 80 percent of all retail sales tax revenue in the United States.

Table 2.1 presents sales tax yield by state for fiscal year 1995, using Census Bureau data after adjustments to correct for certain reporting peculiarities. Although states on average realize about 35 percent of their tax revenue from the retail sales tax, their reliance varies widely. Sales tax reliance is great in states that levy no broad individual income tax, including Florida (57.3 percent), Tennessee (56.9 percent), Texas (60.3 percent), South Dakota (51.6 percent), and Nevada (53.3 percent). However, Wyoming, another state without an individual income tax, raises only 31.2 percent of its tax revenue from a sales tax, while Mississippi, a state *with* an individual income tax, raises 47.0 percent of its tax revenue from its sales tax. States in the Northeast rely less on the sales tax than do those in the West; reliance is particularly low in New York (19.3 percent), Massachusetts (21.4 percent), and the District of Columbia (21.5 percent). There is no ideal mix of taxes that could, or should, be prescribed to states; the mix in any given state is a product of peculiarities of the state's economy, choices in the design of particular taxes to be broad or narrow, and the history of politics of each state. Diverse choice is one valuable attribute of fiscal federalism. All sales taxes offer a large yield with relatively low statutory rates (especially in comparison with European value-added taxes, an alternative indirect consumption tax), reasonably simple collection from retail vendors, and little public objection. It is an important base in American revenue systems and deserves attention and nurturing to protect its critical role in state and local government finances.

⅄ THE GENERAL CASE FOR A RETAIL SALES TAX

Retail sales taxes are generally understood to provide a system for distributing the cost of government according to consumer spending patterns. Some purchases may be exempt for reasons of social or economic policy or because of administrative convenience, but those transactions are understood to be exceptional cases. For economic efficiency and transparency, the structure should require full payment of the tax by the ultimate household consumer, apply to consumption expenditure at a uniform rate, and apply to the amounts actually paid by the final consumer. As a part of the overall revenue structure, the sales tax should be designed to minimize violations of equity standards and to reduce disturbances in the production and distribution channels by which goods and services reach the consumer. Furthermore, the structures should facilitate vendor compliance and administration so that the tax can be collected at the least cost consistent with maintenance of equitable enforcement across taxpayers. As will be discussed later, however, there are tensions in the practical application of this logic in the legislative process.

The retail sales tax can have special advantages in terms of economic efficiency, equity, and governmental transparency. First, assignment of governmental costs according to how much a household chooses to spend on private goods and services surely represents an ability standard much in tune with ideas of consumer sovereignty and of private markets. As Kaldor (p. 47) wrote in 1955, "each individual [measures tax capacity] for himself when, in the light of all his present circumstances and future prospects, he decides on the scale of his personal living expenses. Thus a tax based on actual spending rates each individual's spending capacity according to the yardstick which he applies to himself." Second, use of consumption as a base for taxation may have beneficial efficiency and neutrality effects, particularly as compared with income taxation: "[A] consumption tax is neutral with respect to the intertemporal allocation of consumption because it taxes consumption expenditures independently of their timing. In particular, a consumption tax does not create a wedge between . . . pretax and after-tax interest rates and, therefore, deferral of consumption (i.e., saving) is not penalized" (Escolano 1995, p. 51). Finally, the consumer sees the tax being levied on each purchase and thus is aware of its cost to him or her. The calculation of that cost is not a mystery that is fathomable only to trained tax accountants. The tax can be starkly transparent.

The retail sales tax has a theoretical logic as a way to tax consumption expenditures, but some see (or pretend to see) other objectives for it. For instance, arguments have been made to tax services sold by certain professionals (lawyers, accountants, advertisers, etc.), apparently because many such firms appear to be affluent. Most likely,

Table 2.1 STATE SALES AND USE TAXES, FISCAL, 1995

State	Tax Revenue from Adjusted Sales and Use Tax (in Thousands of Dollars)	Percentage of Total Tax Revenue	Implicit Sales and Use Tax Base as a Percentage of State Personal Income
Alabama	1,430,644	28.2	43.8
Arizona	2,615,311	42.0	60.5
Arkansas	1,301,937	38.4	64.4
California	17,687,262	33.2	38.8
Colorado	1,230,748	27.2	45.7
Connecticut	2,368,000	31.7	37.9
Florida	10,656,548	57.3	54.4
Georgia	3,525,040	37.2	56.3
Hawaii	1,248,411	43.4	106.9
Idaho	575,752	33.2	52.4
Illinois	5,083,281	30.6	32.8
Indiana	2,810,404	37.2	45.2
Iowa	1,462,892	33.2	49.2
Kansas	1,379,070	36.6	50.2
Kentucky	1,987,392	31.6	45.5
Louisiana	1,788,670	38.2	54.3
Maine	650,210	35.9	43.4
Maryland	2,404,465	29.8	36.2
Massachusetts	2,481,300	21.4	29.2
Michigan	5,865,988	33.1	42.8
Minnesota	3,223,664	34.6	48.6
Mississippi	1,691,654	47.0	53.7
Missouri	2,348,110	34.8	47.8

Nebraska	777,024	35.0	44.2
Nevada	1,437,820	53.3	59.3
New Jersey	4,133,278	30.4	29.0
New Mexico	1,311,187	46.1	85.5
New York	6,617,996	19.3	33.0
North Carolina	2,778,242	24.3	45.7
North Dakota	333,673	34.8	55.9
Ohio	4,752,099	31.3	37.9
Oklahoma	1,153,475	26.1	42.1
Pennsylvania	5,550,290	30.4	32.5
Rhode Island	456,610	30.6	27.6
South Carolina	1,829,390	38.4	52.4
South Dakota	358,093	51.6	62.7
Tennessee	3,360,568	56.9	50.7
Texas	12,234,589	60.3	49.3
Utah	1,066,552	39.9	61.8
Vermont	277,306	34.6	44.7
Virginia	2,315,614	26.4	41.7
Washington	4,484,645	44.0	53.4
West Virginia	915,954	33.5	47.2
Wisconsin	2,571,854	28.5	45.1
Wyoming	208,026	31.2	52.4
Total	134,741,038	34.7	
District of Columbia	525,086	21.5	49.3

Sources: U.S. Bureau of the Census, *1995 State Tax Collection Data by State*, unpublished data from the Governments Division of the Bureau of the Census, and data from state tax departments.

Note: The following states do not impose a sales tax: Alaska, Delaware, Montana, New Hampshire, and Oregon.

taxing that which is sold by such entities will mean that the tax will be added to the sales price and be paid by the customers, rich or poor, of the entity, with minimal effect on the net income of the seller. Consumer services may be suitable for inclusion in the sales tax base, but not as an ineffective quasi income tax. Others have seen the retail sales tax as some form of general business tax, a sort of transaction or turnover tax applicable in principle to any exchange that takes place between a buyer and a seller. A general tax on sales transactions would be broader in application, but would lack logical justification on either ability or benefit-received grounds. Indeed, this concept offers no particular basis for determining which exchanges ought to be in the tax base and which ought not, as any transaction is as good as any other for purposes of taxability. Without a clear standard for how the tax intends to distribute the cost of government, the selection of a tax base becomes nothing more than a pure test of political power, almost certainly to the detriment of ideas of fairness and at an economic cost to the taxing unit.

The retail sales tax represents a particular way of applying a general levy on household consumption expenditures. In contrast to either the multistage value-added tax or an approach involving direct filing of tax returns, in which savings throughout the year are subtracted from income to calculate taxable consumption, the retail sales tax applies to consumption by taxing the last transaction in the production-distribution chain, the sale of the final product to the household that plans to consume it. It is a single-state tax, collected bit by bit on each consumption transaction throughout the year. The focus on consumption means that purchases by a business, even a large and apparently prosperous one, ought not be taxed; the taxability of a purchase should depend on whether the purchaser is a household or a business, not on the nature or prosperity of the seller and not on whether the sale is of a good or a service. These are the structural parameters for the design of a tax on consumption administered through an indirect tax on retail sales—a basis for taxation that has some logic as an ability-based tax. The retail sales tax, properly designed, can provide a simple, transparent, and convenient general tax on consumption expenditures. However, the nature of the American retail sales tax emerging from the political and administrative process does not meet the design standard in several important ways. In practical terms, to get the retail sales tax to be a general tax on consumption expenditures is a challenge unmet by the American states, and the challenge is not projected to get any easier in the future.

THE RETAIL SALES TAX AND THE CHALLENGES OF THE TWENTY-FIRST CENTURY

American governments design their sales and use taxes with a wide variety of different structural features, each with somewhat different implications for the distribution of actual tax burdens. The taxes do have several features in common, however. All are levies "imposed upon the sales, or elements incidental to the sales, such as receipts from them, of all or a wide range of commodities" (Due 1957, p. 3), and all are *ad valorem* (in proportion to the value). They all have a system for suspending tax on items purchased for resale and apply to nonfractional rates on retail transactions. And they all encourage separate quotation of the tax in each transaction, facilitate addition of tax to the purchase price by removing the tax amount from gross receipts, and, with the exception of Arizona, prohibit retailers from advertising that they will absorb the tax owed on a transaction. Beyond those common elements, the taxes differ in what transactions they cover and in how states administer them. The overlying federal tax system provides a design template and an administrative starting point with respect to state income taxes, but there is no such federal model for sales taxes and no constraint on states' flexibility to adjust rates in response to additional fiscal demands. The states do copy each other, but sales taxes exhibit considerable individuality in structure and operation. The differences may be seen by comparing sales taxes in Georgia and New York: Table 2.1 shows the implicit sales and use tax base as a percentage of state personal income in 1995 to have been 56.3 percent in the former and 33.0 percent in the latter. Georgia has structured its tax so that it applies to a much broader range of economic activity than in New York, despite the fact that the name of the two taxes is the same. The difference in economic breadth is a direct result of the legislative definition of each tax. Some such legislative choices move a state tax closer to a tax on consumption expenditures and some move it further away. But the array of choices makes for considerable differences in coverage across the states.

Seeing the sales tax as a uniform tax on household consumption provides a clear general template for sales tax structure. Household consumption purchases ought to be taxed, regardless of who the seller or purchaser is and regardless of the nature of the purchase; purchases of business inputs ought to be exempt, regardless of seller or purchaser and regardless of the nature of *that* purchase. The principle of uniform taxation of consumption continues to be difficult in the arena of legislative politics, however, because relieving the tax burden on consumers and removing apparent tax preferences for businesses have considerable political value. In practice, purchases get exempted from taxation because of the nature of the item being purchased (e.g., food for at-home consumption), because of how the item will be used (e.g., items purchased by a vendor for resale), or because of the nature of either the buyer or the seller (e.g., purchases by tax-exempt charitable organizations). Some of these exemptions coincide with the logic of the tax, but some do not; some are adjustments necessary for perceived improvements from revenue policy, but some are not.

Taxing Production Inputs

For a retail sales tax to have the efficiency and equity advantages claimed for a uniform tax on consumption, business purchases must be removed from its scope as completely possible. The reasons are clear. First, not all consumer purchases will have been produced with the same mix of production inputs: "Some goods require, for optimal efficiency in production, more dollars of taxed production inputs per dollar of selling price than other goods" (Due and Mikesell 1994, chap. 3). Families purchasing goods with such high produced input content will bear more embedded sales tax on inputs than others, thus violating the principle of uniform sales tax relative to consumption expenditure. Second, the tax on inputs will distort production decisions. Some purchases will not be made because the sales tax would increase the price of the item, an obvious disincentive to economic development, and vertically integrated firms able to manufacture their own production inputs will have a cost advantage over production chains involving independent firms that must purchase on the open and, therefore, taxed market. Finally, producers in jurisdictions that tax such inputs will be at a competitive disadvantage in relation to those located in areas without such tax requirements. Each problem increases with the statutory rate. They were of less consequence in 1970 when only six states levied rates of 5 percent or more, but of far more significance in 1997 when thirty states levied such rates, and they will become more severe as rates rise with future fiscal demands.

In spite of the strong economic reasons for excluding business inputs, purchases of such items continue to constitute a considerable share of retail sales tax bases. All states do exempt purchases for resale and purchases of items that will become elements of items produced for resale. Those exemptions do raise the taxes above the grossest cascading problems caused by turnover taxes. Most states also exempt industrial and agricultural machinery purchased for production, but some states continue to tax such items or to limit the exemption to purchases made for new or expanded production capacity; most states also tax equipment used in product distribution and marketing. Not all states exempt business purchases of fuels, utilities, or consumables used in the production line, and even fewer exempt such purchases made for other uses in the business (Egr 1996). The reality of the retail sales tax is that a considerable portion of its impact falls on business purchases—estimated to average 41 percent across the states in one study (Ring 1989). That impact will be passed along to consumption spending in an unknown but certainly uneven fashion in the form of price adjustments by businesses. Sales taxes exclude more business input purchases now than was the case a few decades ago. Nevertheless, many inputs remain taxed, causing distortions in production and investment that would not emerge with a general consumption tax.

Why states should continue to discourage investment in production and distribution machinery by adding tax to their purchase price, thus depressing the potential for economic development, remains something of a puzzle. The reasons appear to be both pragmatic and political. First, some items may be purchased either for business use or for household consumption and may, even after purchase and initial use in an exempt fashion, be switched to consumption use. Rather than open an easy avenue for evasion, some states choose to err on the side of protecting their tax base. Second, considerable revenue with generally hidden burden can be extracted by including business inputs in the base; final customers pay, but that part of the tax is included in the pretax price. Finally, many voters and legislators prefer taxes paid by business, apparently under the mistaken impression that this avoids having individuals bear the burden of the tax, or that taxing purchases by businesses provides a means of taxing affluent business owners. Removing business taxes can be portrayed as an unfair loophole in the law, rather than as an adjustment to permit the tax to assign burdens uniformly according to consumption and to reduce economic distortion. Unfortunately, many revenue choices are designed for short-term political advantage rather than with much concern for efficiency, equity, transparency, or long-term economic growth and national and international competitiveness.

The fundamental logic of retail sales taxation is challenged by the inclusion of business purchases in the base. Including these purchases distorts business choices and can harm economic development efforts. Taxation of production machinery and equipment makes business expansion more expensive and certainly presents a barrier to growth. But other inputs should be excluded from the base as well—notably fuels, utilities, and equipment involved in computerization and information technology. States struggle between their desire to reduce the burden placed on business development and their need to maintain and expand their sales tax base to support the operations of the state. The tax paid by businesses is hidden from the view of the business customers who ultimately pay it, being certainly less transparent than the tax added to consumer prices at the cash register; some of that burden may well be exported to people in other states, thus effectively causing some government service to be available at no cost to the local populace. Whether states can more completely suspend tax collection on business purchases is a critical challenge for sales taxes.

Exempting Purchases of Household Goods

Sales tax laws exempt many household consumption purchases. Most of the exemptions seek to improve the perceived equity of the tax, but some reflect an effort to reduce collection problems. Others show the impact of political strength, and some represent a desire to support certain causes. In revenue terms, the most significant is the exemption of food for at-home consumption, around 20 percent of the potential tax base. (The actual impact is dependent on structural choices made in defining the actual base.) Only nineteen states fully tax food purchases; because lower income families tend to spend a higher percentage of their income on food, the exemption reduces the extent of sales tax regressivity. For the same reason, the exemption reduces the relatively higher effective rate otherwise paid by large families and families in urban areas. But it has considerable revenue cost, requires higher statutory rates to produce a given yield, reduces the stability of revenue in times of economic recession, complicates collection by forcing a distinction between food and nonfood items, favors households with a preference for expensive foods, and directs considerable tax relief to high- and middle-income families in an effort to help the poor. Indeed, families in the highest income quintile receive from this untargeted, over-the-counter relief more than twice as much tax reduction as do families in the lowest quintile (Mikesell 1996). And low-income people, especially the elderly, driven by social and housing circumstances to restaurants for many of their meals, receive no relief from the exemption.

Other exemptions include those for prescription medicines (the most widespread of all), residential electricity, clothing, household fuels, commodities subject to selective taxation, and a considerable variety of other items (flags, bibles, nonprescription medicines, etc.). The strongest case can be made for the prescription medicine exemption: Expenditure differs widely among families for reasons other than capacity to pay the tax, spending is driven by adversity, and the exemption can be administered relatively easily. The least sensible of the general exemption categories probably is that for items subject to selective excise taxation. To exempt from general taxation items that are seen to merit a selective tax burden for reasons of economic or social policy simply undoes what the excise tax does. The exclusion of motor fuel, one such exemption found in many states, is the greatest problem, if only because it entails revenue loss second only to the food exemption among the categories of exempt products.

Each exemption of a consumer good reduces the extent to which the retail sales tax will bring the efficiency, equity, and transparency returns of a general consumption tax, by making the tax something other than a uniform tax on household consumption of goods. And each exemption can create fertile ground for more exemptions, to afford relief to populations otherwise left out. Strong state government finances, as experienced in recent years, make such exemptions seemingly easy to afford. The exemptions, however, make those finances more vulnerable to the next economic recession or the next economic disruption in a particular state or region. Resisting general "over-the-counter" exemptions and using targeted relief instead can be a critical foundation for sound governmental finances in the decades to come.

Excluding Service Purchases

A general consumption tax would tax household purchases of both goods and services. The typical state sales tax, however, follows the pattern of the taxes of the 1930s: The base for the tax is defined as tangible personal property. The general excise tax in Hawaii and the gross receipts tax in New Mexico, both of which are broad-concept taxes structured very differently from other sales taxes, included services when the taxes were adopted, and South Dakota later expanded its tax to cover virtually all services. Other states have selectively added services to their taxes, some rather extensively, but the typical tax includes only limited coverage of service purchases. That leaves the sales tax vulnerable to the trend of consumption in the American economy, from purchases of goods to purchases of services: Final expenditures on services increased from 28.1 percent of gross domestic product in 1970 to 39.3 percent in 1996. A number of the fastest-growing areas of service purchases—for example, medical, legal, and financial services—seem to be beyond the reach of sales tax base expansion for social or ethical reasons, and it may not be administratively realistic to tax some services provided in the home. But there remains a block of services sold to households by commercial establishments that appear to be reasonable candidates for taxation.

There are several clear advantages to taxing household purchases of services. First, taxing services will increase the yield from any given statutory tax rate. The fiscal impact depends on what services are added (potentially lucrative medical and professional services are seldom on the list) and what purchases are already in the tax base, but adding services rarely adds much more than 10 percent to revenue. Adding services to the base will make the yield from the tax grow somewhat more rapidly over time, however, because a growing percentage of household spending is on services rather than commodities (Duncombe 1993). Not all service purchases are fast-growing, however, and business purchases of services not suitable for adding to the tax base do grow most rapidly (Dye and McGuire 1992). Nevertheless, taxing household services provides important protection for the sales tax base as consumption patterns change.

Second, taxing services reduces the difference in sales tax paid by families of equal affluence but different preferences for purchasing services as opposed to goods. Taxing both sorts of purchases removes an arbitrary basis for distinguishing between the spending patterns of households. The impact on regressiveness is not so clear. High-income households spend relatively more on services than do low-income households, but that is not the case with respect to the services typically included in expansions of the base to services. Evidence shows that existing taxes with broad-based extension to services leave the tax regressive to income levels of around $30,000. At higher incomes, the tax becomes roughly proportional (Fox and Murray 1988).

Finally, trying to exclude services from sales tax can complicate compliance and administration when a given sale provides both goods and services or when the way sellers deliver a purchase changes. Examples include computer programs (purchase of a physical disk, the service of the program on that disk, or the network download of the program from a remote site), glasses (the physical eyeglasses or the services of the optometrist), motion pictures (sold or rented on videotape, viewed in a theater, or downloaded on command to a home computer from a remote site), and the repair or maintenance of taxable property. States devise rules that may involve separate billing for time and materials and distinctions about what is the "true object" of the transfer, but there can be no single simple answer in a complex and changing society. Making all household purchases taxable, whether goods or services, resolves many issues and simplifies the bookkeeping.

Levying a sales tax on services does cause some problems of policy and practice. Labor contributes a sizable share of value in many service sales, and businesses selling services are often highly specialized, so the firms involved are frequently small. That complicates administrative tasks for tax authorities and increases the chances that firms will have problems in complying with the tax. Furthermore, many services are purchased by both households and businesses. Sellers must distinguish business purchases from household purchases, apply tax to the appropriate purchases and justify exempting the remainder, and segregate receipts into the two categories. To simplify, states usually exclude service purchases, the difficult as well as the easy to categorize.

Aggressive taxation of service purchases would also complicate administration. Administrators would have to define the services that are taxable and register any service vendors who are not already on the taxpayer list because they also sell goods. Problems across state lines would pose an additional difficulty: If an out-of-state accountant prepares an individual income tax return, which state would have a tax claim against that service? Moving the sales tax away from a tax on physical items also complicates audit procedures, because following a trail through input suppliers is less likely to produce meaningful evidence of sales volume on the part of service sellers. Furthermore, many services to households are provided by nonprofit organizations that run hospitals and other health service operations; assist the young, the old, and the poor; provide education or religious services; sponsor cultural or entertainment programs; and so on. Aggressive general taxation of services would bring these entities into the network to the extent that they sell their services. As producers, their purchases, but not necessarily their sales, would logically be exempt. That would depend on choices that the law makes about their customers, a standard especially important with respect to the need to balance competition between proprietary and nonprofit organizations selling a service.

Can states devise a politically feasible approach to taxing consumption services, thus improving horizontal equity and expanding yield at advertised rates, while keeping services sold to businesses out of the base to prevent distortions and economic inefficiencies? If states desire to distribute governmental costs in relation to actual consumer spending, then they must surmount the legislative challenge of bringing household service purchases into the fold while at the same time keeping business services out of the tax. In the politics of taxation, states have found it difficult to make the case for taxing consumer services and not business services, and that problem will continue. Business outsourcing of many activities once done within the firm will make sound tax policy even more difficult; business services—advertising, legal counsel, accounting and information technology, marketing—will grow even more rapidly than the rest of the state economy and will present an attractive target for revenue programs dominated by yield, yet legislatures will need the clarity of vision to keep such services out of the base for the sake of economic development as well as to preserve the basic concept of the tax.[2] It is almost certainly too much to hope for near-general taxation of household services, but the changing nature of the American economy requires greater coverage of services, probably on a selective basis, to maintain the yield and logic of the retail sales tax.

Changing Patterns of Commerce

Retail sales taxes are structured and administered to apply to purchases or sales of tangible personal property (goods) at the destination of those goods. Because constitutional barriers prevented states from applying their tax to purchases made from out-of-state vendors, an early worry was that in-state merchants wold be vulnerable to competition from such purchases—and states also feared that they would lose considerable revenue from such transactions. California and Washington devised a solution: In 1935 they levied a tax on the initial use of goods purchased outside the state and brought into the state for use. The United States Supreme Court agreed that such a "use" tax did not constitute a constitutionally forbidden burden on interstate commerce but was, rather, a tax on the privilege of use after the act of interstate commerce was completed (*Henneford v. Silas Mason Co.* 1937).[3] That allowed levying the tax at the destination when business crossed state lines and preserved the retail sales tax by preventing the most egregious competition based on rate differences.

The problem of enforcement remained, because collecting a use tax directly from purchasers, particularly from individual purchasing households, presents a formidable task. Having out-of-state vendors collect and remit use taxes on behalf of the purchaser—in other

words, handling the use tax in the same manner as the sales tax—
would be a far more effective collection approach. However, federal
constitutional requirements dictate that states cannot require a vendor
to register to collect a tax unless the vendor has a physical presence
in the state (*Quill Corporation v. North Dakota* 1992).[4] That presents
a special collection problem for states with respect to commerce involving mail-order sales, telemarketing, television shopping channels,
and Internet sales. None of these selling mechanisms requires that the
vendor have a physical presence in the destination state, so the vendor
need not register.

States' tax yield is threatened by the growth of business in these
nontraditional formats, given the inability of states to apply their use
taxes in an effective manner. Much use tax revenue goes uncollected
now because states have found no way to induce collection from
individual purchasers nor to enforce collection by out-of-state firms
selling in their jurisdictions. The high voluntary compliance rates for
the retail sales tax represent no more than a dream with respect to
the use tax. The best direct comparison has been done in Washington,
where noncompliance as a share of total liability was estimated to be
1.7 percent for their sales tax, against 40.3 percent for their use tax in
fiscal 1989 (Washington Department of Revenue 1989). The problem
will only worsen as more and better information technology options
become available for concluding transactions without face-to-face
contact between buyer and seller.

States have become especially worried about challenges to the sales
tax arising from emerging information technologies (Collier and Ross-
ner 1995). The new technology provides an alternative telecommunications service (e.g., electronic mail), a new medium for presenting
goods and services for sale (e.g., electronic storefronts or catalogs),
and even a carrier for actual delivery of the service that has been
purchased (e.g., downloaded information, entertainment, or software)
to a destination unknown to the seller. However, such sales simply
add to the decades-old problem caused by the fact that retail economic
activity in the United States does not respect state boundaries.
Administration of use taxes has been inadequate for many years; information technology simply expands and complicates an already difficult task.

Sales through nontraditional formats are certain to grow, especially
as transmission quality improves with respect to direct delivery of
purchased services and as payment mechanisms become more secure
and certain. The physical presence requirement for registration puts
states at a considerable disadvantage. Voluntary registration, financial

inducements for use tax compliance (discounts to pay vendors for the collection service), novel legal theories designed to stretch the boundaries of registration requirements, negotiated agreements with vendor groups, data exchange between states, direct collections from individual purchasers, and so on can nibble at the fringes of the problem, but they promise to remain insufficient to close the use tax compliance gap. In short, states need congressional assistance to establish a registration requirement for major vendors exploiting their markets. Vendors ought not be permitted the outmoded defenses of the complexity and impracticality of the requirement, in light of the several software packages capable of linking destination zip codes and applicable sales/use tax rates, or of the problems from local sales tax jurisdictions, because of the accommodations states have made to avoid causing problems for out-of-state sellers from local sales taxes (Mikesell and Brown 1992).

To protect the sales tax base in the face of changes in the way purchases are made, Congress needs to help the states; otherwise, the retail playing field will not be level, with resulting discrimination, distortion, and adverse effect on yield. Some sales will be from international vendors, and those will be beyond the range of congressional help.[5] But the real need is for federal assistance to open the door with respect to required registration, and Congress ought to help there. These changes in how purchases are made, small though they are now in the totality of consumption expenditure, raise questions about the continued reliability of the sales tax as a source of state revenue, certainly in the long run, unless states get help with their enforcement problem. Can states, frustrated in their efforts to get out-of-state firms to register voluntarily and to induce direct payments from purchasers, convince Congress to establish a legislative formula whereby states may require larger firms to collect and pay their use taxes?

CONCLUSIONS

Retail sales and use taxation, an American innovation, has been critical as a means of financing the expansion of the scope of state government services in the years since the end of World War II. It has been the foundation of state government finances for more than half a century and an important contributor to independent local government finances. It can be defended on grounds of economic efficiency, fundamental equity, relative ease and convenience of collection, and transparency. Its future vitality, however, depends on how states manage the problems of keeping business input costs out of the tax base, keeping household purchases of tangible personal property *inside* the base, and bringing household purchases of *services* into the tax base and the extent to which Congress helps states enforce use taxes on sales from both traditional and novel sellers now outside their registration grasp. Absent a successful resolution of these issues, it is no certainty that this old, reliable method of taxation can survive all these challenges to remain the base for most state fiscal systems.

Notes

1. State tax data in this chapter come from the U.S. Bureau of the Census, from unpublished data graciously provided by the Governments Division of the Bureau of the Census, and from state departments of revenue. The adjustment procedures used to produce the standard-concept sales tax are detailed in Due and Mikesell (1994, chap. 1).

2. Evidence also shows that such extensions are almost certain to add to the regressivity of the tax (Siegfried and Smith 1991).

3. *Henneford v. Silas Mason Co., Inc.*, 300 U.S. 577 (1937).

4. *Quill Corporation v. North Dakota*, 112 S. Ct. 1904 (1992).

5. Internet addresses do not carry zip codes, so there is no way for the seller to know automatically the destination of a pure electronic sale and delivery. When this commerce expands (payment security and other issues limit it now), vendor compliance with the traditional use tax will be nearly impossible on such sales. There are real limits, however, to the range of wants that can be satisfied electronically.

References

Collier, Dennis, and Monroe Rosner. 1995. "Challenges to the Sales Tax from Emerging Information Technologies," *Proceedings of the Eighty-Eighth Annual Conference on Taxation of the National Tax Association*, 242.

Due, John F. 1957. *Sales Taxation*. Urbana: University of Illinois Press.

Due, John F., and John L. Mikesell. 1994. *Sales Taxation, State and Local Structure and Administration*. 2nd ed. Washington, D.C.: Urban Institute Press.

Duncombe, William. 1993. "Economic Change and the Evolving State Tax Structure: The Case of the Sales Tax." *National Tax Journal* 45 (September): 299–314.

Dye, Richard, and Therese McGuire. 1992. "Growth and Variability of State Individual Income and General Sales Taxes." *National Tax Journal* 44 (March): 55–56.

Egr, Mary Jane, et al. 1996. "Sales and Use Tax Considerations for Manufacturing Operations." *State Tax Notes* 10 (May 27): 1613–36.

Escolano, Julio. 1995. "Taxing Consumption/Expenditure Versus Taxing Income." In *Tax Policy Handbook*, edited by Parthasarathi Shome. Washington, D.C.: International Monetary Fund.

Fox, William, and Matthew Murray. 1988. "Economic Aspects of Taxing Services." *National Tax Journal* 41 (March): 19–36.

Kaldor, Nicholas. 1955. *An Expenditure Tax*. London: Allen and Unwin.

Mikesell, John L. 1991. "Fiscal Effects of Differences in Sales Tax Coverage: Revenue Elasticity, Stability, and Reliance." *Proceedings of the Eighty-Fourth Conference on Taxation of the National Tax Association*, 50–7.

Mikesell, John L. 1996. "Should Grocery Food Purchases Bear a Sales Tax Burden?" *State Tax Notes* 11 (September 9).

Mikesell, John L., and Mark Brown. 1992. "How Big Is the Local Use Tax Problem for Mail-Order Vendors?" *State Tax Notes* 3 (August 31).

Ring, Raymond. 1989. "The Proportion of Consumers' and Producers' Goods in the General Sales Tax." *National Tax Journal* 44 (June): 167–79.

Siegfried, John, and Paul Smith. 1991. "The Distributional Effects of a Sales Tax on Services." *National Tax Journal* 44 (March): 41–53.

U.S. Bureau of the Census. 1995 *State Tax Collection Data by State* (http://www.census.gov/ftp/pub/govs/www/sttax95.html).

Washington Department of Revenue. 1990. *Washington State Excise Tax Noncompliance Study*. Olympia: Department of Revenue.

Chapter Three

CAN THE STATE SALES TAX SURVIVE A FUTURE LIKE ITS PAST?

William F. Fox

Retail sales taxes are the most productive state revenue source, perhaps because they score well in surveys of which tax is most acceptable (Advisory Commission on Intergovernmental Relations 1993).[1] While some form of sales taxes is imposed in nearly every country, U.S. states are among the world's heaviest users of a general tax on retail sales.[2] Despite the sales tax's apparent acceptability, however, the thesis of this paper is that it will become a relatively less productive revenue source during the next decade unless federal and state policy actions are undertaken to offset a series of changes that are underway. The combination of an increasing propensity for consumers in one state to purchase goods and services from outside the state and state policy decisions to exempt potentially taxable consumption have already narrowed the sales tax base dramatically, and these trends have not yet abated. During the past fifteen or so years, states have increased their tax rates to offset these tendencies, but it is unlikely that the political capacity to continue raising rates at the same pace exists.

The sales tax grew remarkably as a share of total state tax revenue during its first forty years. Between 1930, when it was first introduced by Mississippi, and 1969, growth resulted from more states adopting the tax, from base increases resulting from growth in the economy, and from rate increases. Forty-four additional states and the District of Columbia adopted sales taxes after Mississippi. Vermont was the last state to enact a sales tax, leaving only Alaska, Delaware, Montana, New Hampshire, and Oregon without one. By 1970 the general sales tax had become the predominant source of state tax revenue, overtaking selective transactions taxes (Ebel and Zimmerman 1992).

The sales tax has continued to rise in importance, its revenue share increasing from 1.8 percent of personal income in 1970 to 2.2 percent in 1996 (see Fig. 3.1). The sales tax remains the largest revenue source, providing 33.3 percent of 1996 state tax revenues, versus 29.6 percent

Figure 3.1 STATE SALES TAX COLLECTIONS AS A PERCENTAGE OF
TOTAL PERSONAL INCOME

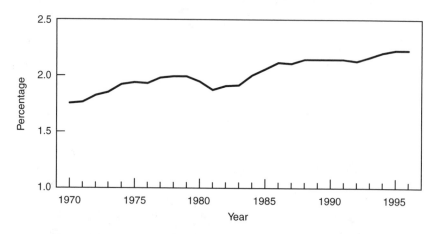

in 1970. However, the relative growth of sales taxes since 1970 is attributable solely to a consistent pattern of rate increases. The median sales tax rate rose from 3.25 percent in 1970 to 5.0 percent in 1996, and only eight states have the same rate as in 1979.[3] The median rate is climbing toward 6 percent, as sixteen states have rates that are at least that high. The tax base, on the other hand, has been narrowing, declining from 58.7 percent of personal income in 1979 to 41.9 percent in 1996. Tennessee provides an example of this pattern. The state's sales tax revenues rose from 2.0 percent of personal income in 1970 to 3.3 percent in 1996, but the increase resulted entirely from the tax rate doubling, from 3.0 percent to the current 6.0 percent. Without the rate increases, revenues would have fallen to about 1.6 percent of personal income.

THE SALES TAX BASE IN TODAY'S ECONOMY

Economists evaluate the sales tax as a tax on consumption, but extensive taxation of business inputs and exclusion of a large share of consumption leave the base dramatically different from that for a pure consumption tax. The sales tax should probably be regarded as a transactions, not a consumption, levy, given the nature of its base. No precise measures of the business share of the base are available, but Ring (1989) estimated the average state's base as comprised of 59 percent sales to residents and 41 percent sales to businesses or non-residents.

Taxable purchases by consumers represent only a share of consumption, since the sales tax in most states remains predominantly what it has always been, a levy on tangible goods. Even some tangible goods sales are outside the base—since, for example, food for consumption at home is not taxable or is taxed at lower rates in twenty-eight states (Missouri and Georgia are in the process of eliminating taxation of food) and prescription drugs are exempt in all states except New Mexico.[4] With the exception of a few states—most notably Hawaii, New Mexico, and South Dakota—most services go untaxed. Many construction, health, and financial services, for example, are exempt in most states.

As noted above, the sales tax base has already declined as a share of the economy. Some of this decline is attributable to policy choices, such as a growing tendency to omit food sales, or to policy inaction. Another contributing factor is a shift in the pattern of consumption expenditures. Services grew from 47.4 percent of personal consumption in 1979 to 57.7 percent in 1996, with a comparable reduction occurring in purchases of goods (see Table 3.1).[5] More rapid inflation for services than for goods is one reason, but there have also been changes in relative consumption patterns. The good news from the states' perspective is that more than half of the rise in services was for medical care and half of the reduction in goods purchased was for food, most of which was for consumption at home. Since neither food nor medical care is taxable in many states, the implication of this shift in consumption patterns for tax bases has been smaller than might otherwise have been expected.

The sales tax's role as the predominant state government tax instrument is threatened by the same types of trends that have characterized the past twenty-five years: changes in consumption patterns and new technologies that lie outside state government control, and policy decisions that are at the discretion of state legislatures. Continued relative growth in the service sector and the expected expansion of electronic commerce threaten to narrow still further the portion of consumption that is taxed and to reduce the sales tax's revenue productivity. Policy decisions, like those enacted in recent years, to exempt additional transactions can exacerbate the natural economic trends that are underway and reduce the base still further.

In the past, these trends have failed to diminish the sales tax's importance because of frequent rate increases. However, rate increases comparable to those enacted during the last several decades

Table 3.1 PERSONAL CONSUMPTION EXPENDITURES, 1979 AND 1996
(in Billions of Nominal Dollars)

	1979		1996	
	Amount	Distribution	Amount	Distribution
Total Expenditure	1,594.0	100.0	5,151.4	100.0
Durable Goods	213.9	13.4	632.1	12.3
Motor Vehicles and Parts	93.5	5.9	252.5	4.9
New Autos	49.3	3.1	81.4	1.6
Used Autos, Net	11.3	0.7	54.9	1.1
Other Motor Vehicles	16.6	1.0	77.3	1.5
Tires, Accessories, and Parts	16.3	1.0	38.9	0.8
Furniture and Household Equipment	82.3	5.2	254.4	4.9
Other Durables	38.2	2.4	125.2	2.4
Nondurable Goods	624.0	39.1	1,542.1	30.0
Clothing and Shoes	101.2	6.3	264.4	5.1
Food and Beverages	324.2	20.3	772.3	15.0
Off-Premise Consumption	221.3	13.9	485.9	9.4
Purchased Meals	96.7	6.1	277.6	5.4
Other Food	6.2	0.4	8.9	0.2
Gasoline and Oil	66.3	4.2	121.8	2.4
Fuel Oil and Coal	14.4	0.9	11.1	0.2
Other Nondurables	118.0	7.4	375.4	7.3
Services	755.6	47.4	2,974.3	57.7
Housing	226.6	14.2	779.4	15.1
Household Operation	100.0	6.3	309.5	6.0
Transportation	59.1	3.7	204.5	4.0
User-Operated	41.7	2.6	163.0	3.2
Local	4.8	0.3	9.7	0.2
Intercity	12.6	0.8	31.9	0.6
Medical Care	158.0	9.9	815.8	15.8
Other	212.0	13.3	865.0	16.8

Source: The WEFA Group, U.S. Long-Term Historical Data, First Quarter 1997.

cannot be relied upon to offset future trends in the base. One indication is that since 1994 fewer states have increased their sales tax rate than in any comparable time period in more than two decades.[6] The ability of states to get by with infrequent increases can be explained by the lengthy economic recovery and good state tax revenue growth, but similar conditions applied in other time periods, such as during the second half of the 1980s. Without the same degree of rate increases or other structural changes, the sales tax may well languish as a revenue source over the long term. The greatest consequences will be in states such as Florida, Tennessee, Texas, and Washington, which have no broad-based state income tax and rely very heavily on sales taxes for revenues.

CHANGING CONSUMPTION PATTERNS
AND NEW TECHNOLOGIES

Two major trends in the U.S. economy have potentially enormous implications for sales taxation: the shift toward increasing consumption of services, and the increasing tendency for transactions to involve vendors and consumers living in different states or countries. These trends are typically recognized in analytical and legislative circles, but state tax structures have not been adequately revamped to take account of their effects. One implication, for example, is that states need to routinely adapt their tax structures to reflect changes in the types of services being consumed and in the means by which services (and goods) are being delivered.

State Taxation of Services

Much of the state tax policy discussion in the 1980s and early 1990s was devoted to whether services should be added to the sales tax base. While a number of states (examples include Indiana, Massachusetts, and North Dakota) seriously considered extending the base to a wide array of services, political forces and economic factors resulted in no significant base broadening, except for Florida's short-lived experiment and Massachusetts legislation that never became effective.[7] Many states were able to add a small number of selected services: The Federation of Tax Administrators (1997) reports that ninety-nine services were added to state bases between 1990 and 1992 and another thirty-nine between 1992 and 1996. All states broadened their tax bases to include canned software, about half of the states to include modified canned software, and about a third to include customized software; other specific services added to tax bases included cable television, pet grooming, amusements, and lawn care. However, those services that potentially offer the greatest revenues, such as construction, health care, and other professional services, generally remain untaxed.

Political opposition is the best explanation for states' failure to move toward service taxation. Differences in the way goods and services are included in the base point up why the political opposition has been so effective. Goods sold at retail are normally contained in the base unless specific exemptions are enumerated. The reverse is generally true with respect to services: Specific services are taxed only if they are individually enumerated. This places state legislatures in the position of selecting individual activities and industries to tax if the base is to be expanded to services. Each chosen industry becomes galvanized against base changes and is often willing to expend considerable resources to defeat the relevant legislation. In contrast, the benefits of base broadening are often more diffuse, and the case for base broadening is left to analysts.

An important lesson is that states could increase their political effectiveness in passing base expansions if they could find a less selective means (and a more general justification) for incorporating services in the base. But well-designed policy requires that decisions on a suitable set of taxable services be made on a case-by-case basis.

One reason to tax services is to minimize the price distortions that arise when one item is taxed and another is not. For example, when the purchase of a refrigerator is taxable and the repair of an existing refrigerator is not, a competitive advantage is provided for repairing existing, rather than buying new, equipment. Another significant advantage of broadening the base is the ability to raise the same amount of revenues with a lower tax rate. Economists have demonstrated that the welfare losses from tax distortions grow more than proportionately with the tax rate, so lower rates can be expected to improve well-being. On the other hand, the administrative costs of taxing many services are significant relative to the revenues raised. Iowa found that the number of vendors rose 60 percent when a number of services were added to the base, and the average tax liability per service vendor was low. Also, some people believe it is unfair to tax certain services, such as selected medical and education services. Finally, many services are heavily consumed by business, thus raising the wholly legitimate concern of tax pyramiding—the multiple taxation of a product as it moves through production to the retail stage.

States have avoided the mistake of including all services in the base, but they have stopped far short of adding all appropriate services, so the states must be more aggressive in expanding the tax base to services than they have been during the past decade. Even a loosely coordinated move of all states toward taxation of services would be helpful in limiting the tax avoidance possibilities that will otherwise develop. Following the logic of a consumption tax structure, services used by final consumers generally belong in the base and those consumed by businesses do not.[8] However, as with implementing the tax on tangible goods, deciding which services should be taxed, which are used by final consumers as opposed to businesses, where they should be taxed, and so forth are difficult tasks for administrators. For example, many services, such as computer and legal services, are heavily purchased by businesses, and attempts to include them in the tax structure would probably lead to a significant increase in business taxation, not taxation of final consumption. The business transactions do not belong in a consumption tax base, but some computer and legal services are used by final consumers and legitimately belong in the consumption base. Construction, telecommunications, personal, computer, and electronic commerce services (such as access to the Internet) are examples of services that states must seriously consider including in their tax bases.

Taxation of services should be approached aggressively but carefully. States should allow exemptions for services that are directly used in production (as opposed to being component parts in production) to avoid dramatically expanding the base to businesses. (Under current law, services used in production generally receive no special exemption from taxation.) Also, tangible goods and services directly used in the production of taxable services should be exempt (again in contrast to state tax laws that normally do not allow such exemptions). Unduly complicated rules, imposed in an effort to prevent any base from escaping taxation, should be avoided. If these guidelines are followed, however, the net additional revenues from including more services will be much smaller than many people anticipate.

New Technologies: Electronic Commerce

In recent years, the focus of tax policy debates has shifted from taxing services to taxing electronic commerce. Electronic commerce does not raise unexplored issues in taxation, though its characteristics exaggerate many problems seen elsewhere.[9] The interstate nature of producing, distributing, and consuming electronic commerce (and many other services as well) is the most problematic concern. Two key aspects of taxing interstate activities are determining which state should legitimately be able to tax each activity and ensuring that states have the capacity to collect sales taxes from the appropriate taxpayers, wherever they are located.

The principle of the retail sales tax is that sales should be taxable in the state where the goods or services are used by the final consumer. Taxes levied at the point of consumption are called destination taxes, and the liability is presumed to exist where the goods or services are enjoyed. With destination taxes, vendors are expected to collect the tax and remit to states based on the location of markets, rather than the location of production. The alternative, levying the tax where goods and services are produced, is called an origination tax. The rationale for destination taxes is to develop a tax that is levied on consumption rather than on production and to avoid the economic efficiency losses and tax avoidance possibilities associated with origination taxes.[10] A significant advantage of destination taxes is that they limit tax competition between states (except with respect to business at the retail level), because the tax burden is identical regardless of where the goods or services are produced.[11] Thus, firms are not advantaged by producing in low sales tax jurisdictions. The high degree of producer mobility on the part of many services and of electronic commerce, which arises because producers often have little need to be geographically near either inputs or consumers, means that states will be unable to retain producers if origination taxes are imposed, since producers of taxable services can be expected to locate in zero tax or very low tax jurisdictions.[12]

Compliance is a potential disadvantage with respect to destination taxes, since firms selling in more than one state must comply with many states' tax structures. But firms producing in more than one state must comply with origination taxes in multiple states, so the compliance advantages of origination taxes may be smaller than anticipated.

Nexus

The most efficient means for collecting the sales tax continues to be taxing vendors of final sales, and destination taxes can be effectively imposed on interstate transactions only if vendors are deemed to have nexus in the destination state. The current nexus standard is heavily based on a taxpayer's physical presence in a state, though emerging nexus theories are being investigated and asserted to reflect the fact of many sales occurring across jurisdictional borders.[13] In many situations, either firms producing goods or services for consumption in other states do not have nexus or there is a question about whether they have it. In cases where nexus does not exist, use taxes must be collected from final consumers, who remit revenues directly to the state. Significant use taxes are obtained from large businesses, but the self-reporting system is cumbersome and difficult to enforce—and, hence, ineffective in the case of most other taxpayers. The very limited extent of self-reporting (with the exception of large businesses) and states' inability to monitor use tax liabilities mean that the use tax cannot be relied upon to collect nonbusiness taxes.[14] The notion that the nexus standard must enable states to fairly and effectively collect taxes on a destination basis is not new, as it dates at least to the 1967 *Bellas Hess* case. However, the problem is growing with movement of consumption toward services and with increased international and interstate trade.[15]

A nexus standard relying on physical presence is simply inconsistent with an economy that no longer connects vendors and consumers via physical contact. A nexus standard for the future must be based on an economic exploitation concept, which means that nexus should be defined to exist whenever a firm exploits a state's market.[16] The basic argument is straightforward: The state that provides the final market for a product is the appropriate site for a destination-based tax regardless of how the sale is consummated. Fortunately, a number of analysts believe that electronic commerce involves sufficient contact so that nexus exists to enable collecting the taxes due on many transactions. However, federal legislation is necessary to achieve an effective standard that provides a broad basis for states to appropriately collect destination-based sales taxes. The states need to make a compelling case to Congress regarding the wide-scale benefits of legislation allowing for an economic concept of nexus.[17] Congress's decision not to act thus far is evidence of the difficulties involved in obtaining such legislation. The legislation is controversial because some businesses see the current physical presence nexus standard as a vehicle for avoiding taxes—which, in turn, creates a price advantage vis-à-vis taxed competitors. But there are many more stakeholders who will be advantaged by a better nexus standard, including companies that are collecting and remitting sales taxes, local vendors, and, of course, state and local government taxpayers—for whom tax rates would fall as tax bases were broadened.

A series of problems will persist unless an economic nexus standard is adopted. First, interstate commerce will continue to be distorted, since firms can vary the consumption tax liability implicit in the goods and services they sell by selecting which side of a state's border to produce on. Neutrality can be achieved only with an economic exploitation definition, so that all like commodities sold in a single market are subject to the same consumption taxes. An example of the current dilemma is that commodities sold by a local vendor are subject to the sales tax, while no sales tax is collected on the identical commodities sold by mail-order vendors that do not have physical presence in the state. Similar distortions exist with respect to electronic merchants unless states aggressively assert their right to collect the taxes. Compact disks or software sold by a local vendor will be taxed, but the same items will not be taxed when downloaded from the Internet. Local businesses are disadvantaged and made less competitive, and state governments lose tax revenue.

Second, firms are encouraged, under the current standard, to reduce their sales tax liability by concentrating their activities in a limited number of low or zero tax rate states. Efficiency losses result, to the extent that siting and production decisions are based on tax, not economic, criteria. Third, the current situation leaves firms unable to anticipate their tax liability with certainty. There is a risk that states will identify new means to assert nexus, leaving firms with large, unexpected sales tax liabilities. Firms stand to benefit if nexus rules are carefully defined so that litigation can be reduced and they can undertake tax planning with greater reliability. Finally, the tax base is narrowed by the inability to collect taxes on many transactions, thereby requiring higher tax rates to raise any given amount of revenue. The higher tax rates also entail greater losses in overall well-being because of greater distortions in people's economic and life-style decisions.

An alternative to defining nexus on a market exploitation basis is for the states to have similar consumption tax structures.[18] Indeed, tax competition will coerce the states toward uniformity to avoid significant losses of capital, economic activity, and tax revenues.[19] As a result, states will increasingly have less control over their sales tax rates and bases, as they feel compelled to keep their tax structures in line with those states imposing the lowest rates. This could result in lower levels of government and provision of public services, with the potential to lessen the economy's capacity to operate efficiently. The base will include a decreasing share of consumption, since the tendency will remain to exempt goods or services that can be most easily purchased outside the taxing jurisdiction. A likely outcome is that, just as it is today, the base will be composed of tangible goods, items that are less expensive (so there is little incentive to travel for their purchase), and goods purchased heavily by lower-income people. The sales tax may thereby become more inequitable in the eyes of many. To offset these revenue and equity problems, there will also be a general propensity for states to tax other, less mobile bases, such as labor. Thus, income taxes could grow in relative importance.

POLICY DECISIONS: NARROWING THE TAX BASE

Redesign of the sales tax base to conform with consumption offers a number of benefits, as has already been described. The aggregate effect of actual state legislative decisions, however, appears to be a *narrow-*

ing of the base, thereby making the sales tax a less productive revenue instrument without achieving consistent movement toward a consumption base. Each piece of legislation appears to be considered as if it were occurring in a vacuum—in particular, without recognition of the substantial cumulative effects of many statutes, each of which on its own often has only small revenue consequences.

On the consumer side, food has been exempted by two-thirds of the states and prescription drugs by essentially all of the states, with the decisions to do so being defended on vertical equity grounds. However, the consequences include a range of serious problems in terms of restricted ability to audit taxpayers, more complicated compliance, reduced horizontal equity, and greater consumption distortions. Economists have argued that indirect taxes like the sales tax are not well suited for achieving vertical equity goals, both because of these problems and on account of the poor targeting of the exemptions to lower-income households. Vertical equity goals are better accomplished through income tax rate adjustments or targeted consumer-type income tax credits.

On the business side, there has been a continual process of granting additional exemptions. Many states have exempted manufacturing equipment during the past several decades: At least thirty-three states currently exempt manufacturing equipment, and a number of other states tax manufacturing equipment at preferential rates. California, Illinois, Minnesota, Texas, Utah, and Washington are examples of states that have recently passed legislation reducing taxation of manufacturing equipment. These exemptions improve the tax's structural design, with the major criticism being that other types of business capital are not exempted as well.

There is an increasing tendency for states to legislate incentives for business. Business purchases should be exempt from a consumption tax structure, but the means through which many exemptions for business have been granted and the specific applications thereof are often questionable. It appears that the tendency to grant special-purpose exemptions in an attempt to attract economic activity is spreading from the corporate income tax to the sales tax,[20] as evidenced by other selected activities routinely being added to the exemption list in every state.

New business exemptions, both for manufacturing capital and for a range of special purposes, are usually defended on the basis of economic development. State legislatures even freely admit that a beggar-thy-neighbor approach to economic development is being undertaken. Often exemptions result from threats by individual firms or industries to relocate (or not locate) unless their activity is exempted. Exemptions are frequently written narrowly so as to limit the application to a small number of firms—which reduces the revenue consequences but makes the tax code a patchwork. As a result many non-neutralities are created, as firms within the same narrowly defined industries are subject to different tax liabilities. Small firms, which are less likely to obtain special tax breaks, are the most likely to be disadvantaged by these practices.

The New York State decision to take the sales tax off clothing for one week during the fall of 1996 and the continuing discussions on permanent removal of clothing from the base are recent examples of a special exemption. The exemption has been justified both as a means to improve fairness and as a way to increase New York's clothing sales at the expense of New Jersey's (where clothing is not taxed). Enactment of permanent legislation in New York would result in the many disadvantages that have previously been discussed. A major concern is that sales tax holidays or exemptions of clothing will grow and narrow the base further.[21] A similar sales tax holiday was considered and, fortunately, rejected in Tennessee during the 1997 legislative session.

Broadening the base to include more consumption expenditures and exempt more business purchases (but to grant only exemptions that are carefully thought out and have broad application) is conceptually appealing, would reduce sales tax cascading, and would limit some incentives for tax avoidance. The experiences of the past twenty-five years, however, make it difficult to be very optimistic about the direction of the sales tax in these regards. Political pressure is pushing states toward a steady narrowing of the base, with respect to both consumers and businesses, but not toward a conceptually improved base. This is discouraging, because state legislatures can control these policy decisions. States have frequently succumbed to political pressure to reduce their bases, while allowing the goals of good tax policy to be relegated to the back seat. It is difficult for the states to argue that Congress is failing to enact needed improvements in the nexus standard when the states themselves continue yielding to political pressures that result in poor sales tax structures. Interestingly, legislatures appear to have been more successful at withstanding pressures to narrow the income tax base by expanding exemptions. Perhaps this is because states can use conformity with the federal income tax as a justification for keeping their structures in place.

LOCAL GOVERNMENT SALES TAXES

Local sales taxes, levied in thirty-one states, comprise about 10 percent of total local tax receipts and are the second-largest local tax source in many states. Sales taxes are small relative to the property tax, but they help diversify revenue structures.

The potential exists for even greater use of local sales taxes, but constraints should be imposed to make them most effective. First, the tax rates must lie within a narrow range, because of the potential for cross-border shopping and destructive tax competition. States would find it best to levy both a minimum and a maximum rate, so that a large local revenue source could be developed without local governments being forced toward the rate selected by the lowest-taxing and least-service-providing jurisdictions. A maximum rate, as is generally legislated by the states, is also important because it limits the welfare loss of the combined state and local sales tax rates.

Second, states must recognize that local sales taxes cannot readily be levied on many services, including some forms of electronic commerce. The administrative and compliance costs of determining the situs of transactions at their destination and the potential to purchase services produced outside the local government's jurisdiction are the major reasons.

The costs of both administering and complying with sales taxes on selected services and some electronic commerce transactions could be lowered by imposing the state's minimum (or average) local tax rate on these transactions and distributing the revenues using a formula. The revenues could be shared in proportion to other local sales tax revenues, other local sales tax bases, or population, or by using another formula enjoying general acceptability. Local sales taxes can be collected directly from electronic merchants who are selling tangible products that are delivered to the final consumer.

LOOKING AHEAD

Current legal restrictions on states' ability to collect destination-based consumption taxes on goods and services produced outside their geographical area are disconcerting, because in an economy that is increasingly mobile and open, consumption taxes appear to be uniquely suited to regional governments. Either nexus standards must be changed from relying on physical presence, or state tax systems will be increasingly distortionary. Specifically, goods and services produced in a state will often be placed at a disadvantage relative to those produced outside. State tax systems will also be less horizontally equitable, because functionally equivalent purchases will frequently be taxed differently, and less vertically equitable in the eyes of many, because taxes will be levied mostly on tangible personal products that are purchased heavily by lower-income people.

An obvious lesson from the past decade is that the sales tax will survive regardless of whether a new nexus standard is legislated or whether states are able to enact taxes on appropriate services and electronic commerce. Of course, implications for the tax are much greater when combined with further, haphazard tax base narrowing. Unless these trends are changed, the result will be a sales tax that remains a levy on tangible personal property. The minimum consequence is that the sales tax will be replaced as the largest state tax instrument, because the current political climate will prevent rate changes from being sufficient to offset relative base declines. More than one-fourth of the tax base as a share of personal income has been lost during the past seventeen years. Over the course of the next seventeen years, the median state sales tax rate would need to rise to over 6.25 percent if the same trend holds and if the sales tax is to be maintained as a percentage of personal income. Similar proportional increases in local rates would need to occur. Based on the current distribution of tax rates, this means the combined state and local sales tax rate would exceed 10 percent in a number of states.

Notes

Author's Note: The author is grateful to Robert Ebel and Matthew Murray for comments on an earlier draft.

1. However, sales taxes do not score as well as state income taxes.

2. More than 90 countries have adopted value-added taxes during the past four decades (Tanzi 1995), often replacing sales or turnover taxes.

3. Connecticut is the only state with a lower sales tax rate than in 1979.

4. Mikesell (1997) provides a thorough review of the current sales tax base.

5. These percentages are only based on services for personal consumption, and do not include business purchases of services.

6. On the other hand, there has been no evidence of taxpayer backlashes against the sales tax, like those that have occurred in some states against income and property taxes. The sales tax rate reduction in Connecticut occurred when its income tax was adopted, not in response to a specific reaction to the sales tax's acceptability. Since 1979, rates have also been lowered (following short-lived increases) in the District of Columbia, Minnesota, New Jersey, North Dakota, South Dakota, and Utah.

7. For discussion of taxing services and the Florida example, see Fox and Murray (1988) and Hellerstein (1988).

8. The distinction between a final consumer and a business that is used in this paper differs from that often used in legislative discussions. The final consumer is one who does not use the service to produce other goods or services. In this context, businesses use services to produce, even if the services do not become a component of the final product or are not used directly in the narrowly defined processes of producing the firm's output. For example, an attorney working on a firm's tax returns is still integral to the firm's activities and this legal service is production, not final consumption.

9. See Fox and Murray (1997).

10. Origination taxes can entail efficiency losses by causing firms to make location decisions based on tax considerations rather than on the lowest production costs. With origination taxes, tax avoidance will result as firms locate or sell in low or zero tax jurisdictions.

11. This assumes that the tax can be effectively administered. The ability to produce services outside the United States is an important potential limitation on the ability to administer destination taxes.

12. Taxes on prepaid telephone cards, which several states have imposed recently, offer an example. Taxation of the point of sale for the cards can be expected to cause vendors to offer the cards for sale from states without a sales tax, effectively shifting the taxable transaction from the state where the call will be made, and resulting in no tax on the card or the call.

13. See Eisenstein (1997) and Grierson (1996) for discussion of nexus.

14. States can use means, such as compacts that allow transfer of audit information, to increase use tax collections for large purchases, but large gaps will still remain.

15. The problem of interstate sales of activities has not become unmanageable at this point. Gramlich (1987) has demonstrated that most goods and services are still consumed in the state where they are produced.

16. Of course, de minimus rules should be developed so that small firms are not required to comply with the tax laws of many states.

17. The Supreme Court ruled in the 1992 Quill decision that limitations on nexus for mail order firms are imposed by the Commerce Clause. Congress has the authority to regulate interstate commerce.

18. See Tanzi (1995) for a discussion of the European Union's attempts to distribute the value-added tax to the country of destination.

19. Public choice economists argue that tax competition is healthy because states are constrained to offer a good return for taxes paid to prevent businesses and individuals from voting with their feet. However, the sales tax incentives discussed here affect the tax structure, not the overall tax level. Ultimately these incentives arise from states' inability to administer a destination tax on some types of consumption, given the current nexus standard. Thus, the benefits anticipated from tax competition will not necessarily result from these incentives.

20. This is not surprising, since Ring's (1989) findings on the percentage of sales taxes paid by business suggest that the initial impact of the sales tax on business is much

greater than that of the corporate income tax. Further, sales tax rate differentials can be very large. These factors suggest that business has a strong incentive to seek sales tax reductions.

21. Six states currently give preferential treatment to clothing purchases.

References

Advisory Commission on Intergovernmental Relations. 1993. "Changing Public Attitudes on Governments and Taxes." S-22, Washington, D.C.: 43.

Ebel, Robert D., and Christopher Zimmerman. 1992. "Sales Tax Trends and Issues." In *Sales Taxation*, edited by William F. Fox, pp. 27–38. Westpoint, Conn.: Praeger Publishers.

Eisenstein, Martin I. 1997. "The Constitutional Limits of Sales Taxation of Cyberspace." *State Tax Notes* (February 24): 601–5.

Federation of Tax Administrators. 1997. "Sales Taxation of Services: 1996 Update." Research Report No. 147 (April).

Fox, William F., and Matthew N. Murray. 1988. "Economic Aspects of Taxing Services." *National Tax Journal* 41: 19–36.

Fox, William F., and Matthew N. Murray. 1997. "The Sales Tax and Electronic Commerce: So What's New?" *National Tax Journal* 50 (September).

Gramlich, Edward M. 1987. "Subnational Fiscal Policy." *Perspectives on Local Public Finance and Public Policy* 3: 3–27.

Grierson, R. Scot. 1996. "State Taxation of the Information Superhighway: A Proposal for Taxation of Information Services." *Loyola of Los Angeles Entertainments Law Journal* 16: 603–55.

Hellerstein, Walter. 1988. "Florida's Sales Tax on Services." *National Tax Journal* 41: 1–18.

Mikesell, John L. 1997. "The American Retail Sales Tax: Considerations on Their Structure, Operations, and Potential as a Foundation for a Federal Sales Tax." *National Tax Journal* 50: 149–65.

Ring, Raymond J. 1989. "The Proportion of Consumers' and Producers' Goods in the General Sales Tax." *National Tax Journal* 42: 167–79.

Tanzi, Vito. 1995. *Taxation in an Integrating World*. Washington, D.C.: Brookings Institution.

Chapter Four

THE FUTURE OF THE STATE CORPORATE INCOME TAX: REFLECTIONS (AND CONFESSIONS) OF A TAX LAWYER

Richard D. Pomp

The corporate income tax is not a major component of most state revenue structures.[1] On average, it constitutes less than 7 percent of state taxes, a nontrivial amount but far less than the 31 percent raised from the sales tax or the 33 percent raised from the personal income tax.[2] Nonetheless, no state is considering the elimination of the corporate income tax. The political reality is that the tax is an accepted feature of nearly every state's revenue structure.

Assuming the tax will be with us into the next century, what role will it play? The tax is under attack, not from its usual critics—taxpayers and economists—but from new quarters and new sources. These new attacks are unlikely to prove fatal, but they have wounded the tax and opened gaping holes in its base, threatening to drain the lifeblood out of the tax.

This chapter examines why the corporate income tax is unlikely to be a major source of increased revenue in most states—at least in the short term. My perspective is that of a tax lawyer. I leave it to the economists to prognosticate about interest rates, wage rates, the changing composition of the economy, and the technological revolution and how these imponderables might affect corporate profits and tax revenue. My threefold thesis is far simpler. First, the changing nature of the state tax profession has resulted in the aggressive exploitation of even the slightest weaknesses in the tax's structure or framework. Second, the current misguided legislative obsession with tax incentives is squandering substantial tax revenue through wasteful and inefficient provisions. Third, modern-day tax planning techniques result in a stealth attack on the tax base. The cost in lost revenue is less visible than from some of the well-publicized tax incentives, but this attack nonetheless results in a bleeding, if not a hemorrhaging, of the corporate income tax base.[3]

My first point is based more on impressionistic than empirical evidence. The second and third points are related, in that many tax planning techniques are facilitated by provisions that legislators adopted to encourage economic development. Tax incentives can have many subtle effects that were not fully understood or appreciated at the time of their adoption. Tax lawyers and accountants, however, are quick to grasp these less obvious implications.

Space limitations prevent a systematic exploration of all of these points. I have limited my discussion, therefore, primarily to issues for which revenue estimates exist and legislative solutions are available. These two criteria have eliminated many current issues, but some of these are discussed elsewhere in this volume. Finally, not wishing to write a primer on corporate tax avoidance, I have relied for illustrations on common tax planning techniques, even if these no longer represent the state of the art.

THE EMERGENCE OF THE STATE TAX PROFESSION: A COMING OF AGE

Once upon a time, issues of state and local taxation played to a small audience. Federal tax matters held center stage; state issues were relegated to the wings. But in the last fifteen years or so, state tax matters have emerged from their secondary status and have moved into the spotlight.

Two federal tax acts helped move state tax issues onto center stage. The first was the Economic Recovery Act of 1981 (ERTA), which gutted the federal corporate income tax by revamping the treatment of depreciation and by introducing safe-harbor leasing. Many of the largest corporations in the United States paid no federal corporate income tax for several years as a consequence of ERTA.

If ERTA's rules on depreciation and safe-harbor leasing had been incorporated into state tax laws, many states would have suffered significant losses of tax revenue without receiving commensurate benefits.[4] Accordingly, many states refused to fully embrace the federal changes and "decoupled" from ERTA's rules on depreciation and safe-harbor leasing.

ERTA had severe repercussions for state tax practitioners. By decreasing the impact of the federal income tax on many corporations, ERTA substantially increased the relative significance and prominence of state taxes, especially in states that had decoupled. In many cases, a corporation's state income tax was greater than its federal tax—a situation that did not escape notice by CEOs, CFOs, or corporate tax managers. Corporations that had typically treated state issues as secondary to federal concerns started to shift their emphasis from compliance to planning.

The second of the two relevant federal changes was the Tax Reform Act of 1986. By lowering federal marginal tax rates, the act increased the after-tax cost of deductible state taxes, thereby generating additional pressure on lawyers and accountants to reduce state taxes through planning. This pressure was exacerbated by increases occurring in state taxes across the country.

The 1986 act also eliminated many of the federal tax lawyer's bread-and-butter issues, altering the complexion of a federal tax practice. Since 1986, my impression is that the real job growth in the tax profession has taken place in state tax practices—and much of that growth has taken place in accounting firms and not in law firms or corporations.

The larger corporations have always had first-rate persons in their state tax departments. But the recent emphasis on downsizing, coupled with a corporate mentality that often views the tax department as overhead and not as a profit center, has kept in-house departments small.

There is a fairly small number of well-known, highly competent law firms with active, full-time state tax practices. They are staffed with the luminaries in the field. These firms, however, are the exception. Many large, prominent firms with traditionally strong federal tax practices have been late in recognizing the importance of the state tax. Such firms have displayed the common bias of federal tax lawyers, who traditionally have looked down on their state counterparts as the Rodney Dangerfields of the profession (Brunori 1997). But the times have changed, and these firms are now playing catch-up. Still, the amount of new hires by law firms pales by comparison with those by the accounting firms.

The bigger accounting firms are no longer content to do compliance work and now have dynamic and growing state practices geared to planning and tax minimization strategies. Actively recruiting from law firms, industry, and government and wooing recent graduates with attractive starting salaries (often commensurate with those offered by law firms), these accounting firms now claim some of the brightest minds in the business, people who combine technical virtuosity with a creativity and a boldness that were more commonly associated in the past with the federal tax bar. With their extensive network of offices, their computer simulation models, their large staffs that can handle an array of state tax issues—from challenges to property tax valuations to unemployment compensation ratings and everything in between—and their increased willingness to become involved in dispute resolution issues, the accounting firms have changed the nature of state tax practice and have emerged as major players.

Unlike most law firms, the bigger accounting firms typically have groups devoted to developing multi-state tax minimization strategies, which go well beyond dealing with only issues of local law. Such strategies typically involve pressing formal rules to their limits, aggressively exploiting weaknesses in state tax structures, shifting income and deductions among the states, identifying and capitalizing on gaps in the interfacing of state laws, restructuring corporate entities, and the use of pass-through entities. The firms market these strategies to corporations, sometimes for a fee based on the tax savings. The firms also apply to state issues many of the techniques that have been developed in international and federal contexts.

The private sector is a repository of some of the finest talent in the tax profession, whose prowess and sophistication I greatly respect. Out of that respect comes my fear for the future of the corporate income tax. Having worked closely over the years with some of the tax maestros in law firms, accounting firms, and corporations, I know the intellectual firepower that the private sector can bring to bear on the corporate income tax. And the tax labors under enough weaknesses without being the target of this formidable firepower.

The corporate income tax is built on a rickety foundation, constructed during the first half of this century to deal with what, by today's standards, seems to be the rather mundane taxation of manufacturing and mercantile activities. Those were simpler times, when substantial sectors of the economy, such as transportation, communications, banking, and power generation, were either regulated or subject to significant federal controls. Multinational corporations and conglomerates were yet to emerge, and few corporations had substantial amounts of foreign income. It was a world in which corporations did not electronically transfer funds around the globe and did not make much use of financial derivatives. Large mail order houses had not yet proliferated, 800 telephone numbers were not widespread, and the Internet did not exist. Limited liability companies, limited liability partnerships, and other pass-through entities were not commonly used.

For much of the early history of the state corporate income tax, taxes were low enough (and state tax administrators passive enough) that litigation was infrequent. Low rates can bury all sins. Moreover, the corporate income tax dealt with changes in the economy primarily through the development of special apportionment formulas in response to the needs of particular industries.

Today's challenges to the tax from an expanding, aggressive, and sophisticated private sector pose a qualitatively different type of problem. The antiquated structure of the tax makes it difficult to repel attacks by tax lawyers and accountants who are using modern weapons.

The first line of defense is the state tax department. Many in such departments can go head-to-head with their counterparts in the private sector. But most state departments are understaffed, overworked, and plagued by turnover. State salary structures cannot easily accommodate the marketable skills and higher opportunity costs of those in specialized areas like taxation. And state tax departments often lose valuable personnel to the private sector. The surprising thing is how much the states manage to accomplish with so few resources.

The second line of defense is, theoretically, the state legislature. The legislature should be busy plugging holes in the tax base, discarding inefficient provisions, modernizing the tax code, and providing tax administrators with the tools they need. As the following section shows, however, too often legislators have retreated from this function, instead becoming one of the forces at work gutting the tax.

TAX INCENTIVES: THE HOLY GRAIL OF ECONOMIC DEVELOPMENT AND JOBS

Legislatures around the country are fixated on the illusion that lower state taxes are the key to economic development. A glut of state tax incentives exists, and there is open and increasing competition among the states to attract new businesses. Between 1977 and 1988, for example, the number of states with corporate income tax exemptions designed to attract footloose corporations increased from twenty-one to thirty-one. By 1988, thirty-two states provided investment tax credits and thirty-five offered job creation credits. Nearly every state enacted at least one new locational tax incentive between 1991 and 1993 (Enrich 1986, pp. 378, 384–89).

The cost of these corporate income tax incentives goes well beyond pocket change. For 1993, for example, New York State reported that its special rules on accelerated depreciation, adopted when it decoupled from ERTA, cost $160 million; its investment tax credit cost $295 million; and its employment incentive credit cost $33 million.

Some jurisdictions have become notorious for their generosity in offering targeted incentives. Tennessee, for example, provided incentives of $150 million to General Motors for its Saturn plant. Indianapolis provided $294 million to attract a United Airlines maintenance facility. Alabama offered more than $300 million in incentives to obtain a Mercedes-Benz plant.[5] Between 1991 and 1993, twenty-five states enacted targeted tax incentives (Brunori 1997). Questions have been raised about whether the states will ever recoup the costs of these incentives.

These estimates of lost revenue can be challenged on the grounds that they do not take into account any of the revenue gained from incentives. In other words, to the extent that the incentives result in economic activity that otherwise would not have taken place, the taxes and other benefits generated by that economic activity should presumably be weighed against the cost of the incentives. Tax exemptions limited to new investment, for example, seem to many legislators to be costless because they think they are merely giving away tax revenue that they otherwise wouldn't have.

Unfortunately, there is scant evidence in the literature to support this romantic view of the cost of incentives. Reasons abound why tax incentives probably reward corporations for doing what they would have done anyway.[6] Moreover, even if one chooses to disbelieve this evidence, it should be obvious that whatever advantage a state achieves is undercut when other states retaliate with competing incentives. One commentator concluded that "[a]ll the evidence points to a single conclusion: state tax incentives are a thoroughly unproven tool for promoting economic development," and that the proliferation of tax incentives "has unquestionably played a significant role in the shrinkage of business taxes from one-half of state tax revenues in the 1950s to only a quarter by 1990."[7]

Of course, legislators may be unaware of this evidence. Or they may simply get caught up in the politics of the situation and fear that being perceived as anti-business or anti-jobs is worse than being seen as promoting highly visible, albeit ineffective, incentives. Politically, doing nothing is sometimes riskier than doing something ineffective, especially when voters may not be in a position to recognize the ineffectiveness. Moreover, the larger corporations and their advisers are increasingly adept at playing off one state or community against another, thereby keeping pressure on legislators to act.[8]

Withal, the use of tax incentives is likely to continue unabated. The states seem incapable of stopping this race to the bottom by agreeing on a truce among themselves. One possible alternative, federal legislation curtailing the use of incentives, also seems remote. A more likely possibility is that the courts will hold that certain incentives unconstitutionally discriminate against interstate commerce.[9]

DOUBLE-WEIGHTED SALES FACTORS AND SINGLE SALES FACTORS: THE GIFT THAT KEEPS ON GIVING

One manifestation of the states' obsession with taxes and economic development is the shift in the weighting of the sales factor in the apportionment formula. For many years, the standard approach was the three-factor, evenly weighted formula adopted by the Uniform Division of Tax Purposes Act (UDITPA) in 1957. The formula was a political compromise between the manufacturing states in the East and the market states in the West.

For a while, this formula proved to be a stable compromise, which furthered the goal of uniformity. For the state corporate income tax to work properly, uniformity is essential; agreement on the apportionment formula is a key ingredient in attaining that uniformity.

The traditional formula is not well suited, however, for taxing some types of nonmanufacturing activities. One of the major challenges to— and successes of—the state corporate income tax has been adjusting that formula for use with respect to other types of business activities. One of the reasons the corporate income tax has been so resilient has been the development of alternative formulas. Today, it is common-place for the states to use specially developed formulas for the taxation of, for example, banking, insurance, financial services, communications, transportation, natural resources, construction, and utilities. Provided the same formula is applied to the same types of activities, the goal of uniformity is furthered.[10]

Over time, however, the consensus underlying the evenly weighted three-factor formula has started to evaporate, undermining the advantages of uniformity and providing inducements for corporations to take advantage of differences among the states. The first inroad was made when the states started to deviate from the traditional formula by double-weighting the sales factor. As of 1997, a majority of states with corporate income taxes double-weight the sales factor under some circumstances.[11]

Compared with an evenly weighted three-factor formula, a double-weighted sales factor increases the tax on some corporations, decreases it on others, and has no effect on corporations that conduct all of their activities in the state. The exact pattern of effects depends on the mathematical relationship between the sales factor and the property and payroll factors. Specifically, corporations whose sales factors are less than the average of their property and payroll factors benefit from a move to a double-weighted sales factor; corporations whose sales factors are greater than the average of their property and payroll factors are disadvantaged (Pomp and Oldman 1997, pp. 701–2).

The motivation for moving to a double-weighted sales factor is typically twofold. First, replacing an equally weighted formula with a double-weighted sales factor reduces the tax on corporations that have a substantial amount of their production activities in a state. Such corporations often have easy access to the state legislature and can threaten to move their facilities and jobs elsewhere. Consequently, they have the political leverage to lobby for what might seem to legislators to be an esoteric change in a technical aspect of the tax. It is widely accepted that Maine moved to double-weighting at the request of the paper industry, Georgia adopted it for its automobile industry, Florida shifted in response to its military contractors, and West Virginia was responding to the request of its mining industry. New Mexico adopted double-weighting primarily for the Intel Corporation.

Moreover, the change will increase the tax on corporations that primarily produce goods out of state and only *sell* to residents of the taxing state. Without any substantial in-state activities, these corporations cannot assert a credible threat to leave the state. Legislators might feel, with justification, that such corporations will continue to sell in the state notwithstanding a change in the apportionment formula. Corporations do not usually bypass a market just because they have to share some of their profits by paying an income tax.

Second, a shift to a double-weighted sales factor is often packaged as an economic development tool. Legislators might view the shift to a double-weighted sales factor as an incentive for corporations with production activities already in the state to expand those activities. Similarly, legislators might feel that they have provided an incentive to out-of-state corporations to shift their production activities to the state.[12]

What legislators do not always fully appreciate is that no serious analytical support exists for the proposition that changes in the apportionment formula will affect a corporation's locational decisions (Pomp 1987, 577–81). Furthermore, double-weighting may actually work to undermine a state's economic development. That is, if the assumption is indulged that changing the apportionment formula can affect a business's locational decision-making, then a double-weighted sales factor could actually be counterproductive, by encouraging certain corporations to move their operations *out* of state.[13]

For example, consider a corporation that sells a substantial amount of its products to a state in which it has little property or payroll. If that state moves from an evenly weighted three-factor formula to a double-weighted factor, the corporation has a greater incentive than previously to move its property and payroll out of the state. Of course, if all states were to adopt double weighting, this corporation would have no incentive to shift its production activities out of state, but then neither would any out-of-state corporation have an incentive to move its activities *into* the state. Put differently, if a majority of the key states were to adopt a double-weighted sales factor, the advantage each was hoping to achieve would be neutralized, leaving a corporations' locational decisions unaffected by apportionment formulas.

The second inroad on the apportionment formula results· from a "More must be better" philosophy. From the perspective of those who lobby for or support a double-weighted sales factor, there is no reason not to weight it even more heavily. If double-weighting is good, triple-weighting must be even better. Or, carried to the extreme, why not use *only* a sales factor for apportioning income?[14] Indeed, the states seem receptive to exactly this thinking. Nebraska and Texas have recently adopted single-factor sales formulas, as has Massachusetts for certain industries.[15]

Unlike these recent converts, Connecticut has used a single-factor sales formula for nonmanufacturing activities for many years. The granddaddy of the single sales factor is Iowa, which adopted it in the 1930s, greatly benefiting two of its major manufacturers at that time, John Deere and Maytag.[16]

Does a shift to a double-weighted or single-sales factor erode the aggregate state tax base? A state that is predominantly a market state will gain revenue, and a state that is predominantly a manufacturing state will lose revenue. Of course, if all states moved from an evenly weighted three-factor formula to, for example, a double-weighted sales factor, and if all states had comparable rates, the aggregate revenue effect would presumably be minimal, because the revenue lost by one state would be offset by the revenue gained by another state.

To illustrate with a simplified example, suppose a corporation has all of its property and payroll in State A and makes all of its sales in State B. If States A and B both use an evenly weighted three-factor formula, and putting aside the effects of Public Law 86-272 (discussed below), the corporation would apportion two-thirds of its income to State A and one-third of its income to State B. If both states now shift to a double-weighted sales factor, the corporation would apportion half of its income to State A and half to State B. Assuming A's and B's rates are comparable, the aggregate amount of corporate income tax revenue would not change; the loss in State A revenue would be offset by the increase in State B revenue.

To be sure, there is a mix of formulas and rates used by the states, so that revenue gains will not always offset revenue losses. But the real kicker is Public Law 86-272, which affords a tax planning opportunity that significantly affects the calculations. This law, adopted in 1959 and originally intended to be a temporary measure, essentially prevents a state from taxing the income of a corporation whose only business activity in that state consists of the solicitation of orders for tangible goods, provided that the orders are sent outside the state for approval and that the goods are delivered from outside the state.

Suppose in the preceding example that the corporation cannot be taxed by State B because of Public Law 86-272. In that case, the reduction in taxes in State A from double-weighting the sales factor will not be offset by any increase in taxes in State B.

The problem of sales occurring in a state in which the corporation is protected by Public Law 86-272 is not unique to double-weighting the sales factor. The problem is inherent in the state corporate income tax and is independent of the type of apportionment formula a state uses. In response to this more general problem, states have developed the so-called throwback rule, which has also been adopted by UDITPA. The UDITPA throwback rule is triggered when a corporation is not subject to taxation in the market state. In that case, the sale is assigned to the state from which the property was shipped (Pomp and Oldman 1997, pp. 709–11).

In theory, a throwback rule should avoid the revenue loss that results when a sale is made in a state in which Public Law 86-272 protects the corporation from taxation. But not all states have a throwback rule. Indeed, some states purposely do not have a throwback rule in order to make themselves attractive to corporations (Simafranca 1995, 1685, 1690).

Even in those states that do have a throwback rule, transactions are often arranged to avoid the triggering of the origin state's rule while avoiding any serious taxation in the destination state. A typical strategy is to establish just enough activity in the destination state of the type that results in the payment of a trivial amount of income tax. In return, the origin state's throwback rule is inactivated.[17]

This type of technique for avoiding a throwback rule works if the origin state uses an evenly weighted formula. Techniques that have been developed in the context of an evenly weighted three-factor formula, however, are even more valuable if the origin state uses a double-weighted sales factor or apportions income on the basis of only a sales factor. The more heavily a state weights the sales factor, the greater the reward for avoiding the throwback rule. Tax planning techniques that might not be cost-effective in the context of an evenly weighted three-factor formula may become worthwhile when a state moves to a double-weighted sales factor or to a single sales factor.

The movement to either a double-weighted sales factor or a single sales factor reflects a shift from origin-based taxes to market-based taxes.[18] The fear that the taxation of origin-based production activities will retard economic development and drive investment elsewhere is a powerful constraint on the state corporate income tax. (The federal debate over replacing the corporate income tax with consumption-based taxes reflects the same concerns.) The incentives used to woo Mercedes-Benz and General Motors are highly visible examples; the shift in the apportionment formula is more technical and esoteric and unlikely to receive the same attention.[19] The net effect is the same, however—a needless loss in corporate tax revenue.

How much of a loss? The aggregate annual revenue effects in states that have deviated from the evenly weighted three-factor formula is around $500 million![20] If the consensus view is right—that these deviations have no role to play in economic development—than legislators have achieved a "lose-lose" situation, no bucks *and* no bang.

TAX PLANNING 101: COMBINED REPORTING, TRANSFER PRICING, AND HOLDING COMPANIES[21]

One of the pervasive problems in tax law is the weight that should be given to the form of a transaction rather than its economic substance. Consider, for example, a U.S. corporation that manufactures in State A, warehouses its inventory in State B, and sells through a sales division in State C. This corporation is conducting a vertically integrated business, the quintessential unitary business. In calculating its State A tax, the corporation would calculate its apportionment percentage by taking into account all of its factors in States A, B, and C. That percentage would be used to apportion its unitary business income to State A.

Suppose that the corporation's nonmanufacturing activities are incorporated in a new U.S. subsidiary. The corporation structure now consists of a parent corporation, which manufactures in State A, and its subsidiary, which warehouses the inventory in State B and sells the product through a marketing division in State C. The parent sells its inventory to its subsidiary at a price set by the parent. That price enters into the calculation of the parent's taxable income. Similarly, the amount paid by the subsidiary enters into its cost of goods sold and consequently affects the calculation of *its* taxable income.

State A confronts a major policy decision. In calculating the taxable income and apportionment percentage of the parent, should the factors and taxable income of the subsidiary be ignored? Or should the formal division of the unitary business into a parent and a subsidiary be ignored and intercompany transactions reversed, in which case the taxable income apportioned to State A would remain the same as it was prior to creating the subsidiary?

States that calculate the taxable income and apportionment percentage of the parent and ignore the taxable income and factors of the subsidiary, with which they have no connection or nexus, are known as separate entity states.[22] In such states, the subsidiary's income and factors have no bearing on calculating the parent's apportionable taxable income. Similarly, the income and factors of the parent have no effect on calculating the subsidiary's apportionable taxable income.

Some states use an alternative approach and ignore the formal corporate structure of a unitary business by treating subsidiaries as if they were divisions or branches of the parent. These states are known as combined reporting states. In them, intercorporate transactions between the parent and the subsidiary are eliminated and the resulting income reported on the books of the subsidiary is added to the income reported on the books of the parent and modified pursuant to state law. Similarly, the apportionment percentage is calculated taking into account the factors of both the parent and the subsidiary.

The majority of states do not require (or impose) a combined report (Pomp and Oldman 1997, 724–32). Yet without a combined report, separate entity states are vulnerable to many orthodox tax planning techniques. First, without combined reporting, corporate tax revenues are linked to the structure of the corporate group. A corporation is likely to pay a different amount of tax if it incorporates a branch or division or liquidates a subsidiary. Indeed, one of the standard simulations a tax planner performs is to determine the tax consequences in separate entity states of corporate restructuring.[23]

Second, without combined reporting, a separate entity state must police transfer prices.[24] In a separate entity state, intercorporate transactions can be used to shift profits from high–effective tax rate states into low–effective tax rate states. For example, consider a parent corporation that manufactures widgets that it sells to its subsidiary. The parent is taxable only in State A, and the subsidiary is taxable only in State B. The income of the parent will be a function of the price at which the inventory was sold to the subsidiary. If State A has a higher effective tax rate than that of State B, the temptation for the corporate group will be to sell the inventory at the lowest defensible price, which would have the effect of shifting profits from the parent to the subsidiary.[25] Computer simulations allow transfer pricing strategies to be implemented for an entire corporate family.

Third, combined reporting states have an advantage over separate entity states in undercutting the use of a holding company to shift profits into other states. One common technique that takes advantage of the lack of combined reporting is the use of a Delaware holding company. Essentially, such a holding company is a Delaware-incorporated corporation whose activities in that state are limited to maintaining and managing intangible assets that generate income, such as capital gains, dividends, interest, and royalties. This income is exempt from Delaware income tax.[26]

One typical use of a Delaware holding company is illustrated by the tax planning strategy of Toys R Us.[27] Toys R Us incorporated a subsidiary in Delaware to which it transferred valuable trademarks and trade names, including the trademark "Toys R Us." The subsidiary executed a license agreement allowing its parent to use the Toys R Us trademark and other trademarks and know-how. In return, the parent paid its subsidiary a royalty, which it deducted in calculating the taxable income it apportioned to the states where it had stores. The desired advantage was to deduct the royalty in calculating apportionable income without paying any state tax on the receipt of the royalty. Indeed, in one year the subsidiary received $55 million of income and paid no taxes to any state.[28]

The licensing of a trademark is only one way of using a Delaware holding company in an attempt to generate a deduction to the payer without subjecting the payee to any tax. Other standard techniques involve loans made by the Delaware corporation to related corporations. The objective is for the payer to deduct the payment of interest in calculating its apportionable tax income while the payee is exempt from taxation by Delaware (or by any other state) on the receipt of the interest. This strategy can be implemented with other types of assets that the holding company can lease to related corporations, such as real and tangible property. Structured properly, funds accumulating in the holding company can be made available to the parent as a loan—generating another round of deductible interest—or, depending on state law, be repatriated as an exempt dividend.

Another strategy is for a corporation to transfer to a holding company stock or bonds that would otherwise generate apportionable business income if held by the transferor; the dividends and interest generated by the transferred assets are tax-free to the holding company instead of generating apportionable business income for the transferor. Any gain on the sale of the stock or bonds would also be tax-free to the holding company.[29]

In a combined reporting state, the (often substantial) income of the holding company would be added to the preapportionment tax base of the taxpayer, and the (often modest) factors of the holding company would be taken into account in calculating the apportionment formula.

A state that does not require related corporations conducting a unitary business to file a combined report is at the mercy of its corporate taxpayers. Transfer pricing, holding companies, and more subtle and less notorious strategies exist for exploiting separate entity states. Once the province of only the most sophisticated practitioners, these tax minimization approaches are now so widespread as to constitute orthodox planning tools.

As if the lack of required combined reporting were not weakness enough, a separate entity state implicitly allows for *elective* combined reporting. This election is not found in the statutes but rather is in the hands (and mind) of the practitioner. That is, a corporate family that wishes to achieve the results of combined reporting can do so by merging certain of its separate entities into other members. The postmerger entity then achieves the same tax result as it would under combined reporting—but the taxpayer chooses when and if to merge and does not have a combined report imposed on it. Obviously, a de facto election that achieves the results of a combined report only adds to the revenue loss that a separate entity state experiences from the use of transfer pricing and holding companies.

It should be borne in mind that corporate restructurings are not casually undertaken, because they involve transaction costs and other legal and business obstacles. The tax savings involved have to be substantial to outweigh these other costs. Accordingly, where tax-induced reorganizations occur, a state can be assured that its loss in revenue from voluntary combined reporting is likely to be significant.[30]

Separate entity states provide taxpayers with the proverbial "Heads I win, tails you lose" option. By controlling the manner in which they report, taxpayers control their tax liability and the state's revenue. And in this situation—which is not the case with respect to other problems in state taxation—the solution of mandatory combined reporting is technically feasible and has already been implemented by a minority of states, including smaller states with limited tax administrations. The obstacle is a political one. Corporate taxpayers typically oppose combined reporting, and legislators do not want to be viewed as anti-business. The loss in corporate tax revenue from the lack of mandatory combined reporting is another example of a self-inflicted wound whose revenue cost is likely to increase over time, as more tax advisers engage in strategies that exploit the weaknesses of separate entity states.

The discussion above has assumed that all of the activities of a corporate enterprise take place in the United States. Suppose, however, that the parent manufactures in State A, a combined reporting state, and sells the manufactured goods to its subsidiary, which is incorporated abroad and conducts all of its activities outside the United States. The reasons that led State A to adopt combined reporting in the domestic setting would seem to be equally persuasive when part of the enterprise conducts its operations abroad. Indeed, in a world where tax havens abound and where transfer pricing can be used to shift profits to exempt offshore corporations, State A might find it logical to use combined reports on a worldwide basis. The alternative is to follow the approach used by the federal government, known as arm's length pricing. This approach is vulnerable to transfer pricing manipulations, and many believe that the IRS does a poor job at controlling abuses.

Worldwide combined reporting has always been controversial. Taxpayers have typically resisted it, citing excessive compliance costs in converting foreign records, accounting concepts, and currencies into state-required formats, especially in situations in which the U.S. taxpayer is owned by a foreign corporation and does not have the right to obtain access to the parent's records. In addition, taxpayers have argued that foreign profit levels, wage rates, and property values cannot be meaningfully combined with their domestic counterparts without resulting in gross distortions. Finally, foreign governments and foreign taxpayers have objected to the use by the states of a computational method that deviates from the arm's length approach used by the United States and other countries.

Despite these objections, a minority of states imposed combined reporting on corporations conducting a unitary business without regard to where the corporations were incorporated or where their activities took place. The Supreme Court upheld this approach in two cases—both involving California, which was then the leading practitioner of worldwide combined reporting.[31] By the time it won the second case, however, California had already abandoned mandatory worldwide combined reporting and made it optional. The retrenchment by California reflected political pressure from the Reagan (presidential) administration (although the implementing legislation was adopted during the Clinton administration), threats by the British to impose retaliatory taxes on U.S.-based companies with U.K. operations, and the fear among California politicians that the state's economic development was being adversely affected by mandatory worldwide combined reporting. And as California went, so did the other states that had required worldwide combined reporting. Even in states that have not followed California in providing an option for worldwide combined reporting, de facto elective combined reporting remains available through corporate restructuring.

Ironically, the states have abandoned worldwide combined reporting as multinational corporations become increasingly common in a shrinking world and cross-national transactions grow in significance, and no reversal seems likely in the short term. International tax lawyers through the years have developed sophisticated schemes for siphoning profits from the United States and squirreling them away in foreign tax havens. The international tax bar has become highly adept at working around the United States' very complicated, highly embroidered anti-tax avoidance rules. Worldwide combined reporting undercuts these efforts. The abandonment by the states of worldwide combined reporting is another self-imposed emasculation of their tax base.[32]

Putting a revenue estimate on the effects of abandoning worldwide combined reporting is difficult. Most of the estimates were done in the 1980s and were controversial.[33] In 1983, the ten states that practiced worldwide combined reporting claimed that it increased their taxes by $500 million to $700 million.[34] Bob Tannenwald of the Federal Reserve Bank estimated that if all states with an income tax practiced worldwide combined reporting, they would increase their tax base by about 13.5 percent compared with domestic combined reporting.[35] In 1996, this estimate would roughly translate into an increase of about $5 billion in taxes.[36]

THE TRANSFORMATION OF BUSINESS INCOME INTO NONBUSINESS INCOME: NOW YOU SEE IT, NOW YOU DON'T

As a matter of constitutional law, a state cannot automatically apportion all of the income of a corporation. A sufficient relationship must exist between the income a state wishes to apportion and the in-state activities of the corporation. The Supreme Court has made it clear that a state can apportion the operational income of a unitary business part of which is conducted in the taxing state, but it cannot apportion the corporation's investment income.[37]

UDITPA is consistent in structure with the Supreme Court's precepts. UDITPA bifurcates a corporation's income into two components: business income and nonbusiness income. These categories seem to parallel the Court's reference in *Allied Signal* to operational income and investment income.

The characterization of income as either business income or nonbusiness income is critical to its treatment. UDITPA apportions business income but allocates nonbusiness income using rules that are best understood as assigning income to the states considered to be the source of such income. Income from intangibles, such as stocks and bonds and patents, copyrights, and other forms of intellectual property, may be properly classified as nonbusiness income in some circumstances, but in other circumstances these categories would constitute business income. States that have not formally adopted UDITPA nonetheless typically follow this general pattern.

One of the orthodox tax planning strategies is to convert income that would clearly be apportionable into income that the taxpayer characterizes as allocable. As a common illustration, suppose the taxpayer is planning to sell part of the assets that it has used in its business and replace them with new assets. Most states would consider the gain on the sale of the old assets to be apportionable business income. Instead, however, suppose the taxpayer transfers the unwanted assets to a newly formed corporation prior to finding a buyer.

After waiting for the stock to become "old and cold," the taxpayer sells the stock to a buyer. Can the taxpayer now report the gain as an allocable capital gain rather than as apportionable business income (Pomp and Oldman 1997, pp. 714–17; Crawford and Uzes 1997)?

This strategy, with a wide number of variations, is commonplace and contributes to the erosion of the tax base. It attempts to exploit weaknesses in a state's definition of business income and is remediable by either legislative or administrative action. The Multistate Tax Commission is currently at work on proposals for updating UDITPA's definition of business income.

CONCLUSION AND PROGNOSIS

Like a dike, the corporate income tax requires constant vigilance, maintenance, and repair. With notable exceptions, many state tax administrations, understaffed and overworked, are not providing that labor. Indeed, many state tax administrations have not even institutionalized any formal training programs for their staffs. Moving instead from crisis to crisis, they tend to climb learning curves more slowly than the private sector and in a less coordinated manner.

Most of the fingers in the dike have come from the Multistate Tax Commission, with its various ongoing and ad hoc projects to modernize the tax. The MTC, however, has a small budget and staff; its effectiveness is attributed to the talents, fortitude, and expertise of its staff and its reputation for excellence. The MTC has the power of persuasion, however, but not the political power necessary for forging a broad political consensus. Without state legislatures willing to excavate the foundation of the tax, patchwork repairs, even by the skilled craftsmen and architects of the MTC, can only plug leaks in the base, not stop hemorrhaging through major cracks.

The problems identified in this chapter are remediable by the states—at least in theory. Combined reporting can be adopted, tax incentives curtailed, and the definition of business income broadened to its constitutional limits. But the current legislative atmosphere, which discourages any reforms that might be perceived as anti-business, makes such remedies seem unlikely of adoption, at least in the short term.

While the politics of tax reform differs from state to state (or, as Tip O'Neill said, "All politics is local"), the country is in an anti-tax mood, and legislators are concerned about appearing pro-business.

Any serious reform of a state's corporate income tax will increase the tax on some groups even if the overall revenue effects are neutral—so a legislature is in the hopeless position politically of being able to reform a tax only if there are only winners, whose taxes go down, but no losers, whose taxes go up.

If only we had known at the beginning of this century what we know now, perhaps the states would never have taken on the administration of a corporate income tax. Imagine that in 1909, when Congress adopted the federal income tax, it had added a few points to the rate and dedicated that revenue to a trust fund for the states. True, there would have been the inevitable fighting about how the revenue should be distributed, but if more revenue were in the pot than the states raise today, each state might be better off regardless of how that debate had been resolved.

Moreover, if the states had a few points of the federal tax explicitly dedicated for their use, they might have become a potent force on the side of reform. At the least, they might have prevented legislation such as the 1981 tax act, which virtually eliminated the federal corporate income tax through generous rules on accelerated depreciation and safe harbor leasing.

Such an approach has missed its day; if anything, Congress may eliminate the federal corporate tax altogether and, by implication, the state tax as well. Congress's current fixation with consumption-based taxes has resulted in various proposals for replacing the federal corporate income tax. Should any of these proposals pass, it would be nearly impossible for the states to continue administering their own corporate income tax. State officials and their representatives view this possibility with dread and horror. But if the states could exact a sufficient quid pro quo from Congress, the net result might not be the end of state sovereignty or of fiscal federalism.

In the meantime, competition among the states for economic development and jobs is likely to stymie serious attempts at reform and will continue to undermine the corporate tax. Ironically, the autonomy that the states have to control their state revenue structures has undermined their sovereign powers of taxation as they race to the bottom.

In principle, Congress could rescue the states by limiting their freedom to use various tax incentives, or by requiring more uniformity in the state corporate income tax. Neither the states nor Congress has shown any interest, however, in such federal intervention. UDITPA is long overdue for revision, but no group has it on their agenda. Short of anything sweeping, the most realistic prognosis for the corporate income tax is that the states will continue to muddle through, at least in the short term, with self-imposed constraints that will keep the tax a minor player while it absorbs a disproportionate amount of intellectual capital in both the public and private sectors.

Notes

Author's Note: I am fortunate to have had an earlier draft closely read by Michael J. McIntyre and Paull Mines. I am lucky to have any ego left. Despite my stubbornness and blind spots, I have responded to most of their comments.

1. The term "corporate income tax" includes any tax that is levied on or measured by net income.

2. See Advisory Commission on Intergovernmental Relations, table 55. The 7 percent average masks wide variations. The figure varies from year to year, but is currently near a historical low. See table 32 in above reference.

3. These observations have implications far beyond a loss in revenue; they have severe equity implications as well. The benefits of tax incentives are highly concentrated among the largest corporations: Two corporations received 40 percent of the benefits of New York's investment and employment incentive tax credits. (See Pomp 1987, 629–39). Similarly, sophisticated tax planning techniques are disproportionately used by the larger, multistate corporations. In most states, the lion's share of the corporate income tax (80–85 percent) is paid by a relatively small number (15–20 percent) of large, multistate corporations. Accordingly, any tax benefits or tax planning techniques concentrated among the larger corporations will have a profound effect on revenue.

4. For background information, see New York State Legislative Commission on the Modernization and Simplification of Tax Administration and the Tax Law, 1984.

5. These incentives are not limited to reductions in the corporate income tax.

6. See Pomp (1987), 393–409, 647–61, and 577–84, Enrich (1996), "Saving the States from Themselves," 382–405, and the voluminous references cited therein. In a nutshell, the corporate income tax is too small an amount compared with a taxpayer's other costs to be significant in making locational decisions.

7. Enrich (1996), 392 and 387, n. 50. At the least, those who advocate using the state corporate income tax to influence business locational decisions, a position that is seemingly inconsistent with an overwhelming body of research, should have the burden of proof of supporting their position with rigorous cost-benefit analyses—rather than with self-serving anecdotes, as is usually the case.

8. For a fuller discussion of the politics of state tax incentives, see Pomp (1987) and Enrich (1996).

9. Enrich provides a blueprint for suits by ordinary citizens and taxpayers challenging their state's use of tax incentives and for suits by one state wishing to challenge the incentives used by another state. For approaches to developing a conceptual framework for distinguishing between constitutional and unconstitutional incentives, see Enrich (1996), and Walter Hellerstein and Dan T. Coenen, 1996, p. 789.

10. As long as businesses can be neatly pigeonholed into categories so that competitors are subject to the same formula, the goal of uniformity is furthered. Today, however, the

traditional boundaries among industries are dissolving, and it is increasingly difficult to categorize taxpayers for purposes of applying the appropriate specialized formula.

11. These states are Arizona, Arkansas, California, Connecticut, Florida, Georgia, Idaho, Illinois, Kentucky, Maine, Maryland, Massachusetts, Mississippi, New Hampshire, New Jersey, New Mexico, New York, North Carolina, Ohio, Oregon, Pennsylvania, South Carolina, West Virginia, and Wisconsin. Other states may weight the sales factor even more heavily (e.g., Minnesota) or use only a sales factor (e.g., Iowa or Nebraska). The single sales factor approach is discussed in the text.

12. Double-weighting can be defended on the grounds that the production states and the market states ought to share equally in the income generated on sales. For example, a corporation that has all of its property and payroll in one state and sells entirely in another will apportion half of its income to each of the two states under double-weighting, which is a defensible normative result and one that has been adopted by the federal income tax. (See Treas. Reg. sec. 1.863-3T [b] [2] [Ex. 2].) Double-weighting, however, is rarely defended on these grounds, and the payroll and property factors are less commonly used by states as tools of economic development. New York excludes from the payroll factor the compensation of general executive officers (NY Tax Law sec. 210 [3] [a] [3]). Those supporting this version of the payroll factor would cite as evidence of its effectiveness the large number of corporate headquarters in New York. More likely, the exclusion of compensation of general executive officers was enacted in response to the lobbying efforts of those already located in New York, albeit packaged in the usual economic development rhetoric.

13. See note 17.

14. Mathematically, a single-factor sales formula can be viewed as a three-factor formula with the sales factor given an infinite weighting.

15. Massachusetts's recent change was made in response to blatant threats by Raytheon, a major Massachusetts employer, to leave the state. The change eliminated three-fourths of Raytheon's Massachusetts corporate income tax. See Enrich, 1995. As this article goes to press, the governor of Illinois has a bill before him calling for a single-factor formula, which is understood to greatly benefit Caterpillar and John Deere. Based on a study funded by the Illinois Manufacturers' Association, supporters assert that adoption of a single-factor formula will create 285,000 new jobs and raise $200 million in additional tax revenue. This estimate is based on the growth in jobs in states that double-weighted their sales factors, without determining whether double-weighting caused that growth.

This type of analysis underscores the need for legislators to be aware of the difference between correlation and causality. It has been suggested that before signing the bill, the Illinois governor "may well ask why there has not been investment growth of this magnitude in Iowa and Nebraska . . ." (Brunori, 1997, p. 1507). The governor might also note that the Illinois Department of Revenue's estimate, which did not take into account any feedback effects, predicted a loss of $46 million. (Ibid.) The bill also calls for eliminating the existing throwback rule. (See text below, p. 00.) It is unclear whether this revenue estimate is only for the shift to a single-factor formula or whether it also includes eliminating the throwback rule.

16. Iowa's single-factor formula was upheld in *Moorman v. Bair*, 437 U.S. 267 (1978).

17. The interaction of Public Law 86-272 and double-weighting can actually discourage an out-of-state corporation from expanding in a state. For example, suppose a corporation ships goods from a state without a throwback rule to customers in State B. Assume the corporation is not taxable by State B because of Public Law 86-272, and that over time its sales in B become substantial. Because State B has become a significant market, the corporation might consider opening an office there. If the corporation opens an office, however, it will lose the protection of Public Law 86-272. And the tax

cost of opening an office will be greater under a double-weighted sales factor (and even greater under a single sales factor) than it would be under an evenly weighted three-factor formula. So if state taxes are assumed to affect locational decisions, a shift in the apportionment formula could actually *discourage* the corporation's expansion.

18. Some of the early apportionment formulas consisted of only a property factor. See, e.g., *Underwood Typewriter Co. v. Chamberlain*, 254 U.S. 13 (1920); *Bass, Ratcliff & Gretton, Limited v. State Tax Commission*, 266 U.S. 271 (1924); *Hans Rees' Sons, Inc. v. North Carolina ex Rel. Maxwell*, 283 U.S. 123 (1931). Other states used both property and payroll. Apparently, states were more concerned then about taxing manufacturing activities than about disincentive effects. The shift to double-weighting and to a single-factor sales formula reflects exactly the opposite concern.

19. Tax expenditure budgets sometimes list the revenue loss from provisions like double-weighting. For a pessimistic view that tax expenditure budgets have not fulfilled the hopes of their supporters, see Pomp, 1993, p. 337.

20. This estimate is based on telephone conversations with revenue analysts in all the states whose apportionment formulas deviate from the evenly weighted three-factor formula. In states in which a deviation is being phased in, the estimate is for the year of full phase-in. The estimates are for the most recent year available which differs from state to state. Nearly all states estimated a revenue loss. A few states estimated that the deviation was revenue-neutral, and a few estimated a small increase in revenue.

21. This section borrows heavily from Pomp and Oldman (1997), pp. 724–32.

22. Sometimes these states are improperly called nonunitary states. This label is misleading, because these states apply formulary apportionment to the business income of a unitary business.

23. This restructuring can usually be accomplished without the payment of federal income taxes because of federal nonrecognition provisions. State law usually conforms with federal law, so that there is no state income tax payable on the restructuring.

24. For a recent survey of the power of state tax administrations to adjust transfer prices and their practices in this regard, see Mary Jane Egr, 1996, p. 1547.

25. Although the example in the text involves the sale of tangible personal property, the same shifting of profits can occur using management fees, consulting fees, royalty payments, interest charges, or payments for goodwill or know-how.

26. Because the use of a Delaware holding company has become so commonplace and is tantamount to waving a red flag in front of an auditor, tax planners have started to use less visible techniques to achieve the same goal.

27. See *Geoffrey, Inc. v. South Carolina*, 437 S.E.2d 13, cert. denied, 114 S. Ct. 550 (1993). For ease of presentation, the facts in the case have been slightly simplified.

28. Ibid. at 13 n. 1.

29. The creation and operation of Delaware holding companies has become a specialty of certain Wilmington-based banks. A pamphlet issued by one of these banks promises to arrange for the rental of office space, a telephone answering service, secretarial help, and accounting and legal services from Delaware's top accounting and legal firms. "By developing relationships with these Delaware professionals, the substance of your Delaware holding company will be further reinforced."

30. With the advent of new forms of pass-through entities and "check the box" regulations, the benefits of a merger may be achieved without the need for an actual corporate restructuring.

31. *Container Corp. v. Franchise Tax Board*, 463 U.S. 159 (1983); *Barclays Bank PLC v. Franchise Tax Board*, 114 S. Ct. 2268 (1994).

32. Worldwide combined reporting is revenue-neutral in principle. After California abandoned its mandatory rules, many corporations elected to file on a worldwide basis. Many of these corporations are based in the United Kingdom, which has been one of the most antagonistic critics of combined reporting.

33. See Norman E. Rusch and J. Lloyd Kennedy, "State Revenues That Would Be Lost by Prohibiting Worldwide Unitary Taxation," *Tax Notes*, December 19, 1983; Norman E. Rusch and J. Lloyd Kennedy, "Once Again, We Question the Alleged Revenue Effects of Restricting Use of the Worldwide Unitary Tax," *Tax Notes*, February 20, 1984; James C. Rosapepe and Gerald H. Goldberg, "The Revenue Effects of the Unitary Method: Two Responses to Shell's Views," *Tax Notes*, January 9, 1984.

34. See Robert Tannenwald, "The Pros and Cons of Worldwide Unitary Taxation," *New England Economic Review*, July/August 1984, reprinted in 25 *Tax Notes* 649 (1984) and in *The Unitary Tax Controversy* (edited by Charles Davenport, 1988) Tax Analysts, Arlington, Va.

35. Ibid. The estimates are based on 1977 data.

36. Not all states practice domestic combined reporting, so the increase would probably be even larger. No good data exist on the revenue effects of domestic combined reporting compared with separate entity reporting.

37. *Allied Signal, Inc. v. New Jersey,* 504 U.S. 768 (1992).

References

Advisory Commission on Intergovernmental Relations. "Significant Features of Fiscal Federalism 1994." Volume 2. Table 55.

Ibid. Table 32.

Brunori, David. 1997. "Behind the Curve: State and Local Taxation in U.S. Law Schools." *State Tax Notes* (May 5).

———. 1997. "Principles of State Tax Policy and Targeted Tax Incentives." *State Tax Notes* (June 9).

Crawford, Ray E., and Russel D. Uzes. 1997. *T. M. Incomes Taxes: The Distinction Between Businesses and Nonbusiness Income*, 1140.

Egr, Mary Jane. 1996. "State Section-482 Type Authority." *State Tax Notes* 11: 1547.

Enrich, Peter D. 1996. "Saving the States from Themselves: Commerce Clause Constraints on State Tax Incentives for Business." *Harvard Law Rev.* 378: 382–405.

———. 1995. "Tax Bill Makes Bad Business Sense." *Boston Globe.* (Oct. 19).

Hellerstein, Walter, and Dan T. Coenen. 1996. "Commerce Clause Restraints of State Business Development Incentives." *Cornell Law Rev.* 81: 789.

New York State Legislative Commission on the Modernization and Simplification of Tax Administration and the Tax Law. 1984. *The Article 9-A Franchise Tax: Should New York Adopt ACRS?*

Pomp, Richard D. 1993. "Rethinking State Tax Expenditure Budgets." *J. of Public Budgeting and Financial Management* 5: 337.

———. 1987. "Reforming a Corporate Income Tax." *Albany Law Rev.* 51: 393–409, 577–84, 629–639, 647–61.

Pomp, Richard D., and Oliver Oldman. 1997. *State and Local Taxation.* 2nd ed. pp. 701–2, 709–11, 714–17, 724–32. Hartford, Conn.

Rosapepe, James C., and Gerald H. Goldberg. 1984. "The Revenue Effects of the Unitary Method: Two Responses to Shell's Views." *Tax Notes* (January 9).

Rusch, Norman E., and J. Lloyd Kennedy. 1983. "State Revenues That Would Be Lost by Prohibiting Worldwide Unitary Taxation," *Tax Notes* (December 19).

———. 1984. "Once Again, We Question the Alleged Revenue Effects of Restricting Use of the Worldwide Unitary Tax," *Tax Notes* (February 20).

Simafranca, Ryan. 1995. "The Double-Weighted Sales Formula—A Plague on Interstate Commerce." *State Tax Notes* 9: 1685, 1690.

Tannenwald, Robert. 1984. "The Pros and Cons of Worldwide Unitary Taxation." *New England Economic Review* (July/August), reprinted in *Tax Notes* 25: 649, 1984, and in *The Unitary Tax Controversy,* edited by Charles Davenport, 1988.

Chapter Five

THE RISE—AND PERHAPS THE FALL— OF BUSINESS TAX INCENTIVES

Peter D. Enrich

Among the most prominent features of state tax policy in recent years has been the proliferation of tax provisions designed to improve the states' business climates and to enhance their ability to attract and retain business investment and the associated jobs. The expanding use of state tax provisions as weapons in the interstate battle to attract economic development poses serious threats both to the integrity of the states' fiscal systems and to the smooth functioning of the national economy. Nonetheless, the powerful political dynamics behind the interstate competition for business suggest that the proliferation of business tax incentives is likely to continue unabated into the next century. The only direction from which I can foresee a substantial possibility of relief from this trend is the Constitution's Commerce Clause, which the Supreme Court has consistently construed as prohibiting state measures that interfere with the free functioning of the national economy—in particular, state tax provisions that discriminate in favor of in-state activities.

States in recent years have shown extraordinary initiative and ingenuity in crafting tax policies designed to influence business decisions about where to site their manufacturing plants, their offices, their warehouses, and their research and development facilities (Wilson 1989; LeRoy 1994). During a recent two-year period, I counted at least thirty-three states that had either enacted or significantly expanded one or more tax incentives with respect to business location. Provisions allowing investment tax credits, selective abatements of property taxes, and credits for targeted expansions of employment are nearly ubiquitous (Chi 1989; Spindler 1994). Incentive packages measured in the hundreds of millions of dollars have become increasingly commonplace in the competition for major industrial facilities. And the trend toward creation of special tax incentives for businesses locating in targeted economic development (or enterprise) zones recently culminated in Michigan's authorization of completely tax-free "renaissance zones."

In addition to the continuing expansion of these familiar categories of tax policies, several significant new trends are evident. A number of states have recently moved beyond incentives aimed directly at businesses, adding incentives for the investors who provide them their capital by providing preferential taxation of funds invested in in-state enterprises. Additionally, states are increasingly crafting incentives that are narrowly focused on particular business sectors—such as aerospace or financial services—that are especially likely to sell their products out of state, thus bringing net revenue into the state economy. Several have specifically restricted certain incentives to businesses that make a specified share of their sales out of state.

One particularly significant trend is the increasing adoption of income tax apportionment methodologies that emphasize the location of a businesses's sales, rather than the location of its property or personnel, in determining the share of the businesses's total income that is subject to the state's income tax. Several states have recently replaced the customary three-factor approach with apportionment rules allocating income exclusively on the basis of where the company's products or services are sold, and a number of others have increased the weight they assign to the sales factor (Simafranca 1995). The effect of these sales-based apportionment rules is to dramatically reduce tax burdens on in-state businesses that sell substantial proportions of their products outside the state, thus providing significant tax incentives for businesses with multi-state customer bases to locate their plant and payroll in the state. While such modifications to income apportionment rules are easily dismissed as technical adjustments, they in fact can substantially affect the tax implications of a multi-state business's decision as to where to locate new property and personnel and, in particular, can create opportunities to shelter significant portions of its income from state taxation by locating in a state with favorable apportionment rules.

A central objective behind all of these policies is to influence business location decisions in favor of the local economy. And a standard argument for their adoption contends that the revenues forgone on account of such tax breaks will be more than recouped by means of the expanded economic activity attracted by the incentives. In reality, however, the effects of these policies are far less benign. The economic benefits that they purport to generate are highly questionable, and the costs they entail, with respect to both state revenues and the national economy, are quite substantial.

Whether state tax policies significantly influence business decisions about where to locate remains the subject of heated debate among the economists who study such issues. One school detects in the numerous statistical analyses a definite, if modest and variable, tendency of lowered tax burdens to generate increased economic activity (Bartik 1991; Papke and Papke 1986). But others conclude from the same evidence that no stable, significant correlation between tax burdens and levels of economic activity has been established (Tannenwald 1996; Carroll and Wasylenko 1994; Lynch 1996). There is general agreement only that state and local taxes are far less significant as determinants of business location decisions than a range of other factors with much larger effects on businesses' bottom lines— factors such as labor costs and skill levels or ready access to inputs and markets (Moore et al. 1991; Schmenner 1982). At most, state taxes will play a role in business decisions only when such other factors are essentially in equipoise.

Even the businesses that are the beneficiaries of state tax breaks repeatedly acknowledge, after the fact, that their location decisions were not guided by the available incentives. Nonetheless, business decision-makers have come to expect governmental concessions as routine fringe benefits of their siting decisions, and they have become increasingly adept at playing the states off against each other in the competition for their investments. Moreover, many state tax breaks are formulated in ways that make them available to an indefinite number of in-state businesses, inevitably including many that were never considering an out-of-state location. Thus, much of the lost revenue from state tax incentives unquestionably reaps no benefit at all in the form of attracted or retained business activity.

Even to the extent that tax breaks do have the capacity to influence businesses' location decisions, their cumulative effects remain deeply problematic. At best, state and local incentives influence only the location of business activity, not its overall level. The jobs and investment that one state attracts would otherwise have located somewhere else. Leaving aside the possibility of some minimal effects on international location decisions, the interstate competition over business incentives is, thus, a zero-sum game, in which one state's gain is another's loss. And even from the perspective of the states that are winners in this game, any gains are likely to be short-lived, because of the accelerating tendency of the states to imitate one another's initiatives, thereby robbing them of any transitory drawing power they may exert.

The only sure winners in this process are the mobile interstate businesses, which are able to benefit from tax concessions virtually wherever they choose to locate and are able to use the interstate competition to lobby states for ever deeper reductions in their tax burdens. The states, faced with the prospect of losing jobs and investment to their more aggressive neighbors, find themselves caught in a vicious cycle of expanding tax breaks for these footloose businesses, a "race to the bottom" that is significantly reducing the proportion of state and local revenues derived from businesses. The ultimate losers are the states' citizens, who are left either with increased tax burdens to offset the breaks granted to businesses or with reduced governmental services.

The interstate competition over business incentives also impairs the efficiency of the *national* economy. If tax incentives achieve their intended effect of influencing business location decisions, that means that businesses are locating their facilities in places that would otherwise not have been economically optimal—places where nontax costs are higher or where nontax advantages are sacrificed. The whole purpose of business tax incentives is to encourage businesses to make choices that would otherwise not be economically rational—that is, to divert resources from their most efficient deployment.

These "first-order" economic distortions can easily be overstated. In fact, to the extent that the states are actively imitating and competing with one another over tax incentives, tax considerations are not likely to be a major factor influencing (or distorting) the location of business investment. But as the interstate competition intensifies, and as states become increasingly skilled in targeting their tax relief exclusively to the most mobile segments of the business universe, significant "second-order" economic distortions become increasingly likely. The cumulative effect of targeted tax breaks will be a substantially lower rate of taxation on investment in highly mobile business sectors, compared with the rate of taxation on other, less mobile sectors. This differential will produce a disproportionately high rate of (after-tax) return on investment in the tax-favored sectors, which will have the effect of diverting capital into these sectors even when that capital could more efficiently be invested elsewhere in the economy.

In short, if the trend of recent years continues and the states continue to vie with one another to offer increasingly generous tax breaks to lure mobile business investment, the consequences are clear. The overall level of business activity will be unaffected, and even its geographical distribution will not be substantially influenced. The tax burdens borne by mobile business sectors will continue to decline, offset by reductions in public services or by increases in others' taxes. Investment decisions will respond to increasingly distorted state tax structures, and both governments and businesses will devote increasing energies and resources to the elaboration and manipulation of an unproductive web of devices whose sole purpose is the displacement of tax-neutral business location decisions.

Faced with these bleak prospects, can we anticipate that state policy-makers will turn away from this losing battle and direct their economic development efforts into other channels? While growing numbers of state legislators and governors have begun to acknowledge the problematic character of the incentives competition, powerful political pressures make its continuation almost inevitable. Notwithstanding the strong performance of economic indicators over recent years, voters remain deeply anxious about their financial security, and they expect state and local governments to place a high priority on economic development and jobs. In this environment, it is very hard for a political leader to oppose highly visible measures that vocal business representatives (and the postulates of supply-side economics) assert will improve the state's "business climate" and help to attract or retain jobs.

In fact, state leaders find themselves in a classic prisoner's dilemma. Each state would be better off in a world where none of the states offered incentives to businesses than in a world where all of them did. But in the absence of a way to ensure that its competitor states would join it in abstaining from the incentives game, the most prudent strategy for each state is to compete as aggressively as it can, even though the foreseeable, ultimate result is less than optimal for all of them.

This calculus is not significantly changed for most decision-makers by the absence of empirical confirmation that tax incentives have a substantial impact on business location decisions. For elected officials, appearances are often as important as reality, and regardless of the actual cause of any subsequent economic gains, the leaders responsible for enactment of an incentive are in a position to take credit for them, whereas those who prevent or eliminate a pro-business policy are apt to bear the political liability of any subsequent job losses. Even if the likelihood of a positive impact is recognized to be slim, the potential political benefits of supporting business incentives, compounded by the risks of opposing them, are typically compelling.

In political terms, tax breaks offer a particularly attractive vehicle with which to offer location incentives to businesses. For the affected businesses, they offer very direct, easily quantified monetary benefits, benefits that typically take the form of guaranteed entitlements for qualifying businesses and that, unlike direct governmental expenditures, are not subject to annual appropriation and legislative scrutiny. At the same time, the costs of a tax break are typically ill-defined and diffuse. No one directly pays for the incentive; rather, its impact appears only in the form of reductions in governmental revenues, reductions whose magnitudes are often not precisely quantified and whose consequences are rarely discussed. The costs of tax breaks are commonly spread out over a number of years, and their ultimate effects, whether in the form of service reductions or increases in other taxes, cannot be directly attributed to a particular incentive policy. Moreover, advocates of tax breaks commonly minimize their costs by arguing that they merely reduce revenues that, without the incentive, would never have been received in the first place—or that their costs will be offset by other taxes on the economic activity they stimulate, arguments that are notoriously impervious to empirical refutation or proof. With such vocal beneficiaries and such diffuse costs, the political appeal of tax incentives is nearly irresistible.

In light of these dynamics, it is easy to predict that the interstate tax competition for business, the proliferation of business tax breaks, and the decline of tax burdens on mobile businesses will all continue to accelerate. Are there any countervailing forces that may reverse or mitigate this movement toward the increasing balkanization of state business taxation?

Perhaps, if governmental policy-making were actually guided by economic analysis, the competition would come to a natural halt when an equilibrium point was reached, at which the costs to government of attracting additional business outweighed the benefits. Economic activity inevitably carries attendant social costs, and economic theorists have observed that it will be rational for states to reduce taxes on mobile capital only to the point at which the remaining tax burden matches the social costs incurred in consequence of local deployment of that capital (Oates and Schwab 1988; McClure 1986). Beyond that point, additional tax breaks would be counterproductive for the state and its citizens.

This notion that the "invisible hand" might regulate the supply of business tax incentives offers little practical comfort, however. For better or for worse, the elected officials who set tax policy are not likely to behave in conformity with the theorems of economic analysis. They are unlikely to have solid information about the full range of costs and benefits that flow from a particular level of economic activity, and are commonly far more cognizant of the potential benefits (which the beneficiaries of a proposed tax break will be sure to highlight) than of the costs (which will typically be widely dispersed, in the form of increased burdens on infrastructure, marginally inflated costs of labor and resources for other businesses, and the like). Even if they had full information, the decision-makers' ultimate calculus is political, not economic, and hence will accentuate the vivid benefits while discounting the politically ephemeral costs. So any equilibrium is likely to be reached only at a point at which real costs far exceed real benefits. In fact, my guess is that many political leaders would conclude, with little hesitation, that the public benefits of new (or retained) business activity are consistently greater than its costs, and would therefore be prepared to eliminate taxation of such activity entirely (and even grant positive subsidies), if that were the price for bringing (or keeping) it in the state.

A more realistic prospect for reining in the incentives competition comes from the increasing efforts in a number of states to design "smarter" tax breaks, which target tax relief more precisely to situations in which it may achieve identifiable economic benefits (Gilbert 1995). Not only have many recent measures focused on specific types of businesses, but a number expressly restrict their benefits to companies that guarantee specified levels of job growth or job quality, and some require a case-by-case finding that the incentive is necessary for the business to choose to locate in the state. Detailed reporting requirements have become relatively commonplace. And, with increasing frequency, tax break legislation incorporates "claw-back" provisions, which terminate—and, in some cases, recoup—benefits provided to companies that fail to live up to commitments they made as conditions for receipt of the benefit.

While these "accountability" measures may mitigate some of the most flagrant problems in the incentives competition, I doubt that they will make a dramatic difference. In fact, more careful targeting of tax breaks may increase, not diminish, the economic distortions produced by disparities in the taxation of competing businesses and alternative investments. Moreover, to the extent that accountability measures increase policy-maker confidence in the efficacy of incentive policies, the growing popularity of such constraints may actually serve to accelerate the adoption of additional location incentives. Many of the apparently most stringent provisions, such as claw-backs, on closer scrutiny reveal niceties of drafting that allow considerable flexibility for recipients, and it is still too early to judge whether states will have the stomach to enforce punitive measures on delinquent companies, who will commonly be able to attribute their delinquencies to unanticipated economic misfortunes that cry out (or so they will argue) for additional assistance, not for penalties. Perhaps the most we can hope from these measures is that, over time, they will shed increasing light on the real costs and benefits that flow from business tax breaks.

Another possible source of restraint is cooperative action among the competing states. The standard solution to any prisoner's dilemma is an agreement between the parties to forgo the choices that end up injuring one another. With growing recognition of the zero-sum character of the interstate tax competition, a number of state leaders have proposed truces among neighboring states, and the National Governors Association in 1993 adopted a resolution encouraging the states to mutually withstand the pressures to engage in bidding wars. Such commitments, however, are legally unenforceable, and the track record to date suggests that they are exceedingly fragile and quickly succumb to competitive opportunities and mutual suspicions.

Congress, by contrast, would have the authority, acting under its Commerce Clause powers, to impose enforceable restraints on interstate tax competition. Several authors have recently suggested that this would be an appropriate and desirable role for the federal government to take on (Burstein and Rolnick 1995; Shaviro 1992; Rivlin 1992). On a number of previous occasions, Congress has stepped in to regulate state taxation of interstate activity, but in each case it has acted to shelter businesses or individuals from problematic state taxation, not to limit state actions favoring preferred businesses. In a period when congressional rhetoric emphasizes devolution and states' rights, it is hard to imagine Congress acting to restrict state powers over the sovereign function of taxation in a manner that most large businesses and many states would actively oppose.

I frankly see little prospect of legislative restraint, whether from the states or from Congress, with respect to the proliferation of competing business tax incentives. If meaningful limits are to be placed on the incentives competition, they will have to come from a different direction. In my view, the most plausible place to look for such relief is the courts, enforcing the Commerce Clause's prohibition on state measures that interfere with the free flow of economic activity within our national common market. To date there have been but a handful of cases in which the Commerce Clause has been invoked to invalidate business location incentives (*Pelican Chapter v. Edwards* 1995; *R. J. Reynolds Tobacco Co. v. City of N.Y.* 1995; *Beatrice Cheese v. Wisconsin Department of Revenue* 1993), but such a use of the Commerce Clause is very much in keeping with its historical function. As the Supreme Court has observed, the Commerce Clause "reflected a central concern of the Framers that was an immediate reason for calling the Constitutional Convention: the conviction that in order to succeed, the new Union would have to avoid the tendencies toward economic Balkanization that had plagued relations among the Colonies and later among the States under the Articles of Confederation" (*Hughes* v. *Oklahoma* 1979, p. 325). The clause was directed against "the mutual jealousies and aggressions of the States, taking form in customs barriers and other economic retaliation" (*Baldwin* v. *G. A. F. Seelig* 1935, p. 522), and "the very purpose of the Commerce Clause was to create an area of free trade among the several states" (*Boston Stock Exchange* v. *State Tax Commission* 1977, p. 328). In short, the vicious cycle of competition over business tax breaks in which the states currently find themselves caught is simply the latest incarnation of the destructive internecine economic struggles against which the Commerce Clause was directed.

As I (Enrich 1996) and others (Hellerstein and Coenen 1996) have described in more detail elsewhere, there is a substantial body of Supreme Court precedent invalidating a wide array of state tax provisions that favor in-state businesses or economic activities over their out-of-state rivals. Repeatedly and consistently, the Court has held that tax incentives that are restricted to transactions or businesses located in the state, and that thereby result in a comparatively heavier tax burden on interstate transactions or on out-of-state businesses, impermissibly discriminate against interstate commerce and are unconstitutional. Among typical provisions the Court has struck down were a New York provision granting income tax credits based on the share of a business's exports that were shipped from a New York site (*Westinghouse Electric Corp.* v. *Tully* 1984), an Ohio provision authorizing a fuel tax credit for ethanol only if it was produced in Ohio or in a state offering reciprocal credits to Ohio producers (*New Energy Corp.* v. *Linbach* 1988), and a Massachusetts provision imposing a levy on milk sold in the state but granting a rebate exclusively to in-state dairies (*West Lynn Creamery* v. *Healy* 1994).

In most of the Court's existing case law, the focus has been on provisions protecting local businesses from interstate competitors, not on provisions encouraging interstate businesses to locate in the taxing state rather than outside of it. But the two sorts of provisions closely resemble one another and at times are indistinguishable. After all, any tax break that favors insiders thereby provides an incentive for others to *become* insiders as well.

In any case, the Commerce Clause's anti-discrimination principles, which the Court has developed in these precedents, appear straightforwardly applicable to measures designed to attract business investment. The central teaching of the case law is that a tax measure discriminates against interstate commerce if it serves to give local commerce, local products, or local activities an advantage over their out-of-state or interstate substitutes. Discrimination is to be recognized by a practically oriented analysis of a provision's purposes and effects. If a measure has the effect of foreclosing tax-neutral decisions about where to do business, if it "exerts an inexorable hydraulic pressure" favoring in-state activity (*American Trucking Associations* v. *Scheiner* 1987, p. 286), then it is discriminatory. Moreover, if a tax provision "facially discriminates"—that is to say, if it expressly provides for preferential treatment of in-state activity—then it is, in the Court's often repeated phrase, "virtually per se invalid" (*Fulton Corp.* v. *Faulkner* 1996, p. 854).

In light of these Commerce Clause principles, a wide range of familiar location incentives are almost certainly unconstitutional. Investment tax credits and targeted jobs credits, which reduce state income tax liabilities on the basis of new investment or employment in the state, offer clear examples. These provisions will sharply differentiate the tax burdens of two similarly situated companies, one of which decides to locate a new facility in the credit-granting state while the other decides to locate elsewhere. The evident purpose of such provisions is to provide an incentive or reward to companies choosing to locate in-state, and the evident effect (to the extent that such provisions have real effects on business decisions) is to tilt corporate location decisions in favor of the state offering the credits. This is precisely the discrimination that the Court's prior cases have condemned. In addition, these credit provisions routinely include express statutory language restricting the credits to investments or jobs located in the granting state and thus fall prey to the rule of "virtual per se invalidity" for facially discriminatory measures.

Similar constitutional problems will attend provisions offering preferential capital gains taxation for investments in in-state companies, and likewise a host of other measures that condition tax relief (whether in the form of property tax abatements, sales tax exemptions, or preferential income apportionment rules) on mandated levels of in-state economic activity. The constitutional flaw afflicting this set of examples is not that they discriminate between in-state and out-of-state taxpayers, but rather that they discriminate among local taxpayers based on their decisions about where to deploy their resources. The ultimate effects, however, are the same: Taxpayers' economic choices are distorted in favor of the taxing state, and those who engage in interstate activity are disfavored relative to those who confine their investments within the state's borders. Again, such measures are typically facially discriminatory. And they also will typically fail the Supreme Court's "internal consistency" test (*Oklahoma Tax Commission v. Jefferson Lines* 1995), which invalidates any tax measure that, even if universally adopted by all the states, would nonetheless impose distinctive burdens on taxpayers engaging in interstate economic activity.

In each case, the fundamental constitutional problem is the same. The central purpose and effect of all these tax provisions is to make in-state business activity more economically attractive than out-of-state alternatives, and each achieves this end by granting preferential tax treatment to local activity. But such preferences discriminate against interstate commerce and establish precisely the obstacles to an open national economy against which the Commerce Clause has consistently been deployed. Under this analysis, a wide range of the state tax incentives used to attract business investment could not survive constitutional scrutiny.

The only reason that the constitutional infirmity of these characteristic location incentives has not been more widely recognized is that, to date, virtually no one has brought Commerce Clause challenges against them to the courts. The bulk of past Commerce Clause tax cases have been initiated by large multi-state businesses challenging protectionist measures that place them at a competitive disadvantage. But these companies are typically not similarly disadvantaged by location incentives. In fact, they are usually the primary beneficiaries of such measures. And when a multi-state company is ineligible for a particular tax break and is thereby disadvantaged, that same company is likely the beneficiary of comparable location incentives in other states and is apt to be very cautious about slaying the goose that is laying its golden eggs.

As we saw earlier, the real costs of the proliferation of business tax breaks, though substantial, are very diffuse and often unnoticed by the citizens, taxpayers, and businesses who pay them in the form of interstate friction, economic inefficiency, and reduced governmental resources. As a result, with rare exceptions, no one has stepped forward to bring Commerce Clause challenges to these measures.

As the incentives competition persists and intensifies, however, constitutional challenges may come from any of a number of directions. With the continuing proliferation and specialization of location incentives, the likelihood increases that particular businesses (perhaps smaller businesses with limited interstate activities and options) will be sufficiently aggrieved by the competitive advantages granted their rivals that they will take up the attack. Similarly, with growing public awareness of the impacts of incentives competition, citizen advocacy groups or public employee unions may decide to take up the cause. While such groups will face significant procedural hurdles in some jurisdictions, in the form of narrow criteria for standing to challenge tax provisions, many states' courts have relatively permissive standards with regard to suits brought by concerned citizens and taxpayers. Finally, as state policy-makers become increasingly troubled by the race to the bottom in which they are caught, it is possible that a state government, rather than escalating the competition by offering further incentives of its own, will choose to challenge another state's incentives in the courts, on the ground that those incentives are luring away its businesses by unconstitutional means.

My hunch is that, in the absence of other meaningful checks on the continued expansion of incentives competition, legal challenges will begin to arise, before too long, from one or more of these sources. And I suspect that a few early successes could breed a rapid outbreak of lawsuits challenging a wide range of business tax breaks.

If such litigation takes off, it will quickly confront the courts with several difficult conceptual challenges. One key question will be what range of tax provisions impermissibly interferes with the free flow of business investment decisions. A number of familiar location incentives, such as property tax abatements for new business facilities or income apportionment rules that are heavily weighted toward the sales factor, do not discriminate against out-of-state or interstate activity in the same straightforward way that an investment tax credit or a targeted capital gains break does. Yet they are essentially equivalent in their purposes and effects to the explicitly discriminatory location incentives—and hence should, arguably, also be found impermissible.

On the other hand, a simple reduction in corporate income tax rates may have a similar purpose and effect of encouraging business investment, but it would seem exceedingly strange to conclude that such a policy choice was constitutionally constrained. Also, a host of state tax breaks directed at ends unrelated to the competition for business investment, such as incentives for pollution control measures or for expanded employee health benefits, are explicitly restricted to in-state activities and investments; yet it would be odd to strike such provisions down for facially discriminating against interstate activity.

Drawing reasonable boundaries for the Commerce Clause's anti-discrimination principle will not be a simple task, and the Court's prior efforts in Commerce Clause jurisprudence suggest that no sharply defined bright-line test is likely to suffice. My advice (Enrich 1996) is that the courts focus their anti-discrimination analysis on the practical question of whether a particular challenged tax provision or practice serves to distort the decisions of economic actors in favor of expenditures on in-state activities. While this question will not provide a black-and-white test for sorting the permissible from the impermissible, it will keep the courts' attention on what the Supreme Court recently described as "the dormant Commerce Clause's fundamental objective of preserving a national market for competition undisturbed by preferential advantages conferred by a State" (*General Motors Corp. v. Tracy* 1997, p. 824).

In the General Motors case, the Court adopted precisely such a practically oriented approach. The Court upheld an Ohio tax provision exempting sales of natural gas by in-state utilities, because the Court's detailed analysis of the economic and regulatory context convinced it that this tax preference did not in practice distort consumer choices between competing in-state and out-of-state suppliers. As the Court recognized, the central concern was not whether consumers purchasing from in-state and out-of-state sellers would face disparate tax burdens, but rather whether the tax provision served to distort economic decision-making (by either purchasers or sellers) in ways that favored in-state activity. The Court found this focus on distorting effects, rather than disparate burdens, to be appropriate because "[t]he dormant Commerce Clause protects markets and participants in markets, not taxpayers as such" (Ibid., p. 825).

Expanding judicial scrutiny of business tax breaks will also raise difficult questions about the differences and similarities between tax incentives and direct governmental subsidies as tools to attract businesses. From a political vantage point, direct subsidies are a somewhat less attractive mechanism than tax breaks for delivering assistance to businesses, particularly because of the heightened and recurrent scrutiny that results from the need for annual appropriation of subsidy funds. Nonetheless, the two devices have essentially equivalent effects on business decision-making and are often viewed interchangeably by state policy-makers. For constitutional purposes, should direct subsidies face the same level of scrutiny as tax incentives?

The Supreme Court, while taking note of this issue on several occasions, has so far avoided deciding it. In one recent case (*West Lynn Creamery v. Healy* 1994), the Court found that a subsidy for local dairy farmers was inextricably linked to the levy on milk producers that funded the subsidy and whose impact on local producers it offset. The Court invalidated the package of levy and subsidy as the functional equivalent of a tax with an exemption for local producers. But in another recent case (*Camps Newfound/Owatonna v. Town of Harrison* 1997, p. 1605), the Court went out of its way to underscore the "important and relevant" differences, for Commerce Clause purposes, between tax exemptions and subsidies.

Some commentators have suggested that cash subsidies, unlike tax breaks, would be sheltered from Commerce Clause attack under the Court's "market participant exception," which allows states to favor local businesses when they engage in proprietary activities, such as constructing public facilities or selling the output of a state-owned cement plant (Hellerstein and Coenen 1996). But the Court's Camps Newfound/Owatonna opinion raises significant questions about such a suggestion, by characterizing what it calls the "narrow" market participant exception as applicable only when a state chooses to enter into a specific market in the role of buyer or seller, a characterization that does not naturally fit a subsidy program aimed generally at economic development. Thus, while Camps Newfound/Owatonna acknowledges the significant differences between tax exemptions and subsidies, it also holds open the possibility of finding, in the future, that some subsidy programs pose the same constitutional problems as discriminatory tax breaks. This is an area where the Court is obviously alert to the questions, but has given little indication so far of the answers.

Finally, if the courts begin to invalidate an array of business tax incentives, it will be interesting to see the effects on the behavior of the various players in the incentives competition. Will the prospect of unconstitutionality deter state legislatures from enacting new incentives, particularly where there is a risk that courts could order substantial monetary relief for taxpayers disadvantaged by an unconstitutional provision? Or will Commerce Clause hurdles simply challenge legislators' ingenuity to craft measures that can pass constitutional muster? Will businesses channel their energies toward obtaining other, less problematic forms of state assistance? And will some of them come to see lawsuits challenging tax breaks that benefit their competitors as a more productive tactic than pursuing breaks for themselves? Will states and businesses, faced with significant but imperfectly defined judicial restrictions on tax incentives, turn to Congress for assistance in clarifying the range of permitted and forbidden interstate tax competition? And will Congress be more inclined to step into this field if its role is that of a facilitator responding to judicial restrictions, rather than that of a regulator of unfettered state action? Only as the answers to these questions unfold will be learn whether judicial intervention can meaningfully abate the economic balkanization caused by the current interstate competition over business tax incentives.

Notes

American Trucking Associations v. *Scheiner*, 483 U.S. 266 (1987).

Baldwin v. *G. A. F. Seelig, Inc.*, 294 U.S. 511 (1935).

Beatrice Cheese, Inc. v. *Wisconsin Department of Revenue*, 1993 W. L. 57202 (Wisc. Tax App. Comm'n, Feb. 24, 1993).

Boston Stock Exchange v. *State Tax Commission*, 429 U.S. 318 (1977).

Camps Newfound/Owatonna, Inc. v. *Town of Harrison*, 117 S. Ct. 1590 (1997).

Fulton Corp. v. *Faulkner*, 116 S. Ct. 848 (1996).

General Motors Corp. v. *Tracy*, 117 S. Ct. 811 (1997).

Hughes v. *Oklahoma*, 441 U.S. 322 (1979).

New Energy Corp. v. *Limbach*, 486 U.S. 269 (1988).

Oklahoma Tax Commission v. *Jefferson Lines*, 514 U.S. 175 (1995).

Pelican Chapter, Associated Builders and Contractors v. *Edwards*, 901 F. Supp. 1125 (M.D. La. 1995).

R. J. Reynolds Tobacco Co. v. *City of N.Y. Department of Finance*, 643 N.Y.S.2d 685 (Sup. Ct. 1995).

West Lynn Creamery, Inc. v. *Healy*, 512 U.S. 186 (1994).

Westinghouse Electric Corp. v. *Tully*, 466 U.S. 388 (1984).

References

Bartik, Timothy J. 1991. *Who Benefits from State and Local Economic Development Policies?* Kalamazoo, Mich.: W. E. Upjohn Institute for Employment Research.

Burstein, Melvin L., and Arthur J. Rolnick. 1995. *Congress Should End the Economic War among the States.* Federal Reserve Bank of Minneapolis (1994 Annual Report Essay).

Carroll, Robert J., and Michael Wasylenko. 1994. "Do State Business Climates Still Matter? Evidence of a Structural Change." *National Tax Journal* 47: 19.

Chi, Keon. 1989. *The States and Business Incentives: An Inventory of Tax and Financial Incentive Programs.* Washington, D.C.: Council of State Governments.

Enrich, Peter D. 1996. "Saving the States from Themselves: Commerce Clause Constraints on State Tax Incentives for Business." *Harv. L. Rev.* 110: 377.

Gilbert, Jennifer L. 1995. "Selling the City Without Selling Out: New Legislation on Development Incentives Emphasizes Accountability." *Urb. Lawy.* 27: 427.

Hellerstein, Walter, and Dan T. Coenen. 1996. "Commerce Clause Restraints on State Business Development Incentives." *Corn. L. Rev.* 81: 789.

LeRoy, Greg, et al. 1994. *No More Candy Store: States and Cities Making Job Subsidies Accountable.* Chicago: Federation for Industrial Retention and Renewal.

Lynch, Robert. 1996. *Do State and Local Tax Incentives Work?* Washington, D.C.: Economic Policy Institute.

McClure, Charles E. 1986. "Tax Competition: Is What's Good for the Private Goose Also Good for the Public Gander?" *Nat'l Tax J.* 39: 341.

Moore, John R., C. Warren Neel, Henry W. Herzog, Jr., and Alan M. Schlottmann. 1991. "The Efficacy of Public Policy." In *Industry Location and Public Policy,* ed. Henry W. Herzog, Jr., and Alan M. Schlottmann. Knoxville: University of Tennessee Press.

Oates, Wallace E., and Robert M. Schwab. 1988. "Economic Competition Among Jurisdictions: Efficiency Enhancing or Distortion Inducing." *J. Pub. Econ.* 35: 333.

Papke, James A., and Leslie E. Papke. 1986. "Measuring Differential State-Local Tax Liabilities and Their Implications for Business Investment Location." *Nat'l Tax J.* 39: 357.

Rivlin, Alice M. 1992. *Reviving the American Dream: The Economy, the States and the Federal Government.* Washington, D.C.: Brookings Institution.

Schmenner, Roger W. 1982. *Making Business Location Decisions.* Englewood Cliffs, N.J.: Prentice Hall.

Shaviro, Daniel. 1992. "An Economic and Political Look at Federalism in Taxation." *Mich. L. Rev.* 90: 895.

Simafranca, Ryan. 1995. "The Double-Weighted Sales Formula—A Plague on Interstate Commerce." *State Tax Notes* 9: 1685.

Spindler, Charles J. 1994. "Winners and Losers in Industrial Recruitment: Mercedes-Benz and Alabama." *St. & Loc. Gov't. Rev.* 26: 192.

Tannenwald, Robert. 1996. "State Business Tax Climate: How Should It Be Measured and How Important Is It?" *New Eng. Econ. Rev.* Jan.–Feb.: 23.

Wilson, Roger. 1989. *State Business Incentives and Economic Growth: Are They Effective? A Review of the Literature.* Lexington, Ky.: Council of State Governments.

Chapter Six

STATE AND LOCAL BUSINESS TAXATION: PRINCIPLES AND PROSPECTS

Thomas F. Pogue

In fiscal year 1994, state and local governments collected $626 billion in taxes. About 30 percent of this total was from taxes that are widely regarded as taxes on businesses: corporation income, franchise, and severance taxes, and taxes on business property and purchases of inputs.[1] These taxes are clearly important sources of state and local government revenue, but they are also controversial. They are costly to administer and comply with, largely because most businesses operate within the jurisdiction of several, if not many, local and state governments. And they are seen by many as barriers to investment, employment, and economic growth. The question of how to tax businesses is far from settled, despite the fact that business taxes have long been an important source of state and local revenue.

The ongoing debate about the role of business taxes points to the issues addressed in this paper. The next section suggests guidelines for business taxation based on traditional efficiency and equity criteria. Taxing businesses, according to these guidelines, rather than being a barrier to economic development, is necessary for efficient resource allocation. Subsequent sections consider several related questions. What will be required to improve business taxation and make it consistent with economic efficiency and a fair distribution of the costs of government? How are business taxes likely to change in the years ahead? Are business taxes likely to become more or less consistent with the guidelines outlined below?

An analysis of these questions requires a working definition of a "business tax." We use the definition offered by Oakland (1992, p. 18): "any tax on a business's purchase of inputs, its ownership of assets, its earnings, or its right to do business." This definition does not include retail sales, social insurance, or personal-income withholding taxes. Collecting these taxes from businesses rather than from individuals is an expedient means of implementing broad-based taxes on individuals' receipt and use of income; it facilitates enforcement and lowers collection costs. In these cases, businesses are essentially acting as collecting agents for government.

GUIDELINES FOR BUSINESS TAXATION

The burden of any tax is the loss of real income it entails. That burden necessarily falls on persons even if the tax is collected from businesses. Since all income generated by business activity accrues to individuals, businesses have no tax-paying capability independent of the persons who transact with them as employees, customers, suppliers, and owners.[2] Business taxes are therefore indirect taxes on individuals. And the question "How should businesses be taxed?" can be restated as "When are the objectives of efficiency and fairness in taxation served by indirect rather than direct taxation of individuals?" Furthermore, business taxation is not necessary in modern economies such as the U.S., since it would certainly be possible to finance state and local government solely with direct taxes. These facts do not mean, however, that governments might just as well tax individuals directly rather than indirectly, via business taxes. Instead, they mean that the case for collecting taxes from businesses should be made on traditional grounds of fairness and efficiency, rather than in terms of the need for revenue or on the basis of the mistaken belief that business taxes do not burden individuals.

The most compelling economic reason for taxing businesses is to charge them for costs they generate but would otherwise ignore in deciding what, where, and how to produce. This can be termed the social cost rationale, because the objective is to confront producers with the full cost to society of the inputs they use in producing goods and services. Under this rationale, business taxes are a means of internalizing the costs of otherwise unpriced inputs used in production. Taxing businesses in this manner, it is argued, is necessary for efficient resource allocation. State and local governments should impose business taxes that are justified by the social cost rationale even if they can raise all needed revenue with direct taxes, and even if existing direct taxes are ideal. There may also be conditions under which augmenting direct taxes with business taxes can compensate for deficiencies in existing direct taxes. The remainder of this section examines in more detail the use of business taxes to internalize social costs and to supplement direct taxes.[3]

Charging for Social Costs

Social costs fall into two broad categories. One is the cost of services supplied by government, examples of which are police and courts to protect property rights and to enforce contracts; waste collection, disposal, and treatment; fire protection; and roads, traffic control, and parking. The second category consists of the external costs generated by production and consumption of goods and services, such as environmental damage from air, water, and soil pollution.

State and local governments provide services that facilitate production of goods and services that businesses sell in the marketplace. If these services were not provided by government, businesses would have to incur the costs of providing substitutes.[4] When governments provide such services without charge, they subsidize private producers, in effect transferring income from taxpayers to subsidized businesses. Depending on market conditions, these governmental subsidies may increase profits, reduce product prices, and/or increase payments to workers and other suppliers.

Providing services free of charge creates two potential problems. First, the resulting subsidies may be regarded as unfair because they transfer income from taxpayers to owners, suppliers, and customers of private businesses. At a minimum, the subsidies are capricious, since individuals' losses as taxpayers and their gains as owners, suppliers, and customers are seldom predictable with acceptable accuracy. Second, the subsidies will vary across business sectors and locations, thereby encouraging a shift of production from lightly to heavily subsidized sectors and locations. This reallocation of production is likely to be inefficient because it is not in response to underlying economic costs and demands.

Using taxes to charge businesses for government-provided services can, in principle, mitigate the unfairness and inefficiency that arises when services are provided free of charge. But to do so, the tax on any given business must be closely related to the costs it generates for government; businesses that generate relatively high (or low) costs should face relatively high (or low) taxes. Furthermore, a business's tax should increase if its operations impose additional costs on government: if it expands, for example, and generates a larger load on a city's waste disposal system or more traffic and wear on city streets. And a business's tax should, likewise, decrease if its activities generate lower costs.

Oakland and Testa (1996, p. 5) argue that taxing businesses for the governmental costs they generate is necessary to implement the benefit principle of taxation. Individuals who buy from, sell to, work for, and own businesses are the ultimate beneficiaries of government-provided services. The benefit principle requires that these individuals also pay the cost of providing those services. But taxing individual beneficiaries directly would be an insurmountable task. It would require knowledge of how governmental services affect the prices paid and wages and profits received by each beneficiary. Economic analysis is simply unable to predict these effects. And even if it could, a government would be unable to tax directly those beneficiaries who reside outside its jurisdiction. But governments can indirectly tax beneficiaries, both resident and nonresident, by taxing businesses for the costs of government-provided services.

The value of governmental services to recipient businesses may exceed, equal, or fall short of the costs incurred in providing those services. If the value of a service is less than the cost of producing it, then taxing in the amount of the cost gives businesses an incentive to seek another supplier or move from the taxing jurisdiction. But that does not mean that the government should charge less than cost; instead, it means that the government is not the least-cost provider of that particular service.

Charging for External Costs

Businesses are also subsidized unless they pay taxes reflecting the external costs they generate. Businesses that generate relatively high (or low) external costs should face relatively high (or low) taxes. Furthermore, a business's tax should increase and decrease with increases and decreases in the external costs of its operations.

For example, if a paper mill disposes of production wastes in a stream, the full social cost of producing that paper includes any loss in the value of the stream to others who use it for recreation, as a source of water, or for other purposes. A tax reflecting other users' losses (the external costs of the mill's operations) can cause the mill to recognize and take account of the full cost of its activities. If such a tax is not imposed, the mill is subsidized.[5] As a result of the subsidy, the market price of the mill's paper may understate the full social cost of producing it. Paper would then appear to be cheaper than it is, the use of paper would be inefficiently high, and the stream's water quality would be inefficiently low. Too many scarce resources would be allocated to paper production and too few to other uses, and the stream would be used too much for waste disposal and too little for other purposes.[6] To the extent that the subsidy is not translated into lower paper prices, it will lead to higher profits for the mill's owners and/or higher payments to the mill's workers and other suppliers. The subsidy may therefore result in gains for owners, workers, and/or other suppliers and losses for other users of the stream. Since these gains and losses may be regarded as unfair, this example illustrates the general point that failing to tax businesses that generate external costs may be both unfair and inefficient.

External costs may result from the consumption of goods as well as their production. For example, consumers of alcohol generate external costs when they cause accidents that damage the property of and cause injury to other persons. Consumption and hence production of alcoholic beverages are subsidized unless the prices of those beverages are high enough to cover such external costs. Excise taxes collected from producers and retailers of alcoholic beverages can be used to increase prices so that they reflect, and thereby cause consumers to consider, the external costs of alcohol consumption.[7] Similarly, excise taxes on motor vehicle fuels can help to internalize the external costs generated by both production and use of those fuels.

TAX-EXEMPT BUSINESSES

Businesses and organizations that are currently exempt from some or all taxes because they are engaged in nonprofit or charitable activities should be taxed in the same manner as for-profit businesses. Even if it is desirable to subsidize the activities of these organizations, it is inefficient and unfair to do so by providing them with free governmental services or allowing them to ignore the external costs they generate. Similarly, governmental enterprises, such as public universities, the post office, and municipal utilities, should pay taxes or fees reflecting any social costs generated by their operations.

Tax-exempt organizations as well as other businesses may produce unpriced outputs—goods and services they do not sell. Examples of such outputs include counseling, education, or job training provided by churches. These outputs are external benefits that may justify subsidies for these businesses and organizations, just as external costs justify taxes. But there is no reason to believe that tax-exempt businesses and organizations generate external benefits that exactly balance the external and governmental costs they generate. Yet, that is the implicit assumption behind current practice. The efficient and fair practice would be to tax on the basis of external costs generated and subsidize in the amount of demonstrable external benefits.

Unprofitable Businesses

Taxing businesses according to the social cost rationale would require that unprofitable as well as profitable businesses be taxed for the external costs they generate and to offset the cost of governmentally provided inputs. This approach to taxation could therefore make otherwise profitable businesses unprofitable, and it could even make some businesses nonviable. Nevertheless, if the underlying objective is efficient resource allocation, taxes should reflect the social costs that businesses generate regardless of the consequences with respect to profitability and viability. Under the social cost rationale, neither ownership nor ability to pay applied to the business itself is an appropriate determinant of business taxes.

Regressivity

If businesses were taxed according to the social cost rationale, the resulting distribution of tax burdens (tax incidence) might well be regressive.[8] But regressivity is not an argument against this approach if the taxes do indeed reflect social costs. For example, when markets operate efficiently, the retail price of bread increases when the price of flour or other ingredients increases, even though the resulting increase in the cost of bread falls relatively heavily on the poor. A policy of providing free flour to bakers so that the poor do not have to pay for the cost of that input would lead to inefficiency. Failing to tax businesses for social costs implicit in their activities because the taxes would be regressive would similarly lead to inefficiency.

Tax Neutrality

The social cost rationale not only implies that businesses should be taxed on the amount of the external and governmental costs they generate, but it also implies that businesses should not be taxed differently unless they generate different external and governmental costs. That is, economic efficiency requires that businesses be taxed uniformly except for differences in taxation that can be related to differences in costs generated. Business taxation meeting this criterion would be neutral because taxes would not prevent businesses from locating where they can operate most efficiently considering all costs of production. Ideally, taxes should be uniform across all locations throughout the United States except where nonuniformity is justified by differences in costs generated.

Coordination of Tax Policy

Neutrality is not achieved if some governments tax businesses according to costs generated while others do not. To achieve tax neutrality, therefore, governments need to coordinate their tax policies to mini-mize interstate and intrastate differences in tax rates and tax base definitions. They also need to forego tax competition, which attempts to attract businesses by making costs artificially low. Tax competition is a barrier to tax neutrality and economic efficiency because it may induce businesses to choose locations at which their production costs are actually higher than at competing locations.

TAX EXPORTING

Tax exporting occurs when taxes levied by a government reduce the real incomes of persons who reside outside the government's jurisdic-tion. Taxes imposed under the social cost rationale may be exported in part as they reduce the after-tax income of nonresident owners and increase prices for nonresident customers of taxed businesses. Such tax exporting can be both fair and efficient because the benefits of government-provided services may also be exported, and because nonresidents may be partly responsible for external costs generated by businesses. However, imposing higher taxes than called for by the social cost rationale in an attempt to enlarge the share of taxes borne by nonresidents may result in inefficient decisions about where to produce.[9]

Augmenting Direct Taxes

Existing direct taxes fail to tax income equitably either as it is re-ceived or as it is spent.[10] Income taxes incorporate numerous tax preferences that result in some income being taxed at relatively low rates or escaping taxation altogether. Similarly, sales taxes do not include all uses of income (i.e., all expenditures). Tax preferences cause resource allocation decisions to be based partly on tax advan-tages rather than on underlying economic demands and costs. The economy is then less efficient because the most valuable products are not produced, and products are not produced at least cost. Tax pref-erences may also be regarded as unfair.

The ideal remedy for these deficiencies would, of course, be to broaden state sales and income tax bases so that taxes depend neither on how income is received nor on how it is spent. That is, taxing businesses is a second-best means of taxing individual incomes, to be resorted to only when existing taxes have serious deficiencies and there are political barriers to eliminating those deficiencies.[11] Such appears to be the case in the U.S. today. In the absence of comprehen-sive tax reform, retaining taxes on business property and income can compensate in a very rough fashion for some of the deficiencies of existing income taxes. Three examples illustrate this point.

First, in the absence of a corporation income tax, taxation of income retained by corporations is deferred until it is paid out as dividends or realized as capital gains upon the sale of corporate stock. And taxes are avoided completely when stock that has appreciated in value because of retained earnings is transferred as part of an estate. As Oakland (1992, p. 25) explains, any single state cannot compensate for this deficiency in its personal income tax by taxing the income of corporations operating within its jurisdiction. The reason is that the corporations operating in any given state are likely to be owned in large part by persons residing throughout the nation. A state's corporation income tax is, therefore, not an effective means of indirectly taxing the retained earnings of its residents. However, if most states were to impose both corporation and personal income taxes, their corporation and income taxes taken together could help to offset the undertaxation of retained earnings in their personal income taxes. Personal incomes may therefore be taxed more fairly, in a very rough sense, when states levy both corporation and personal income taxes than when they levy only personal income taxes.[12]

The second related example is that capital gains in the form of increases in real estate values are not subject to income taxation completely if the assets are transferred as part of an estate. Taxes on business property reflect such increases in asset values and therefore compensate in part for the preferential treatment of capital gains under existing income taxes.[13]

The increase in value of a given real estate property can be divided into two components: the increase due to improvements (buildings, grading, drainage) and the increase in the value of the site. The increase due to improvements is the result of investment by the property owners themselves, but the increase in site value results mainly from investment by others—from public and private investment in neighboring properties. Increases in site value are therefore largely unearned, in the sense that they do not result from investments and actions by site owners. This fact strengthens the case for continuing to tax business property as a means of compensating for relatively light taxation of capital gains under existing income taxes. Indeed, it has been argued that increases in site value should be taxed more heavily than other income—but such increases, like other capital gains, are taxed more *lightly* under existing income taxes.[14]

Third, income generated in a state may flow to nonresidents. Indeed, in today's highly integrated global economy, the lion's share of capital income generated in a state will be dispersed widely, throughout the nation and the world. Some labor income may also accrue to nonresidents, but most of the recipients of labor income generated in a state will also reside there. Governments may wish to tax nonresident income but be unable to do so with direct taxes, because they lack jurisdiction over nonresidents.[15] Such income can, however, be taxed indirectly by taxing businesses. Capital income can be taxed with a business or corporation income tax or as a withholding tax on interest and dividend payments. Labor income can be taxed with a withholding tax on wages.[16]

The equity case for taxing income accruing to nonresidents is perhaps strongest when the income results from the existence or use of resources, such as scenic attractions and mineral deposits, that are unique to a state. Absent business taxation, some of the value of natural resources and amenities, may accrue to nonresident owners and consumers.

THE POSSIBILITIES OF REFORM

Existing business taxes are not consistent with the preceding guidelines. The taxes in use today are not satisfactory means of inducing businesses to take account of either the governmental or the external costs generated by their activities. State corporation income taxes fail because these social costs are not correlated with businesses' profitability. Neither are these costs closely correlated with other business tax bases: gross receipts, franchise, severance, and business property. Existing taxes are therefore non-neutral, because intrastate and interstate differences in tax rates and tax bases are not related to differences in social costs. Furthermore, given the uncertain incidence of most business taxes, they border on the capricious as a means of indirectly taxing individuals. Finally, by all accounts, state and local business taxes are complex, and costly to administer and to comply with.[17]

Any effort to improve on the existing situation must be grounded in a clear concept of the purposes of business taxation. Otherwise, there is little to anchor policy debate, and the complexities and distortions of the present system could be aggravated rather than reduced. Reform efforts could follow two distinct but not mutually exclusive strategies. One would be to develop new taxes and fees to internalize social costs. The other would be to improve existing taxes.

Reform Based on the Social Cost Rationale

If internalizing social costs is accepted as the primary purpose of business taxes, improving existing taxes promises only limited progress. Fundamental reform will require replacing existing taxes with taxes and fees that approximate in amount and distribution the unpriced inputs used by businesses. It will require new approaches to taxing or otherwise charging businesses for the costs of services provided by government. And it will require greater use of taxes to offset external costs.

The social cost rationale implies that business taxation is fundamentally a local concern; decisions about business taxation must be decentralized in the sense that they allow differences between localities in tax rates and even in tax instruments. Local governments need flexibility in how they raise revenue; they need tax options that allow genuinely independent decisions about how to provide and pay for local government services.

Although restructuring business taxation, to be consistent with the social cost rationale, could promote both fairness and economic efficiency, such change is unlikely for two broad reasons. One is the difficulty of implementing taxes that reflect social costs. The other is that policy-makers may fear that basing business taxation on social costs, even if it is possible to do so, would adversely affect economic growth. Let's consider these issues in more detail.

FEASIBILITY

One might argue that the difficulty of first measuring external costs and the costs of governmentally provided inputs and then attributing them to particular businesses severely limits the usefulness and practicality of the social cost rationale as a guide for business tax reform. This is certainly a valid concern, but the difficulties of measuring and attributing costs do yield to analysis and research, as a number of studies have shown.[18] Furthermore, the key question is not whether the external and governmental costs generated by a business can be measured with a high degree of accuracy; almost surely, they cannot. Rather, the question is whether it is possible to devise taxes and fees that are more closely correlated with those costs than existing taxes.

How should businesses be taxed if the external and governmental costs generated by businesses cannot be estimated with sufficient accuracy? The answer, noted above, is that absent demonstrable differences in the external and governmental costs they generate, businesses should be taxed uniformly, which would require a broad-based tax that is more nearly neutral than existing taxes. Oakland (1992, pp. 28–32) and Oakland and Testa (1996, p. 10–12) argue that an origin-based, value-added tax meets this requirement; it is an appropriate general business tax to pay for governmental costs that cannot be allocated with acceptable accuracy among businesses. Replacing general business taxes with a value-added tax deserves careful consideration as a first step toward more neutral taxation of business.[19]

Adverse Effect on Economic Development

Business taxes are commonly seen as barriers to economic development—an increasingly important concern of state and local policymakers. Would business taxes based on the social cost rationale, in fact, inhibit growth? Certainly, a state may be more attractive as a location for production if its government subsidizes production by taxing businesses at less than the cost of the inputs that it provides to them. And some of the state's residents may gain when production is subsidized in this manner—mainly owners of land and other in-place resources that would be in greater demand as the local economy expands.[20] But the state's residents can gain as a group only if some of the taxes required to pay for governmentally provided inputs can be exported to nonresidents. Similarly, levying taxes that do not internalize fully the external costs of production might improve a state's "business climate" and attract some business activity. But it would be potentially beneficial to a state's residents as a group only if some of the external costs are borne by nonresidents. Therefore, it is usually in the self-interest of the residents of a state or locality to tax business as called for by the social cost rationale, even if doing so diverts production from the state.

It might be argued that taxing to internalize social costs would be desirable only if other states also do so. But that is not the case. Regardless of what other governments do, it is not to the advantage of a state's residents, as a group, to subsidize production by failing to tax for costs generated.[21]

Exceptions to this conclusion may, as just noted, arise when external costs and the cost of governmentally provided inputs are borne in part by nonresidents. In these cases, however, what is optimal for individual states is not necessarily efficient from the perspective of the nation. Indeed, to promote economic efficiency in the national economy, the best policy would be for all states to implement taxes called for by the social cost rationale. In contrast, if a state subsidizes business activity by taxing and otherwise charging businesses less than the full cost of the governmental services provided to them, it encourages inefficient resource allocation and distorts interstate commerce just as surely as it would if it were to impose a tariff on imports.

When assessing whether the business taxes levied by a state or locality adversely affect its economic development, the effects of services provided by government should also be taken into account. Relatively high taxes in a state need not be a barrier to business activity if services provided to business are also relatively high in value. Despite this rather obvious fact, analyses of business taxes commonly use equal tax rates as the norm for efficient (nondistorting) taxes. Similarly, the question of whether a tax interferes with interstate commerce is typically resolved without considering whether the tax facilitates provision of services to interstate commerce.[22]

Improving Existing Taxes

Existing business taxes are not closely correlated with the external and governmental costs generated by businesses, and there is little potential for improvement on that dimension. But business taxes could be improved in other respects. Their bases could be broadened, and tax bases and rates could be made more uniform within and across states. The taxes would then be more neutral; they would distort economic decisions less.

To illustrate, consider the two most important taxes: the taxes on business property and corporation income. The same tax rate could be applied to all business property in a state, rather than having the rate vary across local jurisdictions. And assessment practices could be improved to reduce variation in the valuation of business property. From an efficiency perspective, the need for uniform rates and assessment would be greatest in the case of reproducible (mobile) property that can be adjusted in quantity or quality in response to tax differentials. The need for uniformity would be least in the case of land. Indeed, variation in land taxes from one jurisdiction to another would not distort land use decisions as long as tax rates and assessment do not depend on how the land is used. Differences in tax rates on land, which could be capitalized into land values, could, of course, be regarded as unfair.

Similarly, state corporation income taxes would be more neutral if each state would use the same tax rate schedule and the same definition of taxable income. The complexity and lack of uniformity of state corporation income taxes would also be reduced if states would agree among themselves to use simple and uniform rules for establishing nexus and apportioning tax bases. But such cooperation seems unlikely. The experience of more than three decades of negotiation under the Multistate Tax Compact and the Uniform Division of Income for Tax Purposes Act suggests that more direct federal action will be required. For example, states could be required or given incentives to collect their corporation income taxes as a surtax on the federal tax. And rules for apportionment and for determining nexus could be established by federal legislation.[23] These actions would significantly reduce the costs of administering and complying with state corporation income taxes.

THE OUTLOOK FOR BUSINESS TAXES

How are business taxes likely to evolve in the years ahead? My sense, though necessarily speculative, is that the economic and political influences that have shaped business tax policy in recent years are also likely to dominate policy in the future. A large and increasing share of businesses will be footloose or mobile, in the sense that it is economically feasible for them to produce in a number of states and nations. This mobility will foster tax competition, which will continue to be the main political force driving business tax policy. Governments will continue and even increase their efforts to attract mobile businesses with various tax incentives; business taxes will continue to decrease as a share of total taxes. Fundamental tax reform, defined as bringing the tax system more closely into line with standard equity and efficiency criteria, will continue to be an unattainable objective. And business taxes may well become more rather than less complex. Let's discuss these conjectures in more detail.

Business Mobility

Mobile businesses have the option of producing the goods sold in a given market in any number of locations. Shoes and clothing sold in U.S. markets, for example, can be produced domestically in a number of states or abroad in any of several nations. Even perishable fruits and vegetables are produced for U.S. markets in Mexico, South America, Australia, and Asia. Increasing mobility of economic activity is the essential element in the phenomenon commonly referred to as the "globalization" of the economy.

Over the past several decades, domestic and international mobility have been fostered, in the first instance, by decreases in the cost of transportation relative to other costs. International mobility has also been greatly reinforced by political changes. Barriers to international trade, capital flow, and investment have fallen, making it easier for businesses to produce in many countries products that are sold in U.S. markets.[24] And countries that were closed to U.S. business activity one or two decades ago (most notably, China and the former USSR) are now potential sites for producing products to be sold in the U.S. These influences will continue to operate in the years ahead. Continuing integration of the world economy will significantly increase international mobility. And falling relative transportation costs will likely generate some increase in both national and international mobility.

Tax Competition

Business mobility is the source of tax competition; if businesses were not mobile, there would be no reason for tax competition. As national and international mobility increase, so too will national and international tax competition. And the tax policies of individual states will be influenced not just by the policies of other states but also by the policies of other nations. Before outlining the main effects of heightened tax competition, let's consider why tax competition is likely to persist.

Failing to provide tax incentives to mobile businesses when other states and localities do so is widely seen as "unilateral disarmament" in the battle for population and industry. State and local governments will, therefore, continue to be reluctant to individually forego tax competition, fearing that doing so will inhibit economic development. Reducing tax competition will require cooperation among governments—for example, to establish interstate agreements that limit the use of tax breaks and other incentives to attract businesses.[25] But such cooperation will be difficult. Tax competition will persist simply because with increasing national and international mobility, the set of governments that must cooperate in order to eliminate competition is growing—and it includes foreign governments.

Tax competition will, accordingly, ratchet down business taxes. And as state and local governments' ability to obtain general revenue from business taxes diminishes, they will be under pressure to reduce spending and increase other taxes. They will realign their tax systems, decreasing reliance on indirect business taxes and increasing reliance on direct taxes. Business taxes will continue to decrease as a share of total state and local taxes. And local government fiscal capacities will decline as the business property tax base shrinks, which may lead to deterioration in schools and local government services, unless it is offset by expansion of state aid to local governments—especially schools—and by state takeover of previously local functions, such as courts.

Any single state will find it difficult to tax mobile businesses more heavily than other states, unless it also provides services that are sufficiently valuable to offset its relatively high taxes.[26] Tax competition will thus tend to reduce interstate differences in taxes on mobile businesses that are not matched by differences in government-provided services.[27]

Since tax competition typically entails tax abatements and incentives that reduce taxes on capital income, it will also reinforce the shifting of taxes from capital to labor income that has been underway for decades. This redistribution of tax burdens need not be explicitly recognized in tax statutes and administrative rules. As tax breaks are provided, other taxes will have to fill the gap or spending will have to decrease.

The fear that underlies tax competition of driving business away will especially inhibit the use of business taxes to internalize external costs. Business taxes will consequently tend to fall below levels justified by the social cost rationale. Such undertaxation of business will not ordinarily be to the advantage of state residents as a group. But it could, as explained above, benefit some residents (as well as nonresidents) who own immobile resources. Owners of immobile resources will therefore be a source of continuing pressure for business subsidies and, as such, a barrier to implementing taxes consistent with the social cost rationale. Widespread understanding of this fact could be an antidote for the inefficient subsidization of businesses that tax competition is currently generating.

Tax Reform

Although existing business taxes have serious and widely recognized deficiencies, the prospects for significant reform are dim. As explained above, reform based on the social cost rationale will be difficult to implement, and it may be opposed because of presumed adverse effects on economic development. But even less ambitious reform will face several barriers. The most important deterrent to reform is the simple fact that it redistributes tax burdens. Tax reform is not a "win-win" undertaking, since any revenue-neutral restructuring of taxes will almost surely impose losses on many individuals.

These losses are magnified when reform eliminates preferences and distortions that have been capitalized into asset prices.

The prospects for reform are also limited because individual states cannot enact changes that are greatly out of line with what other states are doing. Reform will therefore require either legislation at the federal level or cooperation among states. Finally, state and local policy-makers may see conflicts between their self-interest and tax reform that would make business taxes less complicated and distorting. Reform would rule out manipulation of taxes to alter the location of economic activity and to favor particular constituents, which is an important form of political currency.[28]

Tax Complexity

Businesses today must comply with complex taxes defined by a changing array of statutes, court decisions, and administrative rules. This tax complexity will likely persist—partly because, as noted above, state and local policy-makers see taxes as tools to be used in promoting a variety of objectives. More important, business taxes may become more complex simply because economic enterprises and the products and services they produce are becoming more complex. With respect to a growing set of products and services—for example, financial services and telecommunications—it is difficult to determine where production and use take place. Rules for determining how a business's tax base is divided among states and localities will therefore become increasingly complex and arbitrary.

CONCLUSIONS

The main justification for taxing businesses—the social cost rationale—is to induce them to take account of costs they generate but would otherwise ignore. Indeed, business taxes and fees that reflect nonmarket costs of production are necessary in order for a market economy to allocate resources efficiently. Such taxes and fees are also necessary to ensure a fair distribution of the costs of production—to prevent an unfair subsidy of production by taxpayers and individuals who bear external costs. Therefore, although it would be possible to finance state and local government solely with taxes collected from persons, it would be neither efficient nor fair to do so. And, the need to tax businesses for the costs that their activities generate is not eliminated or reduced by the fact that business taxes are ultimately borne by individuals.

Existing taxes do not meet these requirements. Thorough reform of business taxation will require that the social cost rationale and its implications be widely understood and accepted. It will require research and experimentation to discover observable variables that are closely related to the governmental and external costs that businesses generate. Taxes and fees will have to be more business-specific and locality-specific than existing taxes. They will need to be based on characteristics of businesses' operations rather than the value of their property or the amount of their income. The impact fees that some local governments are imposing on new business developments are a step in this direction.

Whether or not state and local governments implement new taxes and fees to internalize social costs, they could broaden the bases of existing business taxes, especially corporation income and business property taxes. They could also make tax rates and tax base definitions more uniform within and across states. These actions would make existing business taxes more equitable and neutral.

Unfortunately, the prospect that business taxation will evolve along these lines is dim. Instead, business tax policy will be driven by tax competition, which will become more aggressive as business mobility, national and international, increases. The granting of tax preferences in the process of tax competition will narrow, rather than broaden, tax bases and make tax statutes and administrative rules more, rather than less, complex. Tax competition will likely push business taxes below the levels required to offset external and public service costs. It will also tend to shift taxes from capital to labor income and reduce the fiscal capacities of state and local governments, thereby putting downward pressure on spending by those governments.

When state and local governments play the tax competition game, they are attempting to influence how the private sector meets market demands; they are involving themselves in the management of the private sector. Such government intervention is precisely what the former socialist economies of Eastern Europe and the former Soviet Union are trying to reduce. They are trying to eliminate negotiated taxes that favor particular enterprises. The irony is that despite the United States' tradition of free markets and private enterprise, systematic government intervention via tax preferences and other subsidies is pervasive and surprisingly popular.

Notes

1. Oakland and Testa (1996, p. 6) report estimates of the business tax share of total state and local taxes declining from 42 percent in 1957 to 29 percent in 1992. Fiscal year 1993–94 is the most recent year for which data are available on spending by both state and local governments.

2. A business tax—for example, a tax on business property—reduces the income of business owners unless it can be shifted to customers and/or suppliers. Shifting to customers requires that product prices increase in response to the tax; shifting to suppliers (for example, employees) requires that input prices decrease in response to the tax. The extent to which the burden of a business tax can be shifted, therefore, depends on how the tax affects prices and quantities in the product and input markets in which the taxed businesses trade.

3. The literature on business taxation is voluminous, but it deals mainly with the effects of, rather than the reasons for, business taxation. Oakland (1992) provides the most recent examination of the reasons for taxing businesses; others who have written on this subject include Galginaitis (1992), Stocker (1972), Studenski (1940), and Walker (1937).

4. What should be included in government-provided services to businesses is unclear and would surely be subject to debate. A broad definition of such services might well include support for low-wage workers through programs that provide job training and placement, child care, medical care, and low-cost housing. If such needs were not met by government-supported programs, it might be argued, employers would have to provide substitutes or pay higher wages.

5. The tax per unit of paper should equal the marginal external cost of producing paper—the increase in external costs resulting from additional paper production.

6. Stated differently, the production and use of paper are inefficient if users are not willing to pay the full cost of producing it, where full cost includes external costs. In that case, setting prices high enough to cover external costs would reduce the quantity of paper demanded and bought. Similarly, the mill's disposal of wastes results in water quality that is too low if it would be less costly for the mill to alter its waste disposal practices than to compensate other users of the stream for their losses.

7. See Manning et al. (1989) and Pogue and Sgontz (1989) for research on the use of taxes to internalize the external costs of tobacco and alcohol consumption, respectively. See Grossman et al. (1993) for a brief summary of related research.

8. Tax incidence is regressive if tax burden as a percentage of income decreases as income increases. Incidence is progressive if taxes capture an increasing percentage of income as income increases.

9. For example, suppose a business can serve a national market from locations in several states, but it locates in State A, where its costs are minimized. State A might have a cost advantage because its central location minimizes transportation costs or because it has a low-cost supply of a necessary raw material that is costly to ship (such as iron ore). Suppose further that the owners and customers of the business reside mainly in states other than A. Any taxes that State A collects from this business are therefore largely exported. As long as these taxes do not exceed the cost advantages that the business enjoys by operating in State A, the business will remain in A, and the taxes levied by A will not lead to an inefficient allocation of resources. However, if State A tries to collect a larger amount of taxes, the business will relocate. Why? Because taking account of the tax that would be paid in State A, the business's costs are lower at a location other than A. But the actual (social) costs of production are still lower in A than elsewhere. The tax imposed by A artificially increases the costs of operating in A. The attempt by State A to export more taxes therefore leads to inefficient (higher-

cost) production. Of course, this inefficiency does not occur if the business is immobile (tied to the taxing jurisdiction).

10. Equity as defined by the ability-to-pay principle requires that taxes be distributed according to individuals' ability to pay taxes, usually measured by total income or consumption. Equity defined by the benefit principle requires that taxes reflect the benefits that individuals receive from government. Horizontal equity requires that individuals who are equal, in terms of benefits received or ability to pay, bear equal tax burdens. Vertical equity requires that individuals with differing ability to pay (or differing benefits received) bear tax burdens that are "appropriately" different.

11. In underdeveloped economies characterized by poor record-keeping and a large nonmonetary sector, an individual income tax is not feasible; business taxes may be the only effective means of taxing individuals. However, in the present-day U.S. and other modern industrial economies a broad-based income tax is feasible, so the case for taxing businesses solely in order to tax individual incomes rests largely on political, rather than economic, considerations.

12. The better practice would, of course, be to eliminate the tax preference given to retained earnings. That could be done by assigning all corporation income to individual stockholders regardless of whether it is paid out as dividends and taxing that income. The corporation income tax could be retained as a withholding tax.

13. Capital gains as calculated under existing law include increases in dollar value that are due to inflation. Ideally, only the real increase in an asset's value (the increase after adjustment for inflation) should be subject to taxation. Present practice—taxing capital gains at a reduced rate and increasing the basis of the asset to current market value when it is transferred as part of an estate—is not a fair substitute for correctly adjusting for inflation.

14. Henry George, writing in the nineteenth century, was a forceful advocate of the view that land rents and changes in land value are unearned and should therefore be taxed more heavily than other income. See Hansen (1967).

15. Even taxing income at the business level does not assure that a state will succeed in taxing all of the capital income generated within its borders. Businesses may be able to set up transfer-pricing arrangements that shift income generated within a state to related enterprises (subsidiary or parent corporations) in tax-haven countries (or states) that impose no income taxes on resident businesses and individuals.

16. Withholding taxes allow tax rates to vary with the circumstances of individual income recipients. For individual circumstances to be taken into account, it is, of course, necessary for nonresidents to file individual income tax returns in the state or locality from which they receive income.

17. See Slemrod (1996, pp. 357–59) for a very useful discussion of the link between complexity and the total resource cost of collecting revenue, which includes both administrative and compliance costs.

18. Oakland and Testa (1996) estimate how much state and local government spending in 1992 was for general services to business, and conclude that general business taxes exceeded that spending by a substantial margin. Cordes (1992) describes existing state and local environmental taxes and fees. Because it is difficult to determine the amount of tax needed to limit environmental damage optimally, environmental taxes and fees are unlikely, in Cordes's view, to displace regulations and legislative mandates. Bohm and Kelsay (1992) analyze the use of taxes in dealing with a particular environmental problem, municipal solid waste. Pogue and Sgontz (1989) examine the use of taxes to internalize the external costs of alcohol consumption. Summers (1991) argues for greater use of "corrective" taxes on activities that generate external costs, focusing on the case for taxes on the carbon content of fossil energy sources.

19. See also Cline (1988) and Miller (1988) for discussion of state-level, value-added taxes. State-level, value-added taxes would be far from trouble-free; in particular, they would have many of the same apportionment problems as existing corporation income taxes.

20. "Job creation" is commonly asserted to be one of the main benefits of tax incentives and abatements. Such subsidies may generate additional employment within a specific region, but any such increase is likely to come at the expense of employment in other regions. Economic development incentives mainly shift employment among regions, if they have any effect at all. The reason is that total employment in the national economy is determined by the size of the national labor force and the national demand for labor, the latter being determined, in turn, by the demand for goods and services produced by labor. A state's economic development policies cannot influence the total number of jobs in the economy because they cannot significantly affect either the size of the labor force or the national demand for labor. State subsidies of business mainly transfer income (purchasing power) from taxpayers to beneficiaries of the subsidies. Simply transferring income from one pocket to another may shift demand for labor and employment among regions and industries; but it does not add to total demand for goods and services, and therefore does not add to total demand for labor. Some workers may gain from this shifting of employment, but the measure of their gain is not that they now have a job whereas before they did not. Their gain is, instead, the amount by which their wages have been increased by the change in their place of employment.

21. As explained above, a subsidy may be warranted if a business generates external benefits.

22. For more discussion of the effects of taxes on economic development, see the excellent review by Wasylenko (1997) and the studies cited therein, especially Bartik (1994) and Courant (1994).

23. To tax corporations' income, states must establish nexus (i.e., that the corporations have a presence in the state). And the taxable income of multi-state corporations must be apportioned among the states within which they operate; that is, states must have rules that determine how much of the income of each corporation is subject to taxation in each of the states in which it operates. These rules vary from state to state, and they are complicated and subject to continuing litigation. The results are high administrative costs for state revenue departments and high compliance costs for taxpayers.

24. Business mobility has to some degree been subsidized by public policy in several areas. International mobility has been increased by governmental subsidies and loan guarantees that finance overseas investment by U.S. businesses. Public subsidy of transportation has contributed to past decreases in transportation costs. So too has the failure to internalize the air pollution and other environmental costs of the production and use of energy. For more on these subjects, see Lang and Hines (1993), who argue that the underpricing of transportation has led to inefficiently high levels of international trade.

25. The need for such cooperation is recognized in a 1993 report prepared by the National Governors' Association and the National Conference of State Legislatures that advocates "in the long run, moving toward cooperative policy making and consistent tax policies" (Snell 1993).

26. This outcome may be thought of as the Tiebout (1956) hypothesis applied to mobile businesses. Allocative efficiency is not likely to be the result of businesses "voting with their feet," however, for two reasons. Most important, businesses will not move in order to assure that their taxes reflect the external costs they generate. Also, tax competition may result in business taxes that fall short of the cost of government-provided services.

27. A study by Papke (1996) provides some evidence that tax competition has led to similar overall rates of business taxation. Specifically, he estimates marginal tax rates

on new investment in various industrial sectors in the Great Lakes states. These estimated rates are so similar that they provide no basis for businesses to prefer one state over another.

28. See Pogue (1994) for further discussion of how tax reform is inhibited by the political process by which budgetary decisions are made.

References

Bartik, Timothy J. 1994. "Jobs, Productivity, and Economic Development: What Implications Does Economic Research Have for the Role of Government?" *National Tax Journal* 47, no. 4: 847–861.

Bohm, Robert A., and Michael P. Kelsay. 1992. "State and Local Government Initiatives to Tax Solid and Hazardous Waste." In *State Taxation of Business: Issues and Policy Options*, ed. Thomas F. Pogue, pp. 281–309. New York: Praeger.

Cline, Robert J. 1988. "Should States Adopt a Value-Added Tax?" In *The Unfinished Agenda for State Tax Reform*, ed. Steven D. Gold, pp. 235–54. Washington, D.C.: National Conference of State Legislatures.

Cordes, Joseph J. 1992. "State Environmental Taxes and Fees." In *State Taxation of Business: Issues and Policy Options*, ed. Thomas F. Pogue, pp. 271–90. New York: Praeger.

Courant, Paul N. 1994. "How Would You Know a Good Economic Policy If You Tripped Over One? Hint: Don't Count Jobs." *National Tax Journal* 47, no. 4: 863–81.

Galginaitis, Steven. 1992. "What Taxes Do States Impose on Business?" In *State Taxation of Business: Issues and Policy Options*, ed. Thomas F. Pogue, pp. 3–16. New York: Praeger.

Grossman, Michael, Jody L. Sindelar, John Mullahy, and Richard Anderson. 1993. "Policy Watch: Alcohol and Cigarette Taxes." *Journal of Economic Perspectives* 7, no. 4. (fall): 211–22.

Hansen, Reid R. 1967. "Henry George: Economics or Theology?" In *Property Taxation, U.S.A.*, ed. Richard W. Lindholm. Madison: University of Wisconsin Press.

Lang, Tim, and Colin Hines. 1993. *The New Protectionism*. London: Earthscan Publications, Ltd.

Manning, Willard G., Emmett B. Keeler, Joseph P. Newhouse, Elizabeth M. Sloss, and Jeffrey Wasserman. 1989. "The Taxes of Sin: Do Smokers and Drinkers Pay Their Way?" *Journal of the American Medical Association* 261, no. 11, (March): 1604–9.

Miller, Gerald H. 1988. "Virtues of a State Value-Added Tax." In *The Unfinished Agenda for State Tax Reform*, ed. Steven D. Gold, pp. 227–34. Washington, D.C.: National Conference of State Legislatures.

Oakland, William H. 1992. "How Should Businesses Be Taxed?" In *State Taxation of Business: Issues and Policy Options,* ed. Thomas F. Pogue, pp. 17–34. New York: Praeger.

Oakland, William H., and William A. Testa. 1996. "State-Local Business Taxation and the Benefit Principle." In *Economic Perspectives,* pp. 2–19. Chicago: Federal Reserve Bank of Chicago.

Papke, James. 1996. "The Convergence of State-Local Business Tax Costs: Evidence of De Facto Collaboration." *Proceedings of the Eighty-Eighth Annual Conference on Taxation, 1995,* pp. 195–206. National Tax Association–Tax Institute of America.

Pogue, Thomas F., and Larry G. Sgontz. 1989. "Taxing to Control Social Costs: The Case of Alcohol." *American Economic Review* 79, no. 1, (March): 235–43.

Pogue, Thomas F. 1994. "Corporate Tax Policy Issues: Comments." *Proceedings of the Eighty-Sixth Annual Conference on Taxation, 1993,* pp. 50–51. National Tax Association–Tax Institute of America.

Slemrod, Joel. 1996. "Which Is the Simplest Tax System of All?" In *Economic Effects of Fundamental Tax Reform,* ed. Henry J. Aaron and William G. Gale, pp. 355–91. Washington, D.C.: Brookings Institution.

Snell, Ronald, ed. 1993. *Financing State Government in the 1990s.* Washington, D.C.: National Governors' Association and the National Conference of State Legislatures. December.

Stocker, Frederick D. 1972. "State and Local Taxation of Business: An Economist's Viewpoint." In *Business Taxes in State and Local Government,* pp. 37–46. Lexington, Mass.: Lexington Books.

Strauss, Robert P. 1986. "Business Taxes." In *Reforming State Tax Systems,* ed. Steven D. Gold, pp. 2321–58. Washington, D.C.: National Conference of State Legislatures.

Studenski, P. 1940. "Toward a Theory of Business Taxation." *Journal of Political Economy* 47: 621–54.

Summers, Lawrence H. 1987. "Should Tax Reform Level the Playing Field?" (Working Paper No. 2132). Cambridge, Mass.: National Bureau of Economic Research.

Summers, Lawrence H. 1991. "The Case for Corrective Taxation." *National Tax Journal* 44, no. 3: 289–92.

Tiebout, Charles M. 1956. "The Pure Theory of Local Expenditures." *Journal of Political Economy* 64: 416–24.

Walker, M. 1937. *How Should Businesses Be Taxed?* New York: Tax Policy League.

Wasylenko, Michael. 1997. "Taxation and Economic Development: The State of the Economic Literature." *New England Economic Review* (March/April): 37–52.

Wheaton, W. C. 1983. "Interstate Differences in the Level of Business Taxation." *National Tax Journal,* 36: 83–94.

Chapter Seven

PROPERTY, TAXES, AND THE FUTURE OF PROPERTY TAXES

Joan M. Youngman

INTRODUCTION

The political and social turbulence that has buffeted the property tax during the past two decades is not likely to abate in the near future. This turmoil stems from much larger social and political questions concerning the appropriate size and functions of government and the best means of meeting its cost. Property tax collections, imposed at a local level and readily weighed against municipal services, present these issues in an especially compelling form. The clarity and simplicity of the tax allow a high measure of accountability and transparency but exact a stiff political price in terms of taxpayer scrutiny.

The traditional model of property taxation in this country as a local, value-based levy may well be re-formed, if not reformed, in response to political pressure in coming decades. This would be entirely consistent with this country's experience of property taxation—which, far from being static, has undergone continual evolution and taken a variety of forms among the many jurisdictions in which it is imposed.

This process will involve weighing objections to the property tax against a number of important benefits, including its suitability for local government financing, its potential for recovering the costs of infrastructure and other property-related public investments, and the unique advantages of land as an immovable tax base in fixed supply. Nor can such a process overlook the value of a long-standing revenue source to which the economic system has long adapted.[1] The adage that an old tax is a good tax is never more true than when some part of that tax burden may be capitalized into the price paid for a durable good of inelastic fixed supply, such as land. In this situation the current owner may not bear the full burden of the tax, and its abolition may in fact constitute a windfall gain. "[T]he taxpayer, by virtue of the process of capitalization, has bought himself free from any calculable, unequal part of the tax, and as for the general or equal or uniform part of it, he bears that in common with others. So long as the tax does not increase rapidly either generally or locally, the payers of taxes on real property can have no valid claim, on the grounds of justice."[2]

A most compelling question concerns the availability and acceptability of alternative revenue sources that might replace diminished property tax collections. Identifying such alternatives is itself extremely difficult, and few of them would permit continuation of local administration and control. Accordingly, the desirability and feasibility of independent local government figures as an inescapable element of the debate over the future of the property tax.

Any property-related tax has implications beyond the fiscal realm because of its connection to current concerns as to the appropriate division of public and private rights in land and buildings. The contentious and unresolved property rights debate of the past two decades is not unrelated to the contemporaneous and equally volatile property tax revolts of the same period.

From this perspective, discontent with property taxation is connected to a variety of property-related controversies, such as debate over development rights, land use restrictions, environmental protection, and the appropriate charges for private use of federal and state land. Each poses a question as to the extent of a public claim on property under private ownership—or, in the latter case, a private claim of some rights to property under public ownership. The context of taxation raises this issue in a particularly vexatious way, imposing as it does an affirmative payment obligation without regard to cash income and threatening loss of the property if the owner is in default.

Paradoxically, the number and seriousness of the problems confronted by the property tax may enhance its importance to policy debate. The issues it raises must be confronted whether the tax is continued, changed, or abolished, and the high visibility of the tax and highly charged public opinion concerning it present these questions in a concrete and compelling form. The same connection with central problems of public finance and property rights that leaves the tax so prone to public discontent also marks it as a bellwether for social consensus on these issues. The process of determining the appropriate role for the property tax will have implications for these larger debates, and thus affect social and political issues beyond the field of taxation itself.

THE DEFINITION OF "PROPERTY"

The contemporary property tax developed in response to the administrative impossibility of taxing all types of property once intangible assets such as securities and bank accounts grew to a major portion of the total property base. The large-scale elimination of most personalty and intangibles has left the property tax a "residual" levy in more ways than one, deprived of its initial status as a general asset tax and generally limited to a unique and significant but narrow form of wealth.

This evolution in response to necessity is by no means finished, as the current round of measures eliminating vestigial taxes on intangibles demonstrates.[3] It might seem extremely simple to exclude intangibles from the property tax base, but in fact the only simple step is the declaration that intangibles are to be free of tax. Far more intractable is the problem of determining how intangible elements, such as licenses and franchises, influence the valuation of business property, and whether a valuation reflecting this influence constitutes an indirect and impermissible extension of the tax to such intangible items.

If anything, debate on this issue has intensified in recent years as the sums potentially attributable to intangible elements of business property, particularly in the area of telecommunications, have grown. Fiercely contested battles over the valuation of telecommunications property presage similar challenges to the valuation of other business property affected by intangible interests. For example, a 1992 California case upheld a $250 million valuation of cellular telephone property that the taxpayer claimed was worth no more than $111.5 million.[4] After a significant victory by GTE Sprint the following year,[5] the California State Board of Equalization agreed in 1995 to reduce the assessed value of the property of forty cellular telephone companies by $600 million as a means of eliminating intangible values from the tax base (Doerr 1995, p. 1642).

The magnitude of the amounts at stake in this controversy increases the difficulty of resolving an issue rooted in the equivocal definition of property. The ambiguity of the distinction between tangible and intangible property proceeds in part from the nature of real property itself as a set of intangible rights that may relate to a tangible object. It is not possible by fiat simply to remove intangible values from the tax base altogether. Instead, a far more complex and subtle undertaking is required to distinguish those elements of value relating to intangible rights in tangible objects that are appropriately subject to tax from those that are not.

WHY TAX PROPERTY?

Many of the property tax's current woes can be traced to the perceived unfairness of a tax limited to one particular asset. Discontent caused by an ever-closer identification of the tax base with land and buildings may in fact prompt a reconsideration of the underlying rationale for the tax. If so, the drawbacks of a specific tax of this type must be weighed against the economic attributes of immovable property that recommend it for a special form of taxation.

Economists have long held the property tax in far higher regard than does the public at large. The National Tax Association's 1994 survey of its members found 85 percent in favor of retention of the tax as a major source of local revenue, almost exactly the same proportion as had favored that proposition sixty years earlier (Slemrod 1995, p. 121). This stands in stark contrast to the tax revolt fervor of recent years. Economists and political scientists admiring the transparency and accountability of this highly visible tax again find themselves at odds with popular reaction.

By contrast, the ease with which small changes in sales tax levels may raise large revenues, with no annual accounting by the ultimate consumer, makes them nearly irresistible substitutes for direct taxation, as the European experience with the value-added tax has shown. When the poll tax debacle left the United Kingdom in need of a swift alternative revenue source, an increase in the value-added tax from 15 percent to 17.5 percent permitted a reduction of local tax bills by one-third (Farrington 1992, pp. 178, 191). "Any revenue shortfall can be met by an increase in the VAT rates. . . . In this way, there will be a temptation to increase public expenditures, knowing the buoyant VAT is waiting in the wings to help out" (Tait 1988, pp. 226–27).

Ironically, the natural regressivity of sales taxes recommends their combination with wealth and estate taxes[6]—just at a time when both are in political disfavor.[7] The unpopularity of transfer taxes demonstrates that solving the liquidity problems faced by cash-poor taxpayers will not necessarily produce an acceptable source of public revenue. Witness the now-repealed New York state tax on real estate sales of over $1 million, with an exception for certain residential properties, that was vilified as the "Cuomo tax" (Doyle 1997). The feasibility of broad-based transfer taxes is decidedly limited if a tax on nonresidential transfers involving over $1 million cannot find political favor.[8]

What about an annualized transfer tax? California has provided an endlessly fascinating case study of the aftermath of a near-abolition of the property tax. By basing the tax upon acquisition value or pre-1977–78 value and limiting annual increases for inflation to 2 percent, the state has transformed an *ad valorem* system into a kind of transfer tax paid in small increments over the period of ownership. However, it would be a mistake to consider the political success of Proposition 13 any mark of approval for traditional transfer taxes. In 1982, a 64 percent majority approved abolition of the state's inheritance tax (Ascher 1990, pp. 69, 75) even while exempting children's inheritance of their parents' residences from the general rule requiring a step up to market value assessment for property tax purposes upon a change in ownership. This permitted a new form of inheritance, the intergenerational transfer of tax values based on 1975–76 assessments or on purchase prices long past, at the same time that the tax on inheritances was itself eliminated.[9]

California's search for alternative revenue sources has proven equally instructive. Developer fees, special assessments, and parcel taxes have taken root to varying degrees and provoked similar voter antipathy. Parcel taxes, a kind of poll tax for real property, illustrate the unexpected and nearly primitive forms of taxation engendered by the search for a nonproperty tax—and, not surprisingly, have been challenged on the characterization.[10] Interestingly, poll taxes, associated since the time of Adam Smith with rudimentary tax systems unable to do more to distinguish among taxpayers than merely ascertain their existence, demonstrated in the United Kingdom that there are indeed alternative revenue forms more unpopular than property taxes.[11]

The California experience challenges the form of the property tax as based on annual market value. Restrictions on market-value assessments in Oklahoma, Michigan, Florida, and Washington[12] demonstrate the appeal of an alternative that provides certainty as to future tax liabilities. Development fees and parcel taxes offer a different set of benefits and drawbacks. The former offers a relationship to the benefits derived from the extension of local services; the latter, simplicity. Each also exacts a price, however, in terms of equity. The drawbacks of acquisition-value taxation were graphically illustrated in the Nordlinger[13] case, in which the Supreme Court refused to overturn Proposition 13 on constitutional grounds. The opinion recognized that the plaintiff's $170,000 condominium bore property taxes five times those of her neighbors, and equivalent to those paid by the owner of a $2.1 million Malibu beach house (Doerr 1995, pp. 178, 191; Slemrod 1995, p. 121). In his dissent, Justice Stevens cited testimony that discrepancies of this type could exceed a factor of five hundred on vacant land (Anderluh 1995). Development fees may stand in a clear relationship to provision of local infrastructure, but they often impose a differential burden on new buildings, older developments having received the same benefits without having paid any special fee. The simplicity of parcel taxes carries the price of any capitation tax: abdication of any attempt to apportion the cost of local services by reference to either a direct benefit or the taxpayer's financial ability.

These competing pressures greatly complicate the political calculus of property tax reform. While it is possible to predict with confidence that an annual tax on land and building value will continue to elicit opposition, it is not easy to identify acceptable alternative revenue sources. Together with the theoretical and practical arguments in favor of the property tax, this suggests that it will continue to serve as a major element of state and local fiscal structures, although never in a static form.

Values and Valuation

Any value-based tax faces special political challenges because of the special nature of the very term "value." As Justice Brandeis noted, "value is a word of many meanings."[14] Can the valuation process be divorced from value judgments? From one perspective, the answer is obviously yes. The fact that "value" can refer both to objective market price and to a subjective measure of intrinsic worth is a mere coincidence. Once the terms and conditions of a hypothetical sale and the economic and legal constraints on property use are determined, valuation requires an empirical analysis of income, cost, and sales data and the application of professional market judgment.

Inescapably, however, an assignment of value to property touches upon deeper social questions that themselves involve value judgments. This is most clear in the choice of the measure of value upon which tax will be assessed. California has made a value judgment in choosing a tax based on acquisition cost, and preferential income-based assessments for farmland represent a value judgment on the part of voters and legislators. But a debate concerning values also underlies many of the political attacks on the assessment process—the assignment of market values to properties—as well. This is evident whether the property at issue constitutes farmland, forests, open space, historic property, family residences, or the homes of senior citizens.

Uneasiness with the valuation process is particularly acute with regard to the concept of highest and best use. What does it imply when undeveloped open space is assigned a value that assumes that its highest and best use is commercial or industrial? An appraiser might respond that that implies nothing with regard to its social worth, but only represents the use contemplated by the highest bid for a given property. Moreover, those who contend that the assessment process undervalues social and environmental benefits would surely not wish by that logic to assign increased property tax values, and increased taxes, to open space and farmland.

It is relatively easy to predict that this ambiguity concerning valuation will continue to affect the political status of the property tax. It will be far more difficult for tax professionals and theorists to clarify this tangled debate and separate the value-laden choice of a tax base from the process of calculating the most probable price of property of a place under current market conditions.

WHO TAXES PROPERTY? THE UNIT OF GOVERNMENT

A century ago, the property tax provided more than half the revenue supporting state government. If the coming decades witness a reconsideration of the role of the tax, they might well see another shift, in the assignment of its administration and collections.

One impetus for redistribution of tax responsibility could come from measures for school finance reform. To the extent that the issue is the inability of impoverished districts to support quality schools, it is a problem of local taxation, not a problem of property taxation. Modest statewide property taxes may figure in efforts to equalize school funding.[15]

Taxes on business property present additional arguments in favor of shifting some responsibility to a higher level of government. In the first place, such a shift could better reflect regional contributions to business growth and development, not limited to the specific jurisdiction in which the business property is located. It might also reduce the political incentive to favor voting residents over business owners under systems of explicit or "extra-legal" classification, which assign different tax rates to different types of property. This reasoning led to revision of the business property tax rate in Britain, which is now uniform and not subject to local control. Taxes on business property are collected by the central government, then redistributed to localities.

Tax base sharing has in fact attracted a great deal of attention in recent years as a potential means for improving land use decisions as well as redressing disparities in jurisdictions' tax bases. Minnesota's pioneering efforts in this regard have mitigated local competition for siting major facilities, such as the Mall of America, because communities within the metropolitan region may receive a share of the revenue increment attributable to such developments even if they are not located within their boundaries (Orfield 1997). Less ambitious measures, such as the option for affluent Texas school districts to "transfer" a portion of their tax base to poorer districts in order to meet state requirements for school funding equity, illustrate a similar impulse in a more limited fashion (Clark 1993).

This move toward regionalism of necessity confronts some of the same economic and political issues raised by the debate over local government autonomy itself. Bundling local governments together undermines the ability of property owners to choose their jurisdictions of residence as a type of consumer purchase of services in exchange for a tax price. The argument for regionalism is based in part on the argument that state-funded infrastructure has permitted new development, but the resulting expansion of the property tax base has benefited only the localities served by these investments. Advocates of regionalism reject the market analogy, or find a failure in the market process, drawing upon a land-value analysis that claims a portion of private property gains in value for the public, on the basis of public investment.

At the same time that efforts such as these have attempted to broaden the boundaries of tax jurisdictions, tax-restriction measures have led to a proliferation of ever smaller and more private taxing districts, most notably in the form of business improvement districts, homeowner associations, and even gated communities. These organizations combine elements of private voluntary associations with those of public bodies able to assess and collect taxes but not subject to the same constraints—yet another example of reinterpreting the division of public and private interests, and the implications of those classifications.

PROPERTY TAXES AND THE PROBLEM OF SCHOOL FINANCE

For decades now, public debate concerning the property tax has been dominated by the problem of equitable funding for public schools. At present, a new wave of state court decisions has overturned, as unconstitutional, school financing systems that rely primarily on local property taxes. It is clear that the future of the property tax in this country will be significantly influenced by this controversy over the use of tax proceeds. However, it is not easy to predict which of several possible forms this response will take.

One form, of course, could be a radical reduction in property tax collections. This is clearly the outcome contemplated by some parties to the debate, for school finance reform efforts often combine the somewhat contradictory goals of tax relief and increased aid to distressed communities. These otherwise conflicting aims coincide only with regard to the in-common first step: property tax reduction. The additional steps that would be necessary to increase funding for schools in impoverished areas—increasing other forms of taxation in order to replace the lost property taxes, and radically increasing funds for needy school districts— could well lose the political support available for the first step. This is a very troubling possibility, and shows the risks involved in undertaking that tax reduction without assurance that subsequent steps will follow. In some respects, this parallels the debate over the fate of large state mental hospitals two decades ago. Deinstitutionalization of the mentally ill was a goal of those who sought a more humane, smaller-scale, community-based treatment. It was also a goal, however, of those who sought ways to reduce state spending. There was no consensus on the later steps necessary to assure humane care of the mentally ill.

The example of California offers a cautionary perspective on the combination of school funding equalization and tax reduction. *Serrano* v. *Priest*, the first major school finance case filed in state rather than federal court, was also the first in which a school finance system that depended upon the wealth of the local tax base was declared unconstitutional.[16] At the same time, Proposition 13 severely restricted property tax revenue available for all purposes. From 1965 to 1992 the property tax contribution to total state and local taxes in California fell from 49.5 percent to 28.6 percent (Advisory Commission on Intergovernmental Relations 1994). In 1986 the California Supreme Court found the state's school finance system constitutional, as 95 percent of districts fell within a maximum expenditures disparity of $200 per pupil.[17] However, this equalization came at a heavy cost. A report by a research group at the graduate schools of education at Stanford and Berkeley pointed out that in 1965 California ranked fifth among the states in per-pupil spending, while in 1994 it ranked fortieth. An article on this report in the *Sacramento Bee* commented,

"Political support for education in California has been eroding steadily for two decades. . . . Under the current system, the governor and legislature decide how much funding schools get, and the state Department of Education tells them how to spend it" (Anderluh 1995). After a quarter-century, California had squared the circle of equalization, school finance reform, and tax reduction, but at the price of calling into question its long-standing commitment to excellence in public education.

RETHINKING EXEMPTIONS

The interest attracted by the ultimately unsuccessful attempt to drastically restrict charitable and religious exemptions from property taxation in Colorado in 1996 suggests that individual states' reformulation of their tax systems may include restrictions or redefinitions of traditional exemptions. This is a natural response to pressure for both tax restrictions and maintenance of public services. At the local level, cities have exerted increased pressure on exempt institutions to initiate or increase payments in lieu of taxes.[18] At the same time, restricting exemptions, runs counter to the spirit of an era in which private charities are expected to meet some of the obligations shed by diminished government. It is possible that this contradiction may be resolved by greater judicial scrutiny of the extent to which organizations seeking tax exemptions meet statutory requirements, such as relieving the government of burdens it would otherwise bear. Several state courts have issued recent decisions that may indicate a trend in this direction.

The most significant exemption issues may escape new scrutiny extended to religious and charitable property. Instead, they are contained in the definition and measurement of the tax base, through preferential assessment provisions for open space and agricultural land.

Taxing or Untaxing Land?

Two unusual attributes of land recommend it for special tax treatment. The first concerns efficiency. The availability of a tax base in inelastic supply provides a source of public revenue that does not, like most taxes, distort market signals and relative prices. Because the supply of land is not increased or diminished in response to the imposition of this tax, the economy is spared the extra burden of inefficiency accompanying any tax that does affect supply and demand.

The second, closely related, aspect concerns the sources of land value. By definition, changes in the price of unimproved land do not reflect efforts or investment on the part of the owner. A plot of vacant land located in an area that develops over time into the center of a metropolitan region may increase enormously in value during that period without any necessary contribution by the owners. That value increase will reflect instead the influence of community growth, and the concomitant extension of services and infrastructure. Is it appropriate for some portion of that value increase to defray these costs of public investment?

Such a proposal can seem exotic and even radical when considered in the context of Colombian valorization or the 1947 Town and Country Planning Act in Great Britain (Cullingworth 1988; Doehele, Grimes, Jr., and Linn 1979, p. 73). Yet this approach is closely linked to the familiar instrument of special assessments and in fact to the land-based portion of the real property tax itself. Where special assessments in this country are generally limited to recovering the amount expended on public improvements, no such ceiling applies to aggregate property tax collections. Moreover, the tax base is not restricted to value attributable to specific public works projects. From this perspective, the property tax, among the simplest and most long-standing revenue instruments, actually implements a public claim on value derived from public investment more effectively than far more controversial demands framed in terms of property law. This case for land value taxation runs headlong, however, into a precisely opposite policy that has garnered enormous public support in the postwar period: preferential assessment of farmland and open space. Under these approaches, "use-value" assessment, based upon some measure of income produced by the property in its predevelopment state, replaces assessment at market value, which is based upon highest and best use. These provisions, which can produce enormous reductions in property taxes, are effectively limited to land under development pressure. Land that has its most economical use for the foreseeable future for agricultural purposes will command a price based primarily on the agricultural income it is expected to yield. In such a case, current use *is* highest and best use. Only land that may potentially be developed to a different and more lucrative use experiences a dramatic decrease in its assessment under the current-use standard.

In the past several decades, provisions of this type have enjoyed greater popularity, and some variety of them has been adopted in each of the fifty states. They reduce the tax pressure that might otherwise force the sale of agricultural land when the owners would prefer to continue farming it. They do not guarantee the long-term preservation of farmland or open space for the community, nor do they compensate for the reduction in development pressure by encouraging plans for directing future growth. In fact, by easing the incentive for development most where such pressure is greatest, they may encourage sprawl, as new development reaches farther beyond the urban boundary.

This tension between pressure to recover infrastructure costs and popular support for an extremely costly tax preference is likely to influence future policy developments in both taxation and land use planning.

As mentioned above, another possible response to the school finance debate would be some revival of the state property tax, in a reversal of the past century's trend toward assignment of the property tax function to local government. The effort to increase spending in impoverished districts has no necessary relationship to increases or decreases in the property tax. It is a question of the degree of reliance on the local tax base, and of how sufficient funds are to be made available to poor localities. Those who seek property tax relief, however, would be unlikely to support similar taxes imposed by a different level of government and distributed in a different manner.

Although a shift from local to state funding for school budgets has no necessary implications for property taxation, it touches indirectly upon the question of local autonomy that is critical to determining the appropriate role for the tax. A shift to state funding raises two interrelated questions. First, to what extent does local control of schools enhance community support, parental involvement, and educational quality? Second, to what extent can state financing of education coexist with local control?

Uniformity and Multiplicity

The treatment of agricultural and open space land is only one example of the special assessment and taxation provisions that have proliferated in recent years. The fragmentation of the tax base has taken two primary forms. One responded to homeowner fears that court decisions striking down "extra-legal" classification schemes would shift the tax burden from business property to residences. In a number of states, therefore, judicial enforcement of long-ignored uniformity provisions led not to uniformity but to constitutional or legislative enactments permitting nonuniformity. The second involves the past decade's widespread use of tax incentives for business location and expansion, a development that may have culminated with such well-publicized measures as Alabama's offer to Mercedes-Benz.[19] Ironically, this "economic war between the states" shows one of the potential dangers of devolution in a competitive environment, as ever more extravagant incentive packages undercut local government's ability to provide the services and education essential to a favorable business environment in the long run.[20] Pressure for increased funding for needy schools may thus be the catalyst for limiting this diminution of the tax base.

CONCLUSIONS

Projecting what future form the property tax might take requires grappling with an interesting and perplexing set of paradoxes. The tax has a long history in this country and has served as a mainstay of local government finance. At the same time, it is under incessant attack and a frequent target for reduction or outright abolition. Economists may approve a land tax as an efficient revenue source, and political scientists may perceive the benefits of a transparent levy, but popular opinion is firmly opposed nonetheless. At the same time, the experiences of pioneering jurisdictions such as Britain and California that have experimented with the outright abolition of traditional *ad valorem* taxes do not offer great encouragement to states that would follow their example. In fact, the strongest voices against the property tax are currently heard in the school financing debate, where a complex and sometimes contradictory set of policy initiatives coincide only in supporting a reduction in the role of the local property tax in school finance. Beyond that point, a set of goals requiring greater public funds is in conflict with a set calling for tax reduction. Elimination of a revenue source without consensus as to its replacement, or as to the budgetary reductions that can accommodate lower total collections, is fraught with danger, as the California experience has demonstrated.

Moreover, the questions that make the property tax debate so incendiary would not themselves be resolved by its elimination. At the heart of the debate is an enduring conflict over the division of public and private interests in land and buildings. In an economy firmly committed to private property, a public claim on a specified portion of the value of realty is necessarily controversial. This is exactly why the property tax has significance beyond its fiscal role alone, and why its evolution will affect larger political issues as well.

Notes

1. "The property tax does have virtues, so the public interest is in doing what can be done to minimize the defects, rather than merely describing the defects of the institution. The principal virtues are pragmatic rather than philosophical ones. The tax exists; it produces very large revenues; and our society and economy have adjusted to and worked through many of the baleful effects of the tax. . . ." Netzer 1968, p. 29.

2. Jensen 1931, p. 75. This nicely illustrates the difference between a political and an economic argument, for recipients of tax bills are rarely convinced on the basis of incidence analysis that another party has actually shouldered this burden for them.

3. Bowman, Hoffer, and Pratt 1990, pp. 439 and 441, listed twenty-two states with taxes on intangible property. Since that time, such taxes have been repealed or overturned in a number of states. In 1996 the Supreme Court found the North Carolina intangibles tax to violate the commerce clause because it permitted a deduction from the value of stocks held by residents to reflect the fraction of stocks income derived from corporations based in the state. *Fulton Corp.* v. *Faulkner,* 116 S. Ct. 848, 133 L.Ed.2d 796 (1996). After that decision, Georgia repealed its intangible personal property tax as well. ("Georgia Governor Signs Legislation Repealing Intangible Personal Property Tax," 1996, 96 STN 94-2.) For similar disputes in other states, see Sommer 1996, 96 STN 202-9; Bright 1996, 96 STN 191-39.

4. *Los Angeles SMSA Limited Partnership* v. *State Bd. of Equalization,* 11 Cal. App. 4th 768; 14 Cal. Rptr. 2d 522 (1992).

5. *GTE Sprint Communications Corp.* v. *County of Alameda,* 26 Cal. App. 4th 992, 32 Cal. Rptr. 2d 882 (1994).

6. "[A] common recommendation for a comprehensive tax system is a broad-based consumption tax supplemented by a wealth transfer tax." McCaffery 1994, pp. 283, 326.

7. McCaffery 1996, pp. 71, 144–45, writes that a wise observer (whom he characterizes as "Athena") "will soon see that her polis appears deeply opposed to estate taxation; that many years of practice have produced only a porous and potentially counterproductive tax; that other democratic nations, such as Australia, Canada, and Israel, have recently abolished their wealth taxes. . . . Athena will reflect that her people consider it to be natural, reasonable, and even helpful to work hard and save well, holding the wealth in store for a rainy day or a later generation, all the while seeing that the general benefits of enhanced capital stock flow to their fellow citizens." In releasing his proposed 1997–98 budget, New York Governor George Pataki stated, "We eliminate the Estate Tax, which will encourage future retirees to remain here with their children, grandchildren, and lifelong friends. It will also benefit small business owners and family farmers who have lived and worked in New York for generations." *State Tax Notes,* 1997, 72 STN 15-30, Doc. 97-1561. In "The American Dream in Legislation: The Role of Popular Symbols in Wealth Tax Policy," p. 287, William Blatt quotes Joseph A. Pechman: "Although tax theorists almost unanimously agree that taxation of wealth should play a larger role in the revenue system, they have not been successful in convincing Congress."

8. The exception that proves the rule in this case may be resort communities with transfer taxes earmarked for preservation of open space threatened by development. A 2 percent tax for this purpose adopted by Martha's Vineyard and Nantucket in the 1980s may now be doubled, at a time when the average sale price of houses on Nantucket reached $687,000. Arnand 1997. An effort is underway to establish a similar measure in Easthampton and other communities on eastern Long Island. Rather 1997.

9. An amendment to the California Constitution approved in 1996 extended this provision to transfers of real property between grandparents and their grandchildren, when the parents of those children are deceased. See *State Tax Notes* 1996, 96 STN 199-14.

10. The uncertainty of the legal distinction between property taxes, excise taxes, and parcel taxes was illustrated in *Thomas v. City of East Palo Alto*, 53 Cal. App. 4th 1084, 62 Cal. Rptr. 2d 185 (Ct. App. 1997), in which a parcel tax was held to be a property tax and therefore in violation of the California Constitution because not levied in proportion to assessed value.

11. See Smith, pp. 808 ("What are called poll-taxes . . . seem anciently to have been common all over Europe. There subsists at present a tax of this kind in the empire of Russia. It is probably on this account that poll-taxes of all kinds have often been represented as badges of slavery.") and 821 ("Capitation taxes are levied at little expense; and, where they are rigorously exacted, afford a very sure revenue to the state. It is upon this account that in countries where the ease, comfort, and security of the inferior ranks of people are little attended to, capitation taxes are very common."). See also Butler, Adonis, and Travers 1994.

12. See Mayer 1997, 97 STN 103-40; 1996, 96 STN 92-69; *Markham v. Department of Revenue* (Florida Division of Administrative Hearings, Case No. 95-1339RP, June 21, 1995) (which upheld proposed rules to implement an amendment to the Florida Constitution, approved by voters in 1992, by which homestead property would be assessed at its January 1, 1994, value, rising only by the lesser of 3 percent or the annual change in the Consumer Price Index until there is a change in ownership); *Michigan Attorney General Opinion 6851* (1995) (which held Michigan's 1994 constitutional amendments to limit assessment increases to the lesser of the rate of inflation or 5 percent, except upon a change in ownership, inapplicable to public service property).

13. *Nordlinger v. Hahn*, 505 U.S. 1 (1992).

14. *Southwestern Bell Telephone v. Public Service Commission*, 262 U.S. 276, 310 (1923) (dissenting opinion).

15. For example, the 1994 Michigan plan to replace most school property taxes with increased sales and tobacco taxes included a continued statewide property tax of 6 mills to support education.

16. *Serrano v. Priest*, 5 Cal.3d 584, 487 P.2d 1241 (1971).

17. *Serrano v. Priest [III]*, 200 Cal. App.3d 897, 226 Cal. Rptr. 584 (1986).

18. See Glaberson 1996. "In Ithaca, N.Y., state officials recently withheld building permits from Cornell University and in October won an unusual agreement under which the university will increase its annual payments to the city from $147,000 in 1994 to $1 million a year by 2007. Cornell has been making such voluntary payments to the city of Ithaca since 1967."

19. Estimates that Alabama offered between $200 million and $300 million in tax incentives for this plant have been the subject of much commentary. See "Alabama Paid Too Much to Lure Mercedes-Benz, Former Tennessee Governor Says" 1994, 94 STN 214-1.

20. "Corporations have become adept at pitting state and local governments against each other in aggressive bidding wars for tax, financing, regulatory, training, and infra-

structure incentives and concessions. In many cases, these are never recovered in additional business taxes and taxes collected from workers occupying new jobs. Rather than working to present uniform policies to businesses, states have unwittingly been drawn into a series of bidding wars in attempting to attract new industries." Graeser 1994, 94 STN 194-69.

References

Advisory Commission on Intergovernmental Relations. 1994. *Significant Features of Fiscal Federalism*. Volume 2, Table 53.

"Alabama Paid Too Much to Lure Mercedes-Benz, Former Tennessee Governor Says." 1994. *State Tax Notes*. 94 STN 214-1 (November 4).

Anderluh, Deborah. 1995. "New Report Blasts Education in State." *Sacramento Bee*. April 19.

Arnand, Geeta. 1997. "An Island of Community." *Boston Globe*. June 22.

Ascher, Mark L. 1990. "Curtailing Inherited Wealth." *Mich. L. Rev.* 89 (October). pp. 69, 75.

Blatt, William. 1996. "The American Dream in Legislation: The Role of Popular Symbols in Wealth Tax Policy." *Tax L. Rev.* 51 (winter) 287, n. 1.

Bowman, J., G. Hoffer, and M. Pratt. 1990. "Current Patterns and Trends in State and Local Intangible Taxation." *National Tax Journal* 43: 439, 441.

Bright, Joseph C. "Montgomery County, Pennsylvania, Enjoined From Collecting Personal Property Tax." *State Tax Notes* 96 STN 191-39 (October 1).

Butler, David, Andrew Adonis, and Tony Travers. 1994. *Failure to British Government: The Politics of the Poll Tax*. Oxford: Oxford University Press.

Clark, Catherine. 1993. "The Texas School Melodrama." *86th Annual Conference of the National Tax Association Proceedings* 28.

Cullingworth, J. B. 1988. *Town and Country Planning in Britain* 10th ed. London: Unwin Hyman.

Doebele, William A., Orville F. Grimes, Jr., and Johannes F. Linn. 1979. "Participation of Beneficiaries in Financing Urban Services: Valorization Charges in Bogotá, Colombia." *Land Economics* 55 (February). p. 73.

Doerr, David. 1995. California BOE Removes Intangible Values From Cellular Companies' Assessments." *State Tax Notes* p. 1642 (December 11).

Doyle, Christopher L. 1997. "New York's Repealed Gain Tax." 97 *State Tax Notes* (May 20).

Farrington, Colin. 1992. "Development in the United Kingdom." *Review of Urban and Regional Development Studies* 4: 178, 191.

"Georgia Governor Signs Legislation Repealing Intangible Personal Property Tax." 1996. *State Tax Notes* 96 STN 94-2 (May 14).

Glaberson, William. 1996. "In Era of Fiscal Damage Control, Cities Fight Idea of Tax Exempt." *New York Times*. February 21, p. A1.

Graeser, Laird. 1994. "Business Taxes—Quo Vadimus?" *State Tax Notes*. 94 STN 194-69 (October 6).

Hunt, Kenneth. 1996. "Oklahoma Consensus Reached on Property Tax Reforms." *State Tax Notes* 96 STN 92-69 (May 10).

Jensen, Jens. 1931. *Property Taxation in the United States*. Chicago: University of Chicago Press, p. 75.

Mayer, James. 1997. "Oregon Voters Pass Revision of Property Tax Limit." *State Tax Notes* 97 STN 103-40 (May 29).

McCaffery, Edward J. 1994. "The Uneasy Case for Wealth Transfer Taxation." *Yale Law Journal* 104: 283, 326.

————. 1996. "Tax's Empire." *Geo. L. J.* 85 (November), pp. 71, 144–145.

Netzer, Dick. 1968. "The Impact of the Property Tax: Its Economic Implications for Urban Problems." Report of the National Commission on Urban Problems to the Joint Economic Committee of the U.S. Congress (May), p. 29.

Orfield, Myron. 1997. *Metropolitics*. Washington, D.C.: Brookings Institution.

Patakin, George. 1997. *State Tax Notes*. 72 STN 15-30, Doc. 97-1561 (January 23).

Rather, John. 1997. "2% Tax Proposed to Preserve Open Land." *New York Times*. June 15.

Slemrod, Joel B. 1995. "Professional Opinions About Tax Policy: 1994 and 1934." *National Tax Journal* 48: 121 (March).

Smith, Adam. 1937. *Wealth of Nations*. New York City Modern Library, pp. 808, 821.

Sommer, Mark F. "Battle Over Kentucky's Intangibles Tax Continues." *State Tax Notes* 96 STN 202-9 (October 17).

State Tax Notes. 1996. 96 STN 199-14 (October 11).

Tait, Alan. 1988. *Value-Added Tax: International Practice and Problems*. Washington, D.C.: International Monetary Fund, pp. 226–27.

Chapter Eight

THE FUTURE OF THE PROPERTY TAX: A POLITICAL ECONOMY PERSPECTIVE

Steven M. Sheffrin

INTRODUCTION

This paper forecasts trends for the future of the property tax in the United States as we move into the next century. Forecasting is a difficult task, as economists have unfortunately discovered, and forecasting institutional developments is a particularly challenging enterprise. To provide an underlying rationale for my projections, I will rely on what I perceive to be fundamental political-economic trends that are currently influencing the shape of the property tax. I will also draw on some recent developments in areas of public finance closely related to property taxation and incorporate these into my vision of the property tax in the future.[1]

In this paper, I identify four different trends that I believe will fundamentally change the property tax in the next several decades:

- ongoing legal challenges to the use of property taxes to finance schools;
- pervasive tax limitations;
- the growing use of alternatives to *ad valorem* property taxation; and
- pressures for increased "direct democracy" in local public finance.

Despite these trends, other political economy considerations will dictate that the property tax will persist—but it will be capped at relatively low levels and utilized with little local autonomy.

The four trends I outline are interrelated. The property tax has always been an unpopular tax, but it was tolerated because it was a convenient vehicle to enable local autonomy in financing education, a service that the public values highly. Once the legal and moral foundations of using the property tax to finance schools have been undermined, there is no longer a compelling underlying rationale for a broad-based local *ad valorem* property tax. This result is tax limitation movements, directed mostly at property taxation. Local governments initially try to evade these limits by using alternatives to *ad valorem* taxes on property. But as local fiscal systems inevitably become more complex and less transparent, voters will demand more control over these taxes and begin to micromanage local public finances. The final result is what I term a "particularization" of local taxation. Nonetheless, the property tax will persist in a limited form—both because it is a powerful revenue raiser and because the fiscal alternatives are not satisfactory replacements for local governments.

Before turning to this argument, however, it is valuable to look briefly at the historical evolution of the property tax to gain a sense of how radically the property tax has already changed. Probably our greatest danger in making long-term forecasts is to underestimate the capacity for institutional change and merely project minor modifications onto the status quo.

In the last 150 years, there have been dramatic changes in the nature of the property tax. The property tax in the United States originated largely as an *in rem* tax—so many dollars per unit—applied to ownership of very specific types of property, such as cattle, land, and improvements. During the middle of the nineteenth century, states began to include "uniformity" clauses in their constitutions, which were interpreted as calling for comprehensive taxation of all forms of property at a uniform rate. This call for uniformity appealed to widely accepted principles of individualism and also served to limit state legislatures from raising taxes on weak political actors. The uniformity clauses dictated that intangible property (stocks, bonds, mortgages, and other financial instruments) be taxed along with real property and personal property.[2]

In the beginning of the twentieth century, property taxation of intangibles was attacked by both economists and administrators. Economists found that taxation of intangibles, as practiced, inevitably resulted in double taxation, as both an asset and claims to that asset were often subject to tax. Property tax administrators could not track intangible assets as easily as they could tangible assets, with the result that there was widespread evasion of property taxes on intangible assets. By the end of the Great Depression, most states had abandoned or sharply limited taxation of intangibles and had begun to use income and sales taxes as key components of their revenue systems.

This change in the formal structure of property taxation was also accompanied by radical changes in its use by different levels of government. The property tax today is primarily a local government revenue source. Local governments receive the vast majority of property tax revenues—nearly 98 percent. This stands in contrast to the early 1900s, when the property tax provided more than half of state government revenues in the United States.

Several developments led to this change. First, there were political and administrative difficulties with "dual systems" in which local and state governments shared in the property tax. Since local governments did not obtain all the revenue from the property tax, there was a danger that local assessors would underassess property to benefit local property owners at the expense of the state. As a result, in most states, there was a gradual move to separate property into state-assessed property (e.g., utilities) and locally assessed commercial and residential property.[3]

Second, state governments began to take on additional functions that required additional sources of revenue, particularly sales and income taxation. These sources of revenue proved to be extremely elastic. As a consequence, the state share of tax revenue from property taxes declined. Many of these changes occurred in the 1930s; by 1940 the property tax provided less than 8 percent of state tax revenues. By 1980 the share had fallen to 2 percent, and it remained virtually unchanged throughout the decade of the 1980s and into the 1990s.[4]

Although the property tax still dominates local revenue structures, there is a substantial degree of variation in reliance on the property tax by type of local government (counties, cities, school districts, and special districts). Throughout the decade of the 1980s the distribution of the property tax pie has remained fairly stable, with school districts receiving the largest piece, 43 percent. Traditionally, the property tax has been the major source of school finance; this aspect of the property tax, however, is now under sharp attack.

THE CHALLENGE FROM SCHOOL FINANCE

For roughly the past two decades, there has been litigation (much of it successful) challenging the role of the property tax in financing K–12 education. By 1995, forty-three states had experienced legal challenges to their educational systems.[5] The premise of the lawsuits has been that relying on property taxation to finance education unfairly disadvantages students who live in districts in which there are relatively low levels of property tax wealth. Since voters in districts with relatively low property tax wealth must levy a higher rate to raise the same revenue as compared with voters in districts with relatively high property tax wealth, there is a natural tendency toward inequality in educational expenditure across districts. While all states provide some funding to equalize spending, the lawsuits contend that state funding does not provide sufficient equalization.[6]

These lawsuits, both successful and unsuccessful, have prompted state legislatures to reform their educational financing systems. The result of these reforms has been that a higher percentage of funding for education has been undertaken at the state level. Econometric studies generally show that, while reforms do not necessarily reduce total educational spending, increasing the state share of spending does tend to depress spending.[7] Moreover, the states that tried to equalize spending by providing incentives for poor districts to spend more were generally less successful in reducing inequalities.[8]

William Fischel (1989) first drew attention to the link between school finance reform and property tax revolts with his provocative thesis that Proposition 13 in California was "caused" by *Serrano v. Priest*, a successful equalization lawsuit in California. As a result of this ongoing litigation, the California State Supreme Court in 1976 mandated that the legislature reduce inequalities in per student spending across districts to within $100 of the state mean.[9] Fischel argued that this ruling destroyed the previous political and economic equilibrium in the state. Prior to this ruling, citizens would choose to locate in the jurisdiction that offered the combination of taxes and public goods (especially education) that they desired. High-income residents of the state who desired high-quality public services would locate in communities that would vote for high property taxes and high spending. After *Serrano v. Priest*, taxpayers could no longer raise property taxes to increase spending on their own school but would have to increase funding for *all* school districts within the state to increase their own local spending. As a result, the marginal benefit of paying property taxes was significantly reduced, and the rationale for local property taxation was undercut. High-income communities (which were paying substantial property taxes) no longer had an interest in supporting a decentralized property tax system. The result, according to Fischel, was Proposition 13, the landmark tax limitation measure.[10]

In a later work, Fischel (1996) outlined a more indirect connection between *Serrano v. Priest* and the passage of Proposition 13. The California legislature was preoccupied with developing a financing scheme to follow the court mandate. They were reluctant, therefore, to devote the growing state fiscal surplus to property tax relief, which might have averted Proposition 13.

Fischel's thesis has been controversial. But one need not accept Fischel's argument that *Serrano* specifically "caused" Proposition 13 to accept the basic logic of his thesis: The political-economic rationale of a local property tax system is severely undercut if the local property tax cannot be used to finance additional education spending within a community. Although the property tax is used to fund other services, none of the other services has the universal appeal of education.

In the 1990s, two dramatic episodes of property tax reduction in Michigan and Wisconsin centered around educational finance. In both these cases, equalization provided a basic rationale for property tax reduction. Educational reform may have simply served as convenient political cover, however, for an underlying desire to shift the tax base away from property and toward other tax bases.

Over the years, there had been a number of attempts in Michigan to reduce reliance on local property taxes and replace the revenue with other forms of tax. Michigan had one of the highest rates of residential property taxation in the country.[11] Republicans (not typically the party of equalization movements) had been leading this effort in the early 1990s, but with little success. In September of 1993, a Democratic legislator reversed roles and proposed a bill to totally eliminate local property taxes for public schools with no replacement revenue. The political turmoil that ensued led eventually to a legislative agreement to a March 1995 referendum that reduced reliance on the local property tax for education and raised the general state sales tax from 4 to 6 percent.[12] The voters passed this referendum, with the result that the share of K–12 public school funding derived from both state and local property taxes fell from 66 percent to approximately 32 percent by 1995.

In Wisconsin, the legislature was quite explicit in advocating greater state control of education as a means of reducing the property tax burden. In 1993, the legislature imposed revenue caps on school districts to curtail the growth in school property taxes, which had grown at the second fastest rate in the country in the prior decade.[13] Despite this cap, property taxes continued to grow. The legislature then passed a law committing the state to providing two-thirds of the funding for public schools. If the state did not come up with sufficient funds, the legislation authorized strict caps on local districts, which would reduce property taxes substantially. The overall goal of the legislation was to reduce property taxes by 40 percent. Changes in the educational finance system, then, were the route to reduced property taxes.

LIMITATIONS ON THE PROPERTY TAX

With the decreased use of the property tax for educational finance, the tax loses much of its popular rationale. The natural next step would be to see sharp limitations placed on the use of property taxes. In most states these limitations are already in place.

Virtually all jurisdictions that have property taxes have some form of accompanying tax limitations. As of 1991, only six states were free of limitations on property taxes.[14] Such limitations take a variety of forms. There can be limitations on the growth of the property tax base for individual properties or for a given jurisdiction; there can be limitations on rates or on assessments; and there can be limitations on the growth of property tax revenues.

One of the most dramatic limitations on the property tax base came into effect with the passage of Proposition 13 in California. In California, the assessed value of a property can be increased by a maximum of 2 percent a year until the property is sold, at which point it is assessed at market value. If inflation in housing prices exceeds 2 percent a year, then newly purchased properties will be assessed at substantially higher rates than properties that have not been sold.

Studies have revealed that these limitations on assessed value growth have had dramatic effects on effective tax rates.[15] For example, in Los Angeles County in 1992, 43 percent of homeowners had been in their homes since 1975. On average, the effective tax rate for those homeowners was .2 percent, compared with 1 percent for newly purchased homes. In California, the average effective tax rate in the same year was .55 percent, whereas the statutory rate was 1 percent. These disparities in effective tax rates were challenged in the Supreme Court on the basis that they violated the equal protection clause of the Constitution. The Court has generally given wide discretion to states in the design of their fiscal systems, however, and it upheld Proposition 13.[16]

The California system, however, has not been the typical pattern. The majority of property tax limitations place restrictions on the maximum rate of taxation and do not limit increases in assessed value. Only ten states place some limits on assessed value increases.[17] The most recent state to pass a limitation on assessed value was Florida, in 1992. This limitation was 3 percent and applied only to residential property.

Barring a sudden upsurge in real estate prices, it is unlikely that there will be many more states adopting assessment limitations. As long as rates are capped, total property tax revenues will rise with assessments. As long as assessed values do not grow substantially faster than income, the overall burden of property taxation will not change substantially. Further reductions in the property tax burden can be accomplished by lowering the rate limits, as in Michigan. The California experience has been criticized severely for its horizontal inequities among taxpayers and has not, in general, been a positive model for other states.

Limitations on the growth of total property tax levies (without explicit limits on rates or assessed value) are also common among the states. Levy limits can preserve some local autonomy or flexibility. For example, in slow-growing locales with stagnant property values, rate limits would freeze property taxes, but levy limits would permit increases in property tax rates until the levy limit was reached.

Will these property tax limitations persist? The first great wave of limitations was enacted during the Great Depression but gradually disappeared by the late 1930s.[18] The second wave of tax limitations was enacted during the tax revolt era of the late 1970s and followed closely on Proposition 13 in California. These limitations are more likely to remain in place, mainly because the property tax has lost its allure as a source of educational financing and has become a backstop tax for other, less glamorous, local services. Welfare and mental health facilities do not have the same allure as K–12 education. Given, also, its underlying dislike of wealth-based taxes, the public will want to keep sharp limits on property taxation.

ALTERNATIVES TO AD VALOREM PROPERTY TAXATION

One of the key lessons from the tax revolt era is that tax limitations do not prevent the growth of government. Local governments have been ingenious in developing new sources of revenue. Where property taxes have been limited, we see shifts toward alternative revenue sources, such as increased fees and charges, sales taxes, and income taxes. State and local charges and miscellaneous revenue increased from $184 per capita in 1975 to $931 per capita in 1992, exceeding per capita property taxes ($698) and sales taxes ($768).[19] While local governments have witnessed a decline in their own-source revenues financed by property taxation, they have seen an increase in their revenue from fees and charges and miscellaneous revenue and from sales taxes.

Even in California, where there are sharp limitations on the *ad valorem* property tax as imposed by Proposition 13, there has been a growth in other property-related taxes. In addition to expanding their levels of fees and charges, cities and counties have established new "benefit assessment districts" that use flat, per parcel charges (not *ad valorem* taxes) to fund a variety of services, ranging from police and fire support to landscape and lighting. Local governments have been able to establish special assessment districts in California since 1909; but the scope of these assessments was expanded by legislation in 1982 from traditional parks and playgrounds to a variety of basic services, such as lighting, landscaping, and drainage. Not only did the courts permit parcel charges for these services under Proposition 13, but these charges were not included in calculating overall spending limitations that apply to all jurisdictions in California. Since 1982, the growth of these benefit assessment districts has been very rapid. In addition to this innovation, the legislature also permitted localities to levy fees (subject to some limitations) on the transfer of properties.

Each of these revenue sources has its own limitations. Fees and charges cannot greatly exceed the true cost of providing the relevant services without being subject to legal and political challenges. Benefit assessment districts can be financed only by parcel charges, and the revenues can be used only to pay for facilities that provide a special benefit to property owners, as opposed to general benefits to taxpayers. Finally, property transfer fees are partly restrained by state law.

To finance new construction and to provide infrastructure, governments have increasingly begun to rely on other sources of revenue, including fees imposed on new development or, more generally, *exactions*. Exactions are payments or dedications made by a developer for the right to proceed with a project requiring governmental approval and can be in the form of a fee, the dedication of public land, the construction or maintenance of public infrastructure, or the provision of public services. Both cities and counties throughout the country have increased their use of development fees and exactions in recent years.

A recent study examined in detail the magnitude and effects of exactions and fees for Contra Costa County, a county in the San Francisco Bay area that has experienced rapid growth in recent decades.[20] It found that the fees imposed on new construction are quite significant, typically falling in the range of $20,000 to $30,000 per dwelling. In one community, the fees and assessments totaled 19 percent of the mean sales price. These fees and charges do not show up in ongoing city and county budgets; yet they are an important component of the burden placed on property in growing areas.

Another alternative for financing new development has been the growth in assessment districts. California legislators have been particularly ingenious in finding assessment mechanisms consistent with the limitations of Proposition 13. The Mello-Roos Community Facilities Act of 1982 gave counties, cities, and special districts the authority to establish community facilities districts (CFDs) within their jurisdiction. With two-thirds approval of the district's voters, tax-exempt bonds can be issued and special taxes levied. If there are fewer than twelve registered voters residing in the CFD, approval of two-thirds of the landowners in the district is sufficient. It is this latter provision that is responsible for the rapid growth of Mello-Roos districts, as the original landowners create a district to finance infrastructure. Proceeds from the bonds can be used for the full range of public facilities, including schools. Mello-Roos districts have been used throughout California, especially in the fast-growing southern counties.

While city and county officials have been ingenious in developing alternative property-based taxes that appear to circumvent limitations, voters will eventually react to these developments. As the system becomes more complex and less transparent, it is inevitable that city and county officials will want to take advantage of these complexities to fulfill their own private bureaucratic desires as well as for public-spirited purposes. Citizens will begin to feel a loss of control and become suspicious of the motives of public officials. The inevitable result, foreshadowed in California, will be increased voter involvement in the details of local public affairs.

THE ONSET OF DIRECT DEMOCRACY

To illustrate this thesis, I turn now to a discussion of an extremely important constitutional initiative, Proposition 218, that was passed by California voters in November of 1996. Proposition 218 is probably the single most important development in local public finance in California since the passage of Proposition 13, and cities, counties, and special districts are currently grappling with its implications.

The basic idea behind Proposition 218 is to allow voters and property owners to have a greater voice in, and increased opportunities to vote on, specific measures in virtually all areas of local public finance—and, correspondingly, to decrease the discretion of elected officials. I use the term "direct democracy" to refer to this increased use of the ballot with respect to specific fiscal measures, with correspondingly less reliance on representative democracy as embodied in elected officials.

Because Proposition 218 was designed to constrain a system that had become very complex, it is, by its very nature, also complex. The overall structure of Proposition 218, however, is fairly straightforward. It distinguishes between three types of fiscal tools that local governments use—taxes, assessments, and fees—and sets forth the level of direct voter involvement in each type. While Proposition 218 applies to existing as well as future levies, for the sake of simplicity, we will limit our discussion to the rules that apply for new or increased levies.[21]

A tax can be defined as a charge that an individual or business pays that benefits the public broadly.[22] Proposition 13 had created a distinction between a general tax and a "special tax," one whose proceeds are used for a specific purpose. Proposition 218 requires that all general taxes be approved by a majority of the voters, and these elections must be consolidated with those for the officials of the local governing body. Special taxes (as previously required by Proposition 13) require a two-thirds vote. Any tax whose proceeds are dedicated to a specific purpose will be characterized as a special tax even if the funds are placed in the general fund.

Assessments are charges levied on property to pay for a public improvement or service that benefits the property. The rules for assessments were intended to apply to nontraditional uses of assessment districts. Thus, assessments for sidewalks, streets, water, flood control, drainage, and vector control (e.g., mosquito control)—which constitute roughly half of all assessments—were exempt from any new requirements. With respect to all other assessments, local governments must first determine if property owners receive "special benefits" from an assessment. Property owners cannot be charged for "general benefits." For example, a parcel tax that finances libraries or fire protection would be viewed as providing general benefits (available to all citizens, including renters) and would not be permitted under Proposition 218; such benefits must be financed from general funds. Once a local government has determined the share of the assessment that provides special benefits to property owners, it then must set the charges proportionally, based on the benefits to specific classes of property. A majority of voters, weighted by their assessment share, must then approve any new or increased assessment.

Fees are charges imposed on individuals or businesses for services provided directly to an individual or business. Proposition 218 applies only to "property-related" fees, such as those that appear on monthly bills for water, garbage, and sewage, and strict limits are placed on the use of such fees.[23] Local governments must obtain approval from voters to raise fees or institute new fees but have the option of a vote of either two-thirds of the electorate or a majority of property owners (with an option to weight the votes by fee liability).

In their analysis of Proposition 218, the Legislative Analyst Office (1996) speculated that local government could begin to rely more heavily on other revenue sources, such as redevelopment revenues, developer exactions, and general taxes on particular groups (such as hotel occupancy taxes). As they noted, however, there are limits—political, legal, or economic—to increased reliance on each of these sources. Redevelopment revenues are typically diverted from other governmental units; developer exactions are constrained to some degree by law; and increased general taxes, such as hotel occupancy taxes, will reduce business activity and diminish the tax base.

In addition to its specific provisions, Proposition 218 shifts the burden of proof for challenges to fees or assessments to the individual or business. While this will favor taxpayers in specific cases, there are many remaining, open issues. The complexity and comprehensiveness of Proposition 218 have naturally generated a number of difficult questions in terms of its application. Many of these will be settled in court.

Ironically, this movement back to direct democracy hearkens back to the idealized New England town meeting, in which voters could decide on the appropriate levels of taxation for their local services, especially schools. But there are several important differences. First, voter discretion in California applies to virtually all taxes *except* the *ad valorem* property tax. Second, voters have discretion over levies for most categories of local spending *except* for schools, the single most important one. Finally, levies have been "particularized": On any given fee or assessment, a different group (or the same group weighted differently) may be voting. Each assessment or fee will typically stand on its own, and there is less opportunity for the backroom dealmaking and trades that occur naturally in representative bodies across issues or constituencies.

While many of the provisions of Proposition 218 were tailored to the peculiarities of California's complex fiscal system and designed to constrain perceived abuses by local officials, the core idea lying behind this initiative will be transferable to many other states. The dialectic we have examined—school equalization litigation leading to property tax limitations, fiscal innovation by local government leading to a loss of transparency, and subsequent demands for direct control—will occur throughout the country. Initiatives (or state legislation) along the lines of Proposition 218 will, we predict, proliferate in the near future.

Are these developments positive or negative from the point of view of economic efficiency? Whether particularization of local services is efficient depends on whether the services can be treated independently from an economic point of view. If there are no economic interdependencies (such as shared infrastructure), then it would be efficient to let each affected group make its decisions independently. But if there are important spillovers between different types of services, then these services become more like "public goods," and some mechanism is necessary to force the voters to take into account these interdependencies. In recent years, the trend has been to "unbundle" services such as utilities and communications. This trend has typically been viewed favorably by economists. Particularization of local services can be viewed as a parallel trend. It remains to be determined whether the underlying economic assumptions supporting particularization of local services are warranted.

THE PERSISTENCE OF A BASIC PROPERTY TAX

Despite the particularization of property-related taxes, a limited and capped property tax will, I believe, remain an important revenue source for local governments. There are several distinct reasons why the property tax will persist in a limited fashion.

First, the property tax is a proven revenue raiser. Since the value of taxable property is typically a large multiple of current income, even a 1 percent property tax will raise considerable revenue. In states with property, income, and sales taxes, it is quite common for each to raise approximately the same amount of revenue. As long as rates (or overall levies) are capped, the basic property tax can operate silently in the background and not be subject to excessive political controversy.

Second, land, an essential element of the property tax base, is immobile and thus ideally suited for taxation, both from an efficiency point of view and from the perspective of the tax collector. This point has long been recognized, both in economic theory and in the politics of taxation. Property taxation of structures can cause distortions as new construction responds to taxation. But as economic growth occurs and land prices inevitably increase, the property tax is ideally positioned to absorb this increase in value.

Third, the major alternatives to the property tax—sales and income taxes—both have flaws as local taxes. Sales taxes are generally allocated to the jurisdiction where the sale is made. Thus, communities will inevitably compete with each other by offering inducements to sales tax–rich businesses (such as automobile dealers) in order to capture the resulting sales tax. The ultimate beneficiaries of this competition are the businesses, not local governments.

Local income taxes will be limited by household mobility. If a city imposes an income tax when neighboring communities do not, it can anticipate an outflow of residents. Major employment centers can impose wage taxes (to capture commuters as well as residents), but these options are limited for smaller communities with no distinguishing or unique characteristics.

Nechyba (1997) recently analyzed the optimal mix of (flat) income and property taxes for communities when the population is mobile. In a sophisticated general equilibrium model, he found that property taxes would emerge as a dominant tax source for local communities. To understand the logic of his argument, consider a situation in which the stock of housing is given, housing prices are temporarily fixed, and potential residents differ in the ratio of their income to their desired housing value. If a community raised its income tax and lowered its property tax, it would attract residents that have a lower ratio of income to desired house value, since they would experience a tax reduction by moving into the community. An immigrant who displaced an emigrant by moving into his house would have a lower income. The result of these movements of households would be that the community would have a lower income tax base than it had anticipated prior to the change in the mix of taxation, and public services would inevitably suffer. This argument is based on the premise that house prices are temporarily fixed, but Nechyba showed that his conclusion was valid even if house prices are allowed to respond to accommodate changes in demand.

To this point, we have not discussed the possibility that the basic property tax will be classified according to type of property and differing rates applied to each class. Classified property tax systems are common in the United States, especially in many areas of the South. Some states that introduced property tax limitations, such as Massachusetts, have allowed business property to be taxed at a higher rate than residential property. Communities will sometimes take advantage of these laws, as research shows that voters believe that a significant share of property taxes on commercial and industrial properties located in the community are not borne by local residents.[24]

There are natural limits, however, to rate differentials between business and residential property. Interstate and interjurisdictional competition will give businesses leverage to bargain for rate reductions, thereby offsetting, to some degree, pressures for higher rates. Furthermore, if communities become too aggressive in taxing local business, representatives of business interests will appeal to state legislatures, who can then limit such taxation. Local communities may find it in their best interest to commit themselves to equal rates for businesses and residents to afford them the political support they need to resist demands from business for *lower* tax rates for business property.

CONCLUSIONS

As we peer into the future, we still envision a property tax. But the *ad valorem* property tax will no longer be the idealized local tax that economists and political theorists so admire. In the textbook model, the property tax is the main vehicle through which citizens with different tastes for public services can match their demand for public services to their taxes. Variations in property tax rates are most important in financing education, the single most important good with respect to which tastes can differ (in the textbook model). The dialectic we described—the school equalization movement begetting property tax limitations, fiscal innovation by local government leading to a loss of transparency, subsequent demands for direct control—destroys this idealized vision of the property tax.

The main function of the property tax in the future will be to provide a baseline source of revenue for communities, who will have little flexibility with respect to its use. Citizens will use narrowly tailored assessment districts and property-related fees to provide local services—other than education, which will increasingly be centralized at the state level. Since property tax rates will be uniform across the state (and typically across classes of business property as well), states will use this local revenue as a starting point for their system of intergovernmental grants. Since states have great flexibility in the design of their grant systems, they will incorporate local differences in property tax bases (and revenues) into their formulas. In a functional sense, therefore, the property tax will be treated by the state as part of its overall resources. At the beginning of this century, the property tax was an important direct source of state revenue. As we end this century and begin the next, the property tax technically belongs to local government, but it will effectively be treated by states as part of their own financial resources.

Notes

1. This paper does not discuss possible developments in new forms of property taxation engendered by technological developments and the conceptual basis for valuation in these areas. The paper by Joan Youngman in this volume deals with these topics.

2. Glenn W. Fisher (1996) provides a useful discussion of nineteenth-century developments in property taxation, with particular reference to Kansas.

3. For a discussion of some of these developments in California, see Hartley, Sheffrin, and Vasche (1996).

4. Advisory Commission on Intergovernmental Relations (1992), table 65.

5. See Murray, Evans, and Schwab (1995).

6. The lawsuits were brought at the state level because the Supreme Court, in *San Antonio Independent School District* v. *Rodriquez* (411 U.S. 1 [1973]), had ruled, in a 5–4 decision, that educational inequalities did not violate the U.S. Constitution. In general, these lawsuits were brought under "equal protection" clauses of state constitutions. In the State of Washington, a lawsuit was brought under an "ample provision" clause of their Constitution. See Manwaring and Sheffrin (1997) for a discussion of the Washington litigation.

7. See Manwaring and Sheffrin (1997).

8. Hoxby (1996) finds that states that tried to promote equality by "leveling up" were less successful in reducing inequalities than states that "leveled down."

9. Fischel calls this decision *Serrano II* [432 U.S. 907 (1977)].

10. For a complete review of the consequences of Proposition 13 and other tax revolts, see O'Sullivan, Sexton, and Sheffrin (1995).

11. See Ibid., Table 2.1.

12 Other provisions of the referendum are discussed in more detail by Wassmer and Fisher (1996).

13. Reschovsky (1994) provides a detailed discussion of the Wisconsin experience.

14. Advisory Commission on Intergovernmental Relations (1992), table 7.

15. See O'Sullivan, Sexton, and Sheffrin (1995), chapter 4, for an analysis of effective tax rates.

16. See Ibid., chapter 1, for an analysis of the legal arguments.

17. See Sexton and Sheffrin (1995) for an overview of tax limitations and sources for data.

18. See Merriman (1987).

19. Sexton and Sheffrin (1995), p. 1766.

20. Dresch and Sheffrin (1997).

21. For an informative discussion of Proposition 218, see Legislative Analyst of California (1996).

22. Our definitions of taxes, assessments, and fees follow Legislative Analyst of California (1996).

23. At this time, it is an open issue as to whether Proposition 218 applies to metered water, which is more like a commodity than a "property-related" service.

24. Ladd (1975).

References

Advisory Commission on Intergovernmental Relations. 1992. *Significant Features of Fiscal Federalism*, Volume 1. pp. 18, 126–28. Washington, D.C.: Government Printing Office.

Dresch, Marla, and Steven M. Sheffrin. 1997. *Who Pays for Development Fees?* San Francisco: Public Policy Institute of California.

Fischel, William. 1989. "Did *Serrano* Cause Proposition 13?" *National Tax Journal* 42: 465–74.

Fischel, William. 1996. "How *Serrano* Caused Proposition 13." *Journal of Law and Politics* 12 no. 4: 607–36.

Fisher, Glenn W. 1996. *The Worst Tax*. Lawrence: University of Kansas Press.

Hartley, James, Steven M. Sheffrin, and J. David Vasche. 1996. "Reform During Crisis: The Transformation of California's Fiscal System During the Great Depression." *Journal of Economic History* 56, no. 3: 657–78.

Hoxby, Caroline. 1996. *All School Finance Equalizations Are Not Created Equal (Marginal Tax Rates Matter)*. Harvard University, Cambridge, Mass. Mimeographed.

Ladd, Helen. 1975. "Local Education Expenditures, Fiscal Capacity, and the Composition of the Property Tax Base." *National Tax Journal* 28: 145–58.

Legislative Analyst Office of California. 1996. *Understanding Proposition 218*. Sacramento: Legislative Analyst of California.

Manwaring, Robert, and Steven M. Sheffrin. 1997. "Litigation, School Finance Reform, and Aggregate Educational Spending." *International Tax and Public Finance*. Forthcoming.

Merriman, David. 1987. *The Control of Municipal Budgets: Towards the Effective Design of Tax and Expenditure Limitations*. New York: Quorum Books.

Murray, Sheila, William Evans, and Robert Schwab. 1995. *Education Finance Reform and the Distribution of Education Resources.* University of Maryland, College Park, Md. Mimeographed.

Nechyba, Thomas J. 1997. "Local Property and State Income Taxes: The Role of Interjurisdictional Competition and Collusion." *Journal of Political Economy* 105, no. 2: 351–84.

O'Sullivan, Arthur, Terri A. Sexton, and Steven M. Sheffrin. 1995. *Property Taxes and Tax Revolts: The Legacy of Proposition 13.* New York: Cambridge University Press.

Reschovsky, Andrew. 1994. "A Wisconsin Property Tax Primer." *State Tax Notes* (December 5): pp. 1735–43.

Sexton, Terri A., and Steven M. Sheffrin. 1995. "Five Lessons From Tax Revolts." *State Tax Notes* (December 18): pp. 1763–68.

Wassmer, Robert W., and Ronald C. Fisher. 1996. "An Evaluation of the Recent Move to Centralize the Finance of Public Schools in Michigan." *Public Budgeting and Finance* (fall): 90–112.

Chapter Nine

FINANCING PUBLIC EDUCATION IN THE TWENTY-FIRST CENTURY

William L. Waugh, Jr.

By most accounts, public education in the United States is in serious trouble. The perception is that achievement test scores, college entrance examination scores, and graduation rates are declining and drop-out rates are rising while school administrations struggle to control violence and vandalism. While success stories get some attention, the horror stories become national news. In some measure, statistics bear out the generalizations about public school failures, but the reality of public education is somewhat different. Many systems and schools are very effective and many are not. Nonetheless, state legislatures are expanding provisions for charter schools, home schooling, school privatization, contracted instructional programs, and other alternative educational approaches. Concern about the quality of public education is only half the story, however. The *cost* of public education is encouraging scrutiny by taxpayer groups, academic researchers, and the media and is encouraging fundamental reform in the methods of financing public schools.

The strongest impetus for public education finance reform is that education is generally the largest expenditure for a community, and its cost affects the support for other public programs. Deteriorating school buildings, rising maintenance costs, and increasing personnel costs have forced school boards to increase millage rates; in some communities, millage rates have reached their effective limit without producing enough revenue to support the school system. Moreover, while the school board's tax levy does not necessarily count against the limits put on the local government's levy by state law, the public tends to view them as one and is seldom sympathetic to requests for rate increases. And as the costs of public education have increased, cuts have had to be made in other essential government services.

This is not an encouraging place to begin a discussion of public education finance, but it does highlight the two major concerns in the current debate over how to finance public schools: quality and cost.

There is also increasing concern about the general decline of educational opportunity in inner city and rural communities—one that is giving rise to a shift, sometimes legally required, from relying principally on local property tax levies to relying principally on state funding. Expanded federal, private sector, and nonprofit agency roles in funding local schools are also being suggested.

To say that public education is an intensely political, and politically volatile, policy arena is certainly a gross understatement. And the nature of the politics has changed considerably over the last two or three decades. The ideology of management, theories of education, rabid anti-tax sentiment, and simple economics are transforming the debate. State legislators are being seduced by promises of local self-reliance and privatization; state departments of education are being caught up in a frenzy of downsizing; and school boards are buying into the notions of school-based management and system administration by noneducators. Administrative and staff positions are being cut, and growing numbers of superintendents and system administrators are former private sector managers or retired military officers rather than professional educators. The distrust of the traditional education bureaucracies is palpable.

At the same time, local school boards and system administrators are being challenged to improve performance, accountability, and efficiency. Suburban school systems may be faring better on all three counts, but even they are under greater public scrutiny and increased pressure to cut costs. While the wealthier systems have resources with which to address deficiencies, inner city and rural or small-town school systems are being challenged to improve test scores while their budgets stagnate or even shrink. Clearly, the traditional revenue base of public education, the property tax, is proving inadequate for more and more public school systems and is increasingly being challenged politically and legally. All of these issues are central to the debate concerning how to finance public education.

The financing debate ranges from narrow issues of cost-effectiveness to broad concerns about the social goals of public education. It includes concerns about the adequacy of current funding and reflects a growing realization that better financial management will not solve the resource problems of many public school systems—which are less the product of bad management practices than they are the result of political choice. More fundamentally, the debate is focusing on equity in the levels of funding provided to public school systems. This chapter will examine the current debate concerning public education finance, including a brief overview of current policies, and then focus on how those policies may change in the next decade or two. Obviously this is not a perfect world, and what we wish for may not be what we get. Indeed, sound economic reasoning may hold less sway in the debate over how we finance public education than political expedience and public opinion. In short, the issue here is what kinds of financing of public education can we reasonably expect as we move into the twenty-first century, not what methods of financing we *should* adopt.

THE NATURE OF PUBLIC EDUCATION FINANCING

Issues of finance and administration in public education are, in many ways, similar to those involving other kinds of government programs. Determining appropriate levels of funding to support program operations, staff services, facility operations and maintenance, and personnel are familiar issues for most public executives. Public education, however, has its own set of problems, including the relative independence of many public school systems from other structures of local government; the lack of agreement on program objectives, and on what to do with schools and systems that fail to meet performance standards; the impact of changing demographics on resource allocations and funding levels; the nature of public involvement in educational affairs; and the complexity of the financing for public school systems. Large and small school systems have different kinds of problems, as do rural, suburban, and inner city systems.

The relationships between public school systems and local governments differ somewhat from state to state, but most local governments exercise only limited authority, if any, over public school systems. School systems are generally special purpose governments with their own political authority and taxing power, although the revenue-raising power is generally limited by constitutional provision or statute. The federal government has no direct role in public education, but has historically supported programs to serve economically disadvantaged students and to encourage special education, vocational education, and a variety of other programs.

There is a large and growing literature on educational performance, focusing largely on achievement test scores, college entrance examination scores, graduation rates, drop-out rates, and percentages of graduates entering post-secondary education programs, from technical schools to universities. Pupil/teacher ratios are commonly viewed as a very positive indicator of strong educational effort. Indeed, studies indicate a relatively high positive correlation between close pupil-teacher interaction and student performance on standardized tests, although small classes do not necessarily mean close interaction. Increasing numbers of school systems are emphasizing the "value-added" in the educational process and using the success of graduates or changes in test scores or drop-out rates over time as the principal indicators of success. On the input side, there is a similar literature on administrative performance, including teacher/administrator/support staff ratios and the cost-effectiveness of everything from building maintenance to transportation of students to and from school. There are suggested formulas for budget allocations, though differences in energy and transportation costs alone can skew the recommended percentages considerably. And there is a growing emphasis on benchmarking—a product of the quality management movement—as an indicator of cost efficiency (Waugh and Harris 1997).

The "value-added" approach to educational performance and the benchmarking approach to educational administration offer some advantages over previous evaluative methods, but they also present problems for school boards and officials and raise political questions that are difficult to address. They also raise questions about current methods of financing public education. The traditional measures of educational success tend to be much lower in poorer inner city and rural school systems, or precisely in those systems with the least amount of fiscal support. Analyses of system and school budgets in the poorer systems generally show high expenditures for noneducational purposes. Those expenditure levels are frequently assumed to represent gross inefficiencies in system administration, but they may reflect more fundamental differences in the resource bases within school systems. Inner city school buildings tend to be older, and were often built when the most sophisticated classroom technology was a blackboard. The age and design of the facilities limit programmatic flexibility and result in higher maintenance costs. It is also extremely difficult to close or move schools in inner cities because of the importance of these schools to neighborhoods that may already be decaying. Vandalism increases maintenance costs, as well. Personnel costs in inner city and some rural systems also tend to be high, owing to the increased expense of recruiting and retaining experienced teachers. Lower-quality facilities, high percentages of students with special needs, and increased teacher responsibilities outside of the classroom because of having less support staff—all result in a lower quality of working life. In short, teachers have to be paid more because of the working conditions. All of this is to say that relative efficiency is difficult to determine, and other values may be more important to the school system and the community.

THE CRISIS IN PUBLIC EDUCATION FINANCING

Public education in the United States is funded by local and state governments and the federal government, with an increasing amount of support coming from private and nonprofit organizations. Local taxes, whether collected by local or state tax offices, provide the largest share of public school revenue. The federal government provides approximately 7 percent of the total, almost exclusively to support federally sponsored programs of remedial education, job training, and lunch subsidies—i.e., programs targeted for economically disadvantaged students. In legal terms, public education is primarily the responsibility of state government, and there is some expectation that all children within the state will have an equal opportunity to get an education and reasonable equity in the quality of the education that they receive, though not necessarily equality in the results of that education (Jordan and Lyons 1992, p. 3). Local governments, as agents of state government, do not have equal resources to expend on public education, however. Increasing fiscal inequities among school systems are forcing state legislatures to develop allocation formulas to assure that all public school systems in their states have reasonably adequate funding. Legal challenges to funding methods are forcing change, and political pressures to reform education funding are also growing as fiscal crises focus attention on funding inequities.

Legal Challenges

There have been legal challenges to the systems of funding in about thirty-five states since 1970, mostly based on failures to implement provisions of state constitutions regarding educational opportunity for all citizens of the state. In recent years, state courts have raised serious questions about funding methods in the states of Alabama, Idaho, Illinois, Minnesota, Missouri, Ohio, Oklahoma, Pennsylvania, and Virginia. State supreme courts have declared the traditional methods of funding public education unconstitutional in Montana, Texas, Tennessee, Kentucky, and New Jersey. (See Ibid., pp. 5, 55.) For the most part, recent cases have focused on questions about state contributions to poorer systems and subsidies for programs for special needs students (who tend to constitute larger percentages of the students in poorer systems). The basic issues are the adequacy of state and local funding and the redistributive character of state allocations. Some states have provided higher levels of funding to local systems lacking adequate tax bases to raise property tax revenues, but the issue is often hotly contested in state legislatures. It is also uncertain just how much funding is "adequate" and how much tax effort should be required of a community to fund its own school system. And some programs, particularly those for special education and educationally disadvantaged students, simply cost more than regular instructional programs—and states often weight their per pupil allocations to accommodate the higher cost of such programs.

The legal pressure for public education finance reform has built up over the past quarter-century through a series of federal and state court cases. In *San Antonio Independent School District v. Rodriguez* (1973), the U.S. Supreme Court did not accept the argument that unequal funding of Texas school districts constituted a failure to provide "equal protection of the law" and that public education is a fundamental right (Ibid., pp. 68–70). For a time, that decision quieted challenges to the practice of funding public education largely through local property taxes. While the courts were disinclined to accept the argument that inequities in funding constituted a failure to provide "equal protection of the law" under the Fourteenth Amendment, however, other arguments against existing funding methods began to find support in judicial decisions.

In the series of cases involved in *Robinson v. Cahill* (1973 to 1976), the New Jersey Supreme Court followed the lead provided by the *Rodriguez* case but held that the state should determine an appropriate level of support and compel local school boards to raise the necessary revenue. Subsequent cases held that the state needed to set guidelines with respect to the content and quality of primary and secondary education (Ibid., pp. 71–73). And despite the *Rodriguez* decision, the Texas Supreme Court ruled in 1989 that the state's system of funding of public education was unconstitutional and that the state legislature should equalize funding among school systems (Zuchman 1993, p. 751). In large measure, the Texas court's ruling was that per pupil revenue should be substantially equal from one school system to another.

Similar decisions have been rendered in other state courts, and the momentum has clearly shifted. For example, in 1997 the Vermont Supreme Court unanimously ruled that relying on local property taxes to finance public education was unconstitutional. The inequity of local funding was the issue raised by the American Civil Liberties Union in its suit. Representing a group of children, taxpayers, and school systems, the suit argued that students were being denied equal educational opportunity because districts did not have the same capacity to raise property tax revenues. The court has directed the legislature to remedy the problem. Similar rulings can be expected in other states—and the major impetus may be the growing number of fiscal crises in local school systems.

Fiscal Crises: The Michigan Example

While there have been fiscal crises in school systems in a number of states, perhaps the most notable occurred in 1993, in the Kalkaska school district in Michigan. The Kalkaska system was shut down two-and-a-half months early because its funding had simply run out. Voters had rejected an increase in the millage rate, and system officials chose to end the school year early rather than to drastically cut programs, staff, and other expenses (Vergari 1995, 256–57). The shutdown became the occasion for a major media event designed to draw attention to the plight of school systems in the state, and it was supported by education groups from across the state. As a result, later that year, the Michigan legislature voted to stop using the residential property tax to support public education. That decision effectively eliminated two-thirds of the financing for K–12 education (Addonizio, Kearney, and Prince 1995). Faced with budget deficits and a high per capita tax burden, the legislature acted to fundamentally alter the revenue base for public education. Michigan had high property and income taxes, with property tax levies for education ranging from eight to forty-seven mills. Letting local districts set millage rates according to their own preferences meant that the level of funding per pupil became a local choice. As the wealth of more and more districts shrank, however, millage rates had to rise precipitously in order to assure minimum levels of per pupil expenditure. Poorer districts were increasingly unable to raise enough revenue to support their schools, and higher millage rates were not politically or even economically viable options; declining local economies severely limited the ability of communities to pay higher taxes. Alternative revenue sources were needed to assure some modicum of equity among districts, and the relatively low sales tax rate was an obvious choice.

Despite Michigan's having switched (in the early 1970s) from a state funding system that provided a floor or foundation for each district to one that was expected to more nearly equalize funding among districts, the reliance on local property taxes was simply inadequate, and funding inequities were increasing. Efforts by the Republican governor and his colleagues in the legislature to roll back property taxes were unsuccessful until a radical proposal, Act 145, to entirely eliminate residential property tax financing of public education gained legislative approval. The question was how to replace the lost revenue.

Under the new funding method, each district received a per pupil grant equal to the difference between the statewide floor or "foundation" and the revenues raised locally through an eighteen-mill property tax levy on all nonresidential taxable property. The local property tax is essentially the same as a state tax, because of the standardized millage rate. Some state categorical grant programs continue, as well. Still, there have been revenue shortfalls, since the new taxes have not replaced the lost revenue from the old funding method, so there remains an issue of how to add other tax and nontax revenues to the mix. One part of the equalization has meant that parents have to purchase special programs, such as music or sports or computer classes, from outside sources (Wassmer and Fisher 1996). But the funding issue is not settled. It remains uncertain how the state will deal with shortfalls if sales tax revenues decline significantly, and what other kinds of revenue might be earmarked for public education.

THE POLITICS OF PUBLIC EDUCATION FINANCING

The legal and political pressure for education finance reform comes at a time when there is increased interest in tax reform generally. While there appears to be little interest in radically cutting support for public education, bond and tax referenda often do not pass, even though the need for new revenue is manifest. The political support for public education is diluted by middle- and upper-class families enrolling their children in private schools, "white flight" to suburban communities, and "middle-class flight" to communities with lower taxes. But there may be growing support for public education within the business community, as education becomes a central component of more state and community economic development efforts.

The debate over public education financing is encouraging fundamental reform of state and local tax systems. The reliance on local property taxes to fund education is, at best, problematic for local governments as well as for public school systems themselves. Accord-

ingly, there seems to be a growing sentiment among officials, as well
as the public, for reducing local property taxes and shifting to more
consumption—i.e., sales—taxes. While states have only slowly accepted the need to reduce the regressivity of sales taxes by excluding
food, medicine, and basic clothing, the adoption of new sales taxes
may encourage such exclusions.

The reason for the shift to consumption taxes has less to do with
economic reasoning than with the political milieu. States and communities are finding far more support for consumption taxes, particularly so-called "sin taxes" (on, e.g., cigarettes) and lottery and gam-
bling revenue, than for property and income-based taxes. Property
taxes are most burdensome for fixed-income residents and they can
cause distortions in terms of their economic impact (e.g., taxpayers
can move to other districts to avoid the taxes). In many communities,
the millage rates have become so high that officials are having to
seriously consider reductions in homestead and other exemptions.
Finally, property taxes have high administrative costs associated with
their assessment and collection.

Public school systems, as well as general-purpose local governments, are also seeking alternative revenue sources—including selling
unneeded property to finance capital projects, leasing property, engaging in enterprise activities to raise revenue, seeking funding
through nonprofit foundations, and seeking corporate and community
contributions for educational programs—and shifting some of the burden of special programs to users (or, in the case of schools, to parents).
Tax equity may suffer, to the extent that financing will be based less
on ability to pay. But, the increased use of user fees for special programs, such as sports and music, while problematic for disadvantaged
students, does raise the cost of these programs to those receiving the
most benefit. Some school systems are adopting a "bake sale" approach to the financing of amenities and special programs—as well
as to the support of basic instructional programs. Parents are drawn
into fund-raising activities. Some few systems in central cities may
attempt to export some of the burden to those who work and/or shop
downtown, but occupation and "wheel" (commuter) taxes are not very
popular in cities fearful of losing businesses to satellite communities
with lower taxes.

There is also some potential for increased federal support. Federal
funding of the Chapter 1 (formerly Title I) program to increase the
basic skills of economically disadvantaged students may be a model
for other programs targeted at disadvantaged and at-risk students.
Indeed, there are some indications that Congress and the U.S.

Department of Education are becoming more interested in the plight of public school systems, particularly in urban centers. Notwithstanding the debates over "midnight basketball" some years ago, there is an increased focus on the current sad state of public education and its impact on student performance, the employability of high school graduates and drop-outs, and related crime rates. Recent studies by the U.S. General Accounting Office (GAO) (for the Senate and House Committees on Labor and Human Resources) have focused on the deteriorating infrastructure of public schools (1996), the impact of school-based management on budgeting and instruction (1994a), and the impact of regulatory flexibility on instruction and costs (1994b).

A 1995 GAO study of funding equity in Tennessee, Minnesota, and Texas identified some of the implementation problems. It concluded that poor systems were helped by the changes in funding, without damaging educational programs in the wealthier systems, and that there was advantage in tying accountability provisions to the new financing arrangements. A 1997 GAO report concluded that wealthier school systems had about 24 percent more funding per pupil than poor systems. The report went on to recommend a more redistributive state approach to funding and to suggest that states use the study's "fiscal neutrality score, implicit foundation level, and equalization effort" to reduce the gap between wealthy and poor systems.

The recent increases in national economic growth may encourage more investment in human capital to make the United States more competitive internationally. Urban school systems would be logical focal points for such programs (Robinson-Barnes and Waugh 1998).

THE FUTURE OF PUBLIC EDUCATION FINANCING

Legal challenges and fiscal crises have encouraged a reexamination of public education financing, and fundamental change is under way. Clearly, there are also fundamental changes under way in the patterns of spending. Systems are being forced to reduce their ratios of support staff and administrators to teachers, to redirect more of their spending to educational programs, and to cut other operating costs (Jordan and Lyons 1992, pp. 82–90). (As a rule, personnel is the largest controllable part of a system budget, so the largest cut in overhead or administrative costs can be achieved by reducing the numbers of administrators and support staff.) While the gloss is wearing off privatization efforts as officials and the public learn that private sector values are often in conflict with public purposes (see, e.g., Asher, Fruchter, and Berne 1997), the charter school movement is still growing and is slowly merging with the school-based management movement. The adoption of alternative educational approaches and decentralized educational decision-making, however, is at the expense of system and state department of education support services.

Greater cost efficiencies are not the answer for systems without adequate base funding. States and communities are having to find more equitable ways of allocating money to support public education. School boards and local government officials are reducing their reliance on local property taxes and becoming far more creative in their revenue-raising efforts. Sales taxes are a logical and relatively easy choice, although sales tax revenues are not necessarily a stable funding source. More school boards may seek to use sales taxes for special purposes. In 1997, for example, the Georgia legislature approved local adoption of one-cent sales taxes to support school construction. All new sales tax revenues have to be used for capital expenditures, however (e.g., new buildings, renovations, land acquisition, technological enhancement of facilities, and retirement of capital debt) (Evans 1997), so there is little flexibility to address other needs (Waugh and Harris 1997). But the decaying infrastructure has been driving up the costs of public education in Georgia, as well as in other states, and student population growth has been outstripping the available resources. The sales tax revenues at least free up money for other uses. Moreover, the virtues of sales taxes are the ease of administration and reasonably high compliance rates. They are also exportable tax burdens. Estimates are that 40 to 60 percent of the new sales tax revenue for the Atlanta Public School System will come from nonresidents (Evans 1997).

Other options will include student participation fees, contributions by nonprofit educational foundations, and earnings from enterprise activities. The Georgia HOPE scholarship program, paying tuition costs for students who graduate from state high schools with B-averages or better and maintain B-averages in college, is gaining national attention. Lotteries, too, are increasingly attractive choices for state governments. The use of lottery funds to bring schools "on line," with satellite access to distance learning facilities, and to fund computer and other technologies is also getting attention. Similar experiments are likely to be tried in other states.

There is increased interest in linking education finance reform to educational reform, quality management programs, state-sponsored core curricula, and national and/or state performance standards. At a minimum, the development of incentives for outstanding performance at the school and classroom level is being recommended (Jordan and Lyons 1992, pp. 107–21). While there are still questions concerning how to provide economic incentives to improve school and system performance without punishing the students who need the most help, there is a greater willingness to experiment with new funding methods.

How will public education be financed in the twenty-first century? Financing will be far more eclectic than it is today, as states develop "foundation" levels of funding for traditional and special instructional programs, provide supplementary funding to public school systems with higher levels of need, and encourage their public school systems to compete with alternative educational systems like charter schools. Greater focus will be on "value-added" measures, such as national standardized test scores and graduation rates. Financial incentives to reduce drop-out rates, student violence, and other negative indications and behaviors are likely to increase and may find corporate and/or nonprofit sector support. Expenditures are being shifted from administrative overhead to instructional programs, and that trend should continue. As with local government agencies, the public apparently wants a closer connection between inputs, especially tax revenues, and outcomes. There will be increased pressure on school boards and administrators to reach performance goals—and on state and local officials to provide the necessary funding to reach them.

References

Addonizio, Michael F., C. Philip Kearney, and Henry J. Prince. 1995. "Michigan's High Wire Act." *Journal of Education Finance* 20 (winter): 235–69.
Asher, Carol, Norm Fruchter, and Robert Berne. 1997. *Hard Lessons: Public Schools and Privatization.* Washington, D.C.: Brookings Institution Press.
Burtless, Gary, ed. 1996. *Does Money Matter? The Effect of School Resources on Student Achievement and Adult Success.* Washington, D.C.: Brookings Institution Press.
Evans, Sherrell. 1997. "Sales Tax Hike Comes to a Vote." *Atlanta Journal/Atlanta Constitution,* March 9.

Fleeter, Howard B. 1995. "The Impact of Local Tax-Based Sharing on School Finance Equity in Ohio: Implementation Issues and Comparative Analysis." *Journal of Education Finance* 20 (winter): 270–301.

Gess, Larry R., Paul A. Montello, David L. Sjoquist, and John F. Sears. 1996. "Public School Finance: A Rational Response to Reform Pressures." pp. 92–97 in *Proceedings of the Eighty-Eighth Annual Conference of the National Tax Association, San Diego, Calif., October 8–10, 1995,* edited by Robert D. Ebel. Columbus, Ohio: National Tax Association/Tax Institute of America.

Gittell, Marilyn, and Laura McKenna. 1997. "Activist Governors and a New Conservative Direction for Education." Paper presented at the annual meeting of the Urban Affairs Association, Toronto, Ontario, Canada, April 16–20.

Hy, Ronald J., and William L. Waugh, Jr. 1995. *State and Local Tax Policy: A Comparative Handbook.* Westport, Conn.: Greenwood Press.

Jordan, K. Forbis, and Teresa S. Lyons. 1992. *Financing Public Education in an Era of Change.* Bloomington, In.: Phi Delta Kappa Educational Foundation.

McWilliams, Alfred E., Jr., and William L. Waugh, Jr. 1996. *Charter Review Issues: The Atlanta Board of Education.* Atlanta: Research Atlanta/ Policy Research Center, Georgia State University.

Robinson-Barnes, Carla J., and William L. Waugh, Jr. 1998. "The Logic and Pathology of Local and Regional Economic Development Strategies." In *Handbook of Economic Development,* edited by Kuotsai Tom Liou. New York: Marcel Dekker Publishers, forthcoming.

Schwartz, Amy Ellen, Leanna Stiefel, and Ross Rubenstein. 1998. "Education Finance." In *Handbook of Public Finance,* edited by W. Bartley Hildreth. New York: Marcel Dekker, forthcoming.

Strauss, Robert P. 1996. "School Finance Reform: Moving From the School Property Tax to the Income Tax." pp. 84–91 in *Proceedings of the Eighty-Eighth Annual Conference of the National Tax Association, San Diego, Calif., October 8–10, 1995,* edited by Robert D. Ebel. Columbus, Ohio: National Tax Association/Tax Institute of America.

U.S. General Accounting Office. 1997. *School Finance: State Efforts to Reduce Funding Gaps Between Poor and Wealthy Districts.* Washington, D.C.: USGAO, GAO/HEHS-97-31 (February 5).

————. 1996. *School Facilities: Profiles of School Condition by State.* Washington, D.C.: GAO/HEHS-96-148 (June).

————. 1995. *School Finance: Three States' Experiences with Equity in School Funding.* Washington, D.C.: USGAO, GAO/HEHS-96-39 (December).

————. 1994a. *Education Reform: School-Based Management Results in Changes in Instruction and Budgeting.* Washington, D.C.: USGAO, GAO/HEHS-94-135 (August).

_____. 1994b. *Regulatory Flexibility in Schools: What Happens When Schools are Allowed to Change the Rules?* Washington, D.C.: USGAO, GAO/HEHS-94-102 (April).

Vergari, Sandra. 1995. "School Finance Reform in the State of Michigan." *Journal of Education Finance* 21 (fall): 254–70.

Wassmer, Robert W., and Ronald C. Fisher. 1996. "An Evaluation of the Recent Move to Centralize the Finance of Public Schools in Michigan." *Public Budgeting and Finance* (fall): 90–109.

Waugh, William L., Jr., and Robert M. Harris. 1997. *Analysis of the Atlanta Public School System Finances*. Atlanta: Research Atlanta/Policy Research Center, Georgia State University.

Zuchman, Jill. 1993. "The Next Education Crisis: Equalizing School Funds." *Congressional Quarterly* (March 27): 749–54.

Chapter Ten

THE PROGRESSIVITY OF STATE TAX SYSTEMS

Andrew Reschovsky

INTRODUCTION

While there has been a considerable amount of research on the impacts of taxes on the locational decisions of businesses (and, to a lesser extent, of individuals),[1] relatively little academic research has focused on the distribution of state and local government tax burdens. Despite this paucity of research, distributional concerns clearly play an important role in the formation of actual tax policy. Most of the forty-two states that levy an individual income tax have taken various steps to achieve at least some degree of tax progressivity.[2] The majority of states have a system of graduated rates, with nominal rates rising as income rises. Even states with a flat tax rate generally build some degree of progressivity into their tax structure through the use of deductions, exemptions, or credits. Of the forty-five states that levy a general sales tax, most exempt the purchase of various goods and services with the explicit goal of reducing the burden of the tax on those with limited incomes. Furthermore, when state legislatures consider changes in state tax policy, issues of tax fairness almost always play an important role.

Economists, starting with Richard Musgrave (1959) and Wallace Oates (1972), have argued that distributional concerns should be addressed by the federal government rather than by state or local governments. They argue that efforts by state and local governments to levy higher taxes on high-income residents and to distribute public services in a manner favoring the poor will be ineffective because high-income individuals can migrate to political jurisdictions with more favorable fiscal climates. Despite this argument, Congress is actively shifting responsibility for redistributive programs to the states. The result may well be *less* progressive state and local tax systems and reduced spending on the poor and needy.

The purpose of this paper is to review the arguments made by economists about the role state and local tax progressivity should play in a federal system, to assess what is known about the distributional incidence of state and local taxes, and to speculate about whether state and local tax policy is likely to become more or less progressive in the coming decades.

SHOULD STATE GOVERNMENTS USE PROGRESSIVE TAXES?

Aside from the handful of studies that attempt to measure the incidence of state and local taxes, most of the literature addresses one of two questions. One set of papers focuses on the normative issue of whether state and local governments should be concerned with issues of distribution. The second set of papers explores the reasons why some states have more progressive tax systems than others.

In his discussion of the level of government appropriate to carry out various governmental functions, Richard Musgrave (1959) suggested that any efforts at distribution should be carried out solely by the central government. The basis for this prescription, which was more fully articulated by Oates (1972), is that any attempts by governments below the national level to pursue distributional policies, either through spending programs or by the use of progressive taxation, will be doomed to failure because of the mobility of households between jurisdictions. For example, an attempt by State A to levy a progressive income tax as a way of reducing tax burdens on its low-income residents will be self-defeating because high-income residents of State A will migrate to neighboring states with less progressive tax systems, thereby forcing State A to raise tax rates on its remaining residents or to cut spending. It is also possible that low-income households in neighboring states will be attracted to State A because of its progressive tax system.

The Musgrave-Oates argument is most powerful at the local government level, where fiscally motivated interjurisdictional mobility is most likely to occur.[3] The probability of interstate mobility in response to tax rate differentials is much lower—and thus, according to Oates, there is some room for a limited degree of state tax progressivity. As pointed out by Slemrod (1986), the implication of the Musgrave-Oates view is that, to the extent possible, state governments should utilize systems of taxation that link taxes paid to the benefits received from state expenditures. In cases where benefit taxes or user fees are not appropriate—e.g., to finance services targeted to the poor or finance goods produced with decreasing costs—the Musgrave-Oates view provides no direct guidance. By implication, if taxpayer mobility prevents states from using progressive taxation, states can, at best, resort to a system of taxes that is proportional to income.

State policy-makers often support the expansion of taxes on business as an alternative means of increasing the progressivity of state tax systems. As pointed out forcefully by Oakland (1992), however, the incidence of business taxes rarely falls on the (presumably) rich owners of business. Oakland argues that as capital is mobile, the burden of taxes on business—at least those taxes that exceed the value of public services provided—will fall on immobile factors of production (for example, labor) or immobile individuals.

In several recent papers, Oates and Schwab (1988, 1991) present a model in which individuals are immobile and local governments compete to attract mobile capital by providing a mix of services that will be attractive to business. They demonstrate that in a competitive environment, all taxes will become benefit taxes and businesses will pay taxes that are equal to the value they place on the public services they receive. Any attempt by local governments to raise taxes on business above the value of services received will lead capital to flee to another jurisdiction. Although one can question the realism of a number of the assumptions Oates and Schwab use in their model, these questions don't seriously call into question their conclusion that competition for business capital severely limits the use of ability-to-pay taxes by local governments.

In a recent paper, Feldstein and Vaillant (1994) suggest that not only will progressive taxation by state governments be completely ineffective in redistributing income, but by increasing the cost of hiring high-skill workers, it will lead to economic inefficiencies. They argue that a progressive state tax system will cause high-skill residents to migrate to lower-tax states. As a consequence, pre-tax real wages will rise in the high-tax state and fall in the lower-tax state until after-tax wages are equal in all locations. The authors attempt to test this proposition by regressing gross wages on a set of human capital attributes of individuals and a measure of the effective tax rates they face. They argue that their empirical results not only support their gross wage-adjustment hypothesis, but indicate that gross wages adjust to tax rate changes very rapidly—within a period of a few years.[4]

In my view, the results of the Feldstein-Vaillant paper are far from convincing. While there is a body of evidence suggesting that interstate capital mobility is rapid, there is little collaborating evidence of substantial labor mobility in response to tax rate changes. As the authors acknowledge, the use of state-level tax rate data requires that all intrastate differences in variables that may affect gross wages are ignored. This opens the possibility that gross wages are determined in part by other factors correlated with effective tax rates.[5] Also, owing to data limitations, the authors are unable to provide accurate measures of effective property and sales tax rates. Finally, as I will discuss below, it is possible that the causality runs the other way, with exogenous changes in the economic circumstances of various economic interest groups leading to political reactions that result in changes in the tax rates faced by those groups.

The view that progressive taxation by subnational governments is either infeasible or inefficient has not gone unchallenged. Pauly (1973) presented a model based on the premise that people receive utility from providing support for the poor who live in their community. He demonstrates that under these circumstances, redistribution policies pursued by local or state governments can be efficient. Timothy Goodspeed (1989) demonstrates in the context of a general equilibrium model that local governments can employ progressive income taxes with only relatively minor losses of economic efficiency. Although Goodspeed's work is theoretical, it does open up the question of what exactly are the consequences of the use by subnational governments of redistributive taxes. We know very little about how responsive inter- and intrastate residential location decisions are to the degree of progressivity of state and local tax systems. There is no convincing evidence that the locational decisions of individuals are highly sensitive to interstate tax rate differentials.

In a recent paper, Chernick (1997) directly explores the hypothesis that the progressivity of state tax systems has a negative impact on the rate of growth of states' economies. If a highly progressive state tax system induces either labor or capital to migrate to other states, the economic effect of these responses is likely to be revealed in the form of slower growth in state personal income. Specifically, Chernick assumes that once one controls for the average value of state spending and the generosity of state welfare programs, a more progressive state tax system will lead to a larger divergence between the taxes paid and the benefits received by high-income households. This divergence between taxes and benefits may increase the incentive for high-income families to migrate, and the departure of a state's most productive workers is likely to lead to slower state economic growth. Chernick tests this hypothesis using data from all fifty states and finds no statistical support for a relationship between tax progressivity and economic growth. This finding suggests that state governments do, in fact, have some latitude in their ability to utilize progressive taxes.

Regardless of the theorizing of economists, a number of state governments have implemented progressive state income tax systems. One important reason that states have adopted progressive income taxes, however, is the fact that state income tax payments are deductible from federal adjusted gross income. Taxpayers who itemize deductions on their federal returns are able to reduce their federal taxes by the amount of their state income tax payment times their federal marginal tax rate. For example, for a taxpayer with a $1,000 state income tax liability facing a federal marginal tax rate of 31 percent, deductibility of state income taxes will in most cases reduce the taxpayer's federal tax liability by $310.[6] Each extra dollar of state income tax will cost this taxpayer only sixty-nine cents, with the remaining thirty-one cents being exported to taxpayers around the country. From the state's perspective, deductibility reduces the burden of the state income tax on all state residents who itemize. And as both the probability of itemizing and federal marginal tax rates increase as income increases, the benefits of deductibility are greater for those with higher incomes.[7]

Deductibility thus creates an incentive for state governments to increase the progressivity of their state income taxes. By lowering the effective burden of state income taxation, deductibility reduces the incentive of high-income taxpayers to migrate to other states with lower tax rates or to oppose increases in tax progressivity.[8] In a model explaining differences across states in the distributional incidence of state and local taxes, Chernick (1992) finds evidence that deductibility has a strong positive effect on the progressivity of state and local tax systems. This suggests that deductibility of state and local taxes provides a mechanism for the federal government—in the form of a "fiscal bribe" to high-income taxpayers—to encourage redistribution by subnational governments.

The passage of the Tax Reform Act of 1986 (TRA86) provided a useful test of the assumption that the deductibility of state and local taxes reduces fiscally motivated migration. TRA86 eliminated the deductibility of sales taxation and reduced the value of deductibility to most taxpayers by reducing marginal tax rates. The top marginal income tax rate was nearly cut in half; it was reduced from 50 percent to 28 percent. This reduction in the value and scope of deductibility might suggest that TRA86 will result in an increase in the migration of high-income itemizers from state and local governments with progressive tax systems and/or redistributive public services. This issue is addressed in papers by Gramlich (1985) and by Chernick and

Reschovsky (1987). Gramlich suggests that the deductibility of property taxes provides an incentive for high-income taxpayers to live in mixed- or low-income central cities. The reduction of marginal tax rates raises the tax cost of local government relative to the benefits received and thereby encourages high-income taxpayers to move to homogeneous high-income suburban communities.[9] Gramlich estimated that TRA86 would create a fiscal incentive to move from a central city to the suburbs equal to about 5 percent of city government tax payments; he concluded that an incentive of this magnitude would be too small to generate much migration by high-income taxpayers. While Chernick and Reschovsky agree with Gramlich's general conclusion, they provide estimates that suggest that TRA86 will create incentives to move from New York City to its Connecticut and New Jersey suburbs equal to 10 to 15 percent of the state and local tax liabilities of high-income New York City residents. They suggest that these estimates provide an upper-bound estimate of the likely impact of changes in deductibility on incentives to migrate.

Even if tax-motivated migration is limited, the fear of losing high-income residents may motivate state governments with progressive income tax systems to reduce tax rates on the rich. John Shannon (1991) has argued that states tend to act like ships in a wartime convoy, with no single ship daring to get too far out front. This analogy suggests that while states differ in the effective tax rates they levy on high-income residents, interstate competition for these potentially mobile residents deters them from setting tax rates that are too far out of line with tax rates in other states. History appears to support this contention. A number of states with progressive income taxes, including New York, California, Minnesota, and Wisconsin, have recently reduced their top marginal income tax rates.

At the same time, the fiscal map of the United States includes a number of adjacent states that have a long history of strikingly different state tax systems. For example, Vermont has a quite progressive state income tax system, while neighboring New Hampshire does not have a broad-based income tax at all; Oregon has an income tax with a top marginal rate of 9 percent, while Washington has no income tax; and the top marginal rate in the District of Columbia, 9.5 percent, is nearly double the 5 percent top rate in Maryland.

One might ask why the low-tax states have not exploited their neighbors' high rates and enacted income taxes or, if they have an income tax, raised their rates. One possible explanation has been provided by Howard Chernick's (1991) "tax haven" theory. He argues that low-progressivity states adjacent to high-progressivity states provide a tax haven for high-income households who work in the high-tax state and live in the low-tax state. The low-progressivity states have little incentive to enact an income tax because they would most likely have to grant credits to their residents who worked and paid taxes in neighboring states. Thus they risk alienating their high-income residents in return for only a modest amount of additional revenue.

WHAT DETERMINES THE PROGRESSIVITY OF STATE TAX SYSTEMS?

While the debate over the appropriateness of progressive taxes at the subnational level continues unabated, a small literature has emerged that attempts to explain why the degree of tax progressivity varies among the fifty states. Ettlinger et al. (1996) demonstrate that a number of states have highly regressive state and local tax systems, while a few states have mildly progressive systems. They calculate that in several states (Washington, Florida, and South Dakota), the state and local tax burden on the poorest 20 percent of families is about four times higher than the burden on the richest 1 percent.[10] Several states (Delaware, Montana, and Vermont) have mildly progressive tax systems, in which the burden on the richest taxpayers is slightly higher than the burden on the poor.

The literature that attempts to explain interstate differences in tax progressivity includes papers by both political scientists and economists. A paper by David Lowery (1987) finds that an important determinant of tax progressivity is the early adoption of broad-based sales and income taxes. This finding begs the question, since it provides no explanation of the factors that determine the timing of state adoption of broad-based taxation. Two recent papers, by Morgan (1994) and Berch (1995), attempt with limited success to explain the degree of progressivity of state and local tax systems. Morgan finds that states with higher newspaper circulation per capita tend to have more regressive tax systems. He argues, not very convincingly, that this variable may be a proxy for middle-class opposition to progressive taxation. Berch finds that tax progressivity in 1985 is very important in explaining tax progressivity in 1991. He also finds weak support for the hypothesis that states in which the Democratic party has a stronger hold on the governorship will have more progressive tax systems.

Several recent papers explain the design of tax policy as being motivated by the vote-maximizing behavior of governments and the attempts by fiscal interest groups to influence state government decisions about the distribution of tax burdens. Hettich and Winer (1988) and Winer and Hettich (1992) posit models in which governments want to design tax policies that minimize political opposition without creating major increases in the costs of implementing tax policy. Inman (1989) incorporates distributional objectives into a model of the tax choices of large American cities. In his model, both tax burdens and the political costs borne by various interest groups are important determinants of tax policy.

Chernick (1992, 1994) and Chernick and Reschovsky (1996) develop a series of models to explain differences in the progressivity of state tax systems. They estimate their models using data from a 1991 tax incidence study by the Citizens for Tax Justice—the same data set used by both Morgan and Berch.[11] In Chernick's model, politicians raise a given amount of revenue by choosing a set of tax instruments that maximize their chances of getting reelected. In order to minimize the political costs of any tax, politicians attempt to set tax rates so as to equate the net benefits of government received by each fiscal interest group. Variables describing the distribution of income in each state serve as proxies for the role that these fiscal interest groups play in determining state tax policy. Chernick and Reschovsky's (1996) empirical results provide limited support for the thesis that interest groups play a role in determining tax incidence. They also find limited support for the importance of political ideology, with states that have more liberal congressional delegations having somewhat more progressive state tax systems. In addition, their results show that the greater the proportion of taxpayers who itemize, the greater the progressivity of state and local tax systems. It appears that when a change in deductibility (in the form of higher federal marginal tax rates) reduces the net state tax burden on high-income taxpayers, states offset this change by increasing gross state income tax rates. This behavior implies that states do in fact have a target distribution of net tax burdens, which, if disturbed, leads to offsetting adjustments. Chernick and Reschovsky's results also suggest, however, that there are limits to the amount of redistribution that is possible through state and local tax systems. If tax liabilities on the rich diverge too much from the benefits they receive from public spending, high-income taxpayers will exert political pressure on state and local governments to reduce tax progressivity.

Chernick (1994) and Bahl et al. (1996) argue that within these limits there remains room for some degree of redistribution by state governments. Both of these studies find evidence that states with progressive tax systems also tend to have spending patterns favoring the poor.

ARE STATE AND LOCAL TAX SYSTEMS PROGRESSIVE?

There have been relatively few studies of the distribution of state and local tax burdens that have been national in scope. Perhaps the best-known studies were conducted by Joseph Pechman and his colleagues at the Brookings Institution (Pechman and Okner 1974; Pechman 1985). One of the most comprehensive studies was one conducted by Donald Phares (1980). Both the Brookings studies and Phares present a set of results based on a range of tax incidence assumptions. Citizens for Tax Justice (CTJ), a Washington-based research and advocacy organization, has conducted several studies of the distribution of state and local tax burdens. Their most recent study, *Who Pays? A Distributional Analysis of the Tax Systems in All Fifty States* (Ettlinger et al. 1996), is based on 1995 data and was completed in collaboration with the Institute on Taxation and Economic Policy (ITEP). Finally, Gilbert Metcalf (1994) conducted a study of state and local taxes taking a lifetime incidence approach.

In addition to these national studies, there have been a number of state-specific tax burden studies, often conducted as part of comprehensive studies of state tax systems. One of the early studies that served as a model for studies in other states was the *Wisconsin Tax Burden Study* (1979). (More recent studies have been conducted in a number of other states, including Minnesota, Arizona, and Massachusetts.) As a way of summarizing what we know about the distribution of state and local tax burdens, I will summarize and compare the results of two recent national studies that come to strikingly different conclusions: the Citizens for Tax Justice–Institute on Taxation and Economic Policy study and the Metcalf study.

In order to conduct a study of the distribution of state and local tax burdens, an analyst must make five major decisions. First, a decision must be made about which taxes to include. Metcalf restricts his analysis to the three most important taxes used by state and local governments: the general sales tax, the individual income tax, and the residential property tax. The CTJ–ITEP study is more comprehensive;

in addition to the taxes analyzed in the Metcalf study, it includes selected sales and excise taxes, nonresidential property taxes, and the corporate income tax.

Second, a decision must be made about the population of taxpayers to be included. Metcalf analyzes tax burdens on all households, while the CTJ–ITEP study restricts its tax burden analysis to nonelderly married couples.

Third, a decision must be made about the time frame over which the analysis is to be conducted. The typical distributional analysis, including most of those cited above and the CTJ–ITEP study, is based on annual data on both taxation and income. A growing number of economists, however, have argued that it is inappropriate to determine tax incidence on the basis of annual data.[12] They argue that most people with low incomes are only temporarily poor, and if consumption decisions are generally made on the basis of lifetime incomes, then calculating tax burdens based on data from a single year will yield tax burdens for low-income people that are substantially higher than burdens calculated on the basis of lifetime or permanent income. Metcalf's approach is to calculate tax burdens by combining tax base or tax payment data for a single year with a measure of lifetime income.

Fourth, analysts must decide how comprehensive a measure of income to use as a foundation for calculating tax burdens. Ideally, one wants to use as broad a measure of "ability to pay" as possible. For example, the Office of Tax Analysis of the U.S. Department of the Treasury uses the concept of "family economic income" in its distributional analyses. "Economic income" includes, in addition to cash income, nontaxable transfer payments, such as Social Security and AFDC; employer-provided fringe benefits; Individual Retirement and KEOGH account deductions; tax-exempt interest; and the imputed rent on owner-occupied housing. The income measure used in the CTJ–ITEP study is less comprehensive than economic income: The imputed rent from homeownership and the value of fringe benefits. To operationalize a lifetime approach to tax incidence, Metcalf needs a measure of lifetime income. A number of recent studies have used longitudinal data on individual or household income to impute lifetime income.[13] Metcalf's approach is to use total consumption expenditures in a single year as a proxy for lifetime income.[14] He argues that if one ignores bequests and if consumption is smooth over the life cycle, then annual expenditures provide a good measure of lifetime income.

Finally, any study of the distribution of tax burdens must start by making assumptions about the *incidence* of each tax. Because taxpayers often change their behavior in response to taxes, the taxpayers who bear the actual burden of a tax may well be different from those from whom the tax is collected. Metcalf and the CTJ–ITEP make identical, and conventional, incidence assumptions with respect to the individual income tax and the sales tax: namely, that the burden of the income tax falls on taxpayers and the burden of the sales tax on consumers. Metcalf assumes that the entire burden of the residential property tax falls on the owners of capital, while the CTJ–ITEP study assumes that the property tax on owner-occupied housing is borne by homeowners and the property tax on residential rental property is split evenly between tenants and landlords.[15]

Given the fact that Metcalf and the CTJ–ITEP took very different approaches in their studies of state and local tax burdens, it is not at all surprising that they came to strikingly different conclusions about the progressivity of state and local taxes. Table 10.1 summarizes the results of the two studies. The CTJ–ITEP ranks nonelderly married couples by income quintiles and calculates average tax burdens for each quintile.[16] Metcalf ranks households by annual consumption expenditure quintiles and defines burdens as taxes divided by expenditures.

CTJ–ITEP reports quite conventional results: The sales tax is regressive, with the burden in the bottom quintile 2.5 times the burden in the top quintile; the personal income tax is progressive, with the burden in the top quintile 2.25 times the burden in the bottom quintile; and the residential property tax is regressive, with the burden in the bottom quintile 2.35 times the burden in the top quintile. In fiscal year 1994, these three taxes accounted for about 65 percent of all state and local government tax revenue. The right-hand column of table 10.1 demonstrates that the distribution of burdens from the sum of the three taxes is regressive: The average burden in the bottom quintile is 1.5 higher than the average burden in the top quintile.

In sharp contrast to these results, Metcalf finds that the sales tax is progressive and the income tax is progressive over the bottom four quintiles, while the residential property tax is close to proportional, with the average burden in the bottom quintile only 6 percent higher than the average burden in the fourth and fifth quintiles. Metcalf demonstrates that his results are primarily attributable to his lifetime perspective. When he calculates sales tax burdens based on annual income, he finds that the tax is regressive over the entire income

Table 10.1 AVERAGE STATE AND LOCAL TAX BURDENS
Taxes as a percentage of income (CTJ-ITEP) on consumption expenditures (Metcalf)

Quintiles	General Sales Tax		Personal Income Tax		Residential Property Tax		Total of Three Taxes	
	CTJ-ITEP	Metcalf	CTJ-ITEP	Metcalf	CTJ-ITEP	Metcalf	CTJ-ITEP	Metcalf
Bottom	3.5%	1.2%	1.2%	1.0%	4.0%	3.4%	8.7%	5.6%
Second	2.9	1.4	2.1	2.1	2.6	3.7	7.6	7.2
Third	2.4	1.6	2.6	2.7	2.4	3.0	7.4	7.3
Fourth	2.0	1.7	2.6	3.0	2.1	3.2	6.7	7.9
Top	1.4	1.7	2.7	2.6	1.7	3.2	5.8	7.5

Source: Author's calculations from data in CTJ-ITEP (1996) and Metcalf (1994).

Notes: In the CTJ-ITEP study, burdens are calculated for non-elderly married couples, and couples are arranged in quintiles of 1995 income. The burdens in the Metcalf study are calculated for all households, and these households are ordered by quintiles of 1989 annual expenditures. Income and property tax burdens are net of federal deductibility. Metcalf's income tax burdens were calculated after dropping households with negative income tax liabilities.

distribution, with a pattern of burdens looking very similar to those reported by CTJ–ITEP. Likewise, the pattern of property tax burdens based on annual income is regressive above the third income quintile, even though Metcalf assumes that the entire incidence of the property tax falls on the owners of capital.

What conclusions should state policy-makers draw from the results presented in table 10.1? If lifetime incidence is the appropriate basis on which to analyze the distribution of tax burdens, then, as Metcalf demonstrates, both sales and income taxes are progressive, and the choice between them can be made on grounds other than tax fairness. There is quite widespread agreement among economists that the use of annual data biases tax incidence studies in the direction of regressivity. This bias occurs because for some people high tax burdens reflect temporarily low income, while consumption of taxable items is based on higher, long-term income. For example, temporary unemployment will reduce income but may have relatively little impact on spending; the result is a temporarily high tax burden. Likewise, if spending decisions by students or by retired elderly persons reflect their long-term or normal income, they will appear to have high tax burdens during the period that they are students or retired and particularly low burdens during their peak earning years.

The question we want to ask is whether lifetime tax incidence is the correct way to deal with the bias generated by relying on annual data, or whether lifetime incidence calculations create their own set of biases. A major problem in conducting lifetime incidence studies is that it is not possible to observe any individual's lifetime income, and a great number of assumptions are necessary in order to estimate lifetime income. Metcalf's approach is based on the assumption that while most households' income varies from year to year, their consumption expenditures remain quite constant over time. In fact, this is a poor assumption. People tend to have occasions for nonrecurring, often unanticipated expenditures, such as an illness that requires out-of-pocket medical expenses, a special vacation trip, or a daughter's wedding. In years when these expenditures occur, using annual expenditures as a measure of lifetime income will lead to a downward bias in tax burdens.

For annual consumption expenditures to be a good proxy for lifetime income, households need to be able to finance spending in a year when income is low by drawing on past savings or by borrowing against future income. For households that have no savings and are unable to borrow, changes in consumption are more likely to track changes in annual income than changes in lifetime income.

If liquidity constraints caused by the absence of savings or the inability to borrow affected only a small portion of the population, they might not be important to the lifetime income issue. But the low level of wealth in at least the bottom two quintiles of income distribution suggests that a substantial number of people are likely to face such constraints Wolff (1994). For a large fraction of the population, then, annual consumption is likely to be a poor proxy for lifetime income.

The assertion that annual expenditures are a good proxy for lifetime income is also predicated on the assumption that over the course of a lifetime all income is consumed—an assumption that will be valid only if individuals make no bequests. Although research on bequests is limited, a careful study by Menchik and David (1982) provides evidence that bequests are a rising share of lifetime income as income rises. Thus, the failure to categorize bequests and gifts as consumption expenditures will overstate tax progressivity as measured by Metcalf by biasing tax burdens upward at the top of the income distribution.

The conclusion that Metcalf's results overstate the progressivity of state and local taxes does not imply that the CTJ–ITEP study provides an accurate picture of the incidence of state and local taxes. Likewise, the difficulty of measuring lifetime income should not be interpreted as meaning that the measurement of tax incidence using annual data on income and taxes provides accurate estimates of tax burdens. As long as incomes vary over time and at least some economic decisions are made on the basis of a household's long-term economic position, the use of annual data will bias tax incidence studies toward regressivity. One way to correct for this annual income bias while avoiding most of the problems of trying to measure lifetime income is to use data on individuals' or households' income and tax payments over a period of (at least) several years.

In a recent paper, Chernick and Reschovsky (1997) use eleven years of income and gasoline consumption data for a sample of individuals to calculate "intermediate-term" gasoline tax burdens. They find that the use of intermediate-term data reduces, but does not eliminate, the regressivity of the gasoline excise tax. One reason why the gasoline excise tax remains regressive is that over an eleven-year period there was a rather limited amount of income mobility. Chernick and Reschovsky report that over 85 percent of individuals with incomes in the bottom quintile of the 1982 annual income distribution remain in the bottom third of income distribution when income is measured as average income in the eleven-year period between 1976 and 1986. For these individuals, tax burdens measured using data from a single year provide a quite accurate measure of their overall tax burden. However, for the relatively small number of individuals whose income in 1982 was only temporarily low, the use of annual data in calculating tax burdens substantially overestimates the regressivity of gasoline tax.

Chernick and Reschovsky (1993) also analyze the incidence of the residential property tax on homeowners and of the sales tax on restaurant meals. They find that although the use of annual data biases tax incidence toward regressivity, both taxes remain regressive when tax burdens are calculated using eleven years of data regarding both incomes and tax payments.

The regressivity of the residential property tax as reported in the CTJ–ITEP study reflects not only the use of annual data, but the assumption that homeowners bear the full burden of the tax. While this assumption has been used frequently in studies of property tax burdens, it probably does not reflect the view about property tax incidence held by many (if not most) economists. Under this so-called "new view," the property tax is seen as a combination of a national tax on capital and a local "excise tax" reflecting deviations in local property tax rates from the national average. The incidence of this excise tax depends on the relative mobility of capital, labor, and the consumers of housing. Given the fundamental uncertainty about relative mobility, it is probably not correct to assume that the full burden of the property tax (on owner-occupied residential housing) falls on housing consumers (as in the CTJ–ITEP study), nor that the full burden falls on the owners of capital (as in the Metcalf study). A middle-ground assumption would presumably result in a pattern of property tax incidence somewhere between the two sets of results displayed in table 10.1.

I conclude from this discussion that neither of the two studies is correct. The average incidence of the sales, income, and residential property taxes falls somewhere between the CTJ–ITEP and the Metcalf results. Based on Howard Chernick's and my finding that bias created by using annual income in tax incidence studies is quite small, my best estimate is that the average burden of the three taxes is somewhat regressive, particularly over the bottom half of the income distribution.

A final note: The data in table 10.1 are national averages and as such give more weight to the bigger states, many of which place an above-average reliance on the income tax. Thus, while for the nation as a whole the incidence of the income, sales, and residential property taxes may be only slightly regressive, in the majority of states the composite incidence of these three taxes is clearly regressive.

THE PRESSURE ON STATES TO INCREASE TAXES

The continued strength of the economy in mid-1997 has been reflected in budgetary surpluses in many statehouses across the country. Despite the current rosy fiscal climate in many states, fiscal storm clouds are brewing on the horizon. Events largely outside the control of state and local governments will create extraordinary pressures on state and local governments to raise taxes. These pressures will be apparent even if the economy continues to perform strongly into the next century. And if the economy slows at some point in the next decade, the need to raise taxes will be even greater.

The balanced budget legislation passed by Congress in August 1997 mandates substantial cuts in federal funds currently provided to state and local governments. The bill requires that nondefense discretionary programs, which include federal grants to state and local governments, be 10 percent lower by the year 2002 than they are under current law (Center on Budget and Policy Priorities 1997). Nondefense discretionary programs also include spending on the FBI and the Secret Service, on federal prisons, on veterans' hospitals, and on the IRS. As it is very unlikely that financing for these functions will be reduced, it is almost inevitable that balancing the federal budget will require cuts in federal grants to state and local governments that are in excess of 10 percent. These grants are concentrated in two areas. They provide assistance to individuals and families with low incomes, by distributing grants for a range of services including housing, education, and job training. And they contribute funding toward the building and maintenance of states' physical infrastructure, with the single largest grants financing highway maintenance and construction.

It is difficult to predict the extent to which state and local governments will replace lost federal grants with locally raised revenues. Although there exists a large body of empirical literature on the response of governments to the receipt of grants, there has been very little study of how governments respond to a reduction in grants.[17] Researchers have found that, on average, a lump-sum grant of one dollar results in an increase in spending by the recipient government of about fifty cents. This finding flies in the face of the predictions of economic theory that the receipt of a lump-sum grant is equivalent to an increase in income, and thus will induce quite small (in the range of five-to-ten-cent) increases in spending. The empirical evidence that money has a tendency to "stick where it hits" has been dubbed the "flypaper effect."[18] A couple of recent studies, one of county governments in Pennsylvania (Stine 1994) and another of school districts in New Jersey (Goodspeed 1996), have provided limited evidence of a "reverse flypaper effect." In both cases, the response to a reduction in grants has been considerably less than a dollar-for-dollar increase in local property taxes. Gamkhar and Oates (1996) also provide evidence of a reverse flypaper effect, with state and local government expenditures falling in response to cuts in federal grants by roughly the same amount as they rise in response to an increase in federal grants. Much more work, however, needs to be done before we can predict with confidence how state and local governments will respond to reductions in federal grants.

Although most of the attention in Washington is on achieving a balanced budget by the year 2002, the major impact of federal budgetary policy on state and local governments will be felt in the years *after* 2002. The Balanced Budget Act of 1997 includes changes in the taxation of capital gains, changes in the estate tax and the corporate alternative minimum tax, and an expansion of Individual Retirement Accounts, all of which have been structured so that the major revenue losses will occur in the years after 2002. According to the Joint Committee on Taxation, the tax provisions in the new legislation will result in a net tax cut of $95 billion between 1997 and 2002 and $180 billion between 2002 and 2007. In the subsequent ten years, from 2008 through 2017, the revenue cost of the new legislation is likely to grow to more than $500 billion (Lav 1997). In addition, a substantial portion of these revenue losses is attributable to tax provisions—such as the establishment of "backloaded" Individual Retirement Accounts (IRAs), which, once enacted, cannot be easily undone.[19]

It is exactly during this period that federal spending on Social Security, Medicare, Medicaid, and federal employee retirement programs will begin to grow rapidly, as the baby boom generation begins to retire. Current estimates indicate that unless policy changes are made in the interim, by the year 2012 total federal government spending on Social Security benefits will exceed tax payments into the Social Security trust fund (Advisory Council on Social Security 1997). Although the Advisory Council was unable to come to an agreement about how to solve Social Security's long-term financing problems, they were unanimous in their assessment that *some* policy changes, which might include a modest increase in payroll taxes, will be necessary in the next couple of decades. It is also possible that additional taxes will be necessary in order to partially finance the rising costs of the Medicare program.

The growing revenue costs of the tax provisions included in the balanced budget agreement, along with the fiscal demands on the Social Security and Medicare systems as the baby boom generation retires, have serious implications for state and local governments. Unless Congress is willing to enact large federal tax increases, state and local governments should anticipate major reductions in federal grants that currently help fund state and local government programs in education, health care, social services, environmental protection, and transportation. In 1996, these grants equaled 24 percent of state and local government expenditures (Office of Management and Budget 1997). Thus, substantial reductions in federal funds would initiate major fiscal crises in most states. It is also likely that fiscal pressures on the federal government will lead to a range of cuts in federal government programs that themselves provide resources to needy individuals. A consequence of these cuts in federal programs will be a shifting of the costs of providing services to the needy directly to state and local governments. The states—and, in particular, local governments—cannot avoid these extra costs, even if they choose not to replace federal assistance to the needy with state or local dollars. If cuts in federal support lead to increases in the incidence of homelessness, or increases in the crime rate or in the number of medically uninsured individuals, local governments will be forced to respond to these problems. In other words, local citizens and their governments will be unable to avoid the consequence of federal fiscal policies.

The devolution of fiscal responsibilities from the federal government to state and local governments has been occurring for nearly two decades. The pace of devolution quickened with the passage in 1996 of welfare reform legislation. This legislation shifts the ultimate responsibility for the economic welfare of individuals facing severe economic hardships from the federal to state and local governments. Under the new legislation, Aid for Families with Dependent Children (AFDC) matching grants were replaced with block grants. These block grants, which will remain unchanged over time and will be largely invariant with respect to the number of people in need of assistance, are called Temporary Assistance to Needy Families (TANF) grants. Because caseloads have fallen in almost all states over the past few years, the new welfare legislation will actually provide states with substantially more federal funds during 1997 and 1998 than they would have received under the prior law. Although the new block grants are providing most states with adequate funds to begin establishing new, work-focused welfare programs, it is highly unlikely that block grant funds will be adequate when, as inevitably will happen, the economy slows down and unemployment rates begin to rise.

Because the size of the welfare block grants will remain largely unchanged as the economy weakens, state governments will be forced to bear the entire cost of maintaining an economic and social safety net for their citizens.[20] The fiscal situation of states will be further complicated by the fact that real state tax revenues usually decline, sometimes precipitously, during recessions. For example, Steven Gold (1995) calculated that during the last recession real state tax revenues, after eliminating the effects of legislated tax increases, fell in every quarter between the fourth quarter of 1990 and the second quarter of 1992.

WILL STATE TAX SYSTEMS BECOME MORE OR LESS PROGRESSIVE?

I have argued in the previous section that efforts to balance the federal budget, the rising costs of Social Security and Medicare as the baby boom generation begins to retire, the long-term revenue impacts of federal tax cuts, and the switch from AFDC matching grants to block grants for the financing of welfare will all increase the revenue demands on state and local governments. Most states will probably respond with a mix of spending cuts and tax increases. In this section, I speculate about whether these state responses will result in an increase or decrease in the progressivity of state tax systems.[21]

Because competitive pressures limit the use of progressive taxes by subnational governments, Richard Musgrave (1997, p. 157) argues that devolution will lead directly to the increased use of regressive state and local taxes. "The case for (against) devolution, therefore, also serves as a case against (for) progressive taxation. Though hidden between the lines, this is a major issue on the tax side of the devolution debate."

Although it is too early to tell, there are some indications that state governments will respond to devolution by shifting responsibilities for some public services to county and perhaps even municipal governments. Except in the unlikely cases when these shifts in responsibilities are fully state-funded, these lower-level governments will need to raise additional revenues from local sources, and the property tax remains by far the dominant source of own-raised revenue. The net effect of this shifting of responsibilities then, will be less progressive state and local tax systems.

There is very little systematic evidence available that helps us predict how state and local governments will respond to the need for additional revenues. One recent example, however, is the way in which the State of California responded to its most severe economic downturn since the 1920s. In fiscal year 1992, California faced the prospect of a budget deficit of over $14 billion, an amount equal to one-third of its general fund expenditures in that year. In order to close the deficit, the state pursued a range of budgetary strategies, including large spending cuts, tax increases, and the shifting of expenditure responsibilities to county governments (Chapman 1995). The tax changes included a progressivity-enhancing increase in the income tax (by increasing marginal tax rates on high-income taxpayers) and a progressivity-diminishing one-and-one-quarter-cent increase in the sales tax rate. Since the sales tax increases generated about four times more revenue than the income tax increases, the net result of the tax increases was a reduction in the progressivity of the state tax system. (The two additional income tax brackets were temporary, in any case, and have since been repealed.) Although there have been some changes in the sales tax since 1992, the overall rate has not been reduced. In addition, county governments were given new responsibilities in the areas of mental health, public health, and social services and were provided with the revenue from one-quarter of a cent of the sales tax increase. Chapman reports, however, that the new revenues were inadequate to meet the spending required by the shifting of responsibilities to the counties.

Another example comes from Wisconsin, where a recent study compares the incidence of state income, sales, and excise taxes in 1974 with the incidence of these taxes in 1995 (Reschovsky and Reuter, 1997). The authors find that over this period, the burden of these taxes on nonelderly married couples become somewhat less progressive, with average burdens rising the most in the second and middle quintiles of the income distribution.

With the passage of the Tax Reform Act of 1986, the federal government reduced the income tax burden on the poor. The recent expansion of the Earned Income Tax Credit has further reduced the federal tax liabilities of low-income families. And in the decade since 1986, a number of states have taken steps to increase the income tax threshold—the minimum income level at which individuals must pay income tax; other state efforts to reduce the tax burden on the poor include property tax relief in five states and the establishment of state earned income tax credits (Liebschutz and Gold 1995). Using data from 1988, however, Chernick and Reschovsky (1990) document the existence of high state and local tax burdens on the poor and near-poor. And McNichol and Lazere (1997) report that in 1996, of the forty-two states with a personal income tax, twenty-four of them levied taxes on two-parent families of four with incomes below the poverty line, and twenty-two levied income taxes on poor single-parent families of three.

Predicting whether states will continue efforts to reduce tax burdens on the poor is difficult. In most states, income tax provisions that provide tax relief for low-income taxpayers, such as personal exemptions, deductions, and credits, are not indexed for inflation. The result is that unless legislatures take explicit steps to offset the impact of inflation, tax burdens on the poor rise over time. The elimination of matching grants for welfare may, as suggested by Liebschutz and Gold (1995), increase the willingness of states to provide tax relief for the poor. They argue that as long as the federal government paid at least fifty cents of each extra dollar of state spending on welfare, states had an incentive to expand welfare spending rather than provide tax relief for the poor. The switch to block grants eliminates this incentive and suggests that states may be willing to provide tax relief rather than direct cash assistance to the poor. Depending on how it is structured, tax relief may have an advantage over cash assistance, if it encourages work effort.

Tax changes at the federal level can either encourage or discourage increases in tax progressivity on the part of state governments. As part of the Tax Relief Act of 1997, the tax rates on realized capital gains were reduced. It is likely that many states will adopt these changes. The adoption will be automatic in states whose state income tax systems are directly linked to either federal tax liabilities, federal taxable income, or federal adjusted gross income. In states that are not automatically coupled to the federal tax code, there will be considerable political pressure to adopt the federal changes in the treatment of capital gains. Given that capital gains are concentrated among high-income taxpayers, any capital gain tax cuts enacted by state governments will certainly reduce the progressivity of state tax systems. On the other hand, a recent study by Howard Chernick (1994) suggests that state governments offset the distributional impacts of federal tax changes. Thus, to the extent that changes in the federal income taxation of capital gains reduce the effective tax rates on high-income individuals, states may be provided with the political room to *increase* state tax rates on these individuals, thereby retaining the distribution of overall tax burdens that existed prior to the federal tax changes.

There is considerable interest in this country in "fundamental tax reform."[22] A number of proposals have been made to replace both the individual and corporate income taxes with various forms of consumption taxation. Although it is by no means certain that any of these consumption tax proposals will be enacted, if the federal government did in fact abandon the income tax, there would be strong pressure on state governments to switch to the use of consumption taxation or, at a minimum, to reduce their reliance on the income tax. Not only do most of the tax reform proposals call for the elimination of deductibility for state income taxes, but the administration of state income tax systems would become much more difficult once the Internal Revenue Service no longer shared compliance data with state revenue departments.

CONCLUSIONS

Hardly a year passes without changes being made in some element of each state's tax system. When the economy is weak and state revenue growth slows, states tend to raise rates or expand tax bases, while in periods of sustained economic growth, states tend to reduce tax rates and expand deductions, credits, and tax base exclusions. With this continual flux in state tax systems, it is not surprising that issues about the fairness of state taxes are frequently on the political agenda in statehouses across the nation.

The determination of the distribution of the burdens of state tax systems is difficult and fraught with measurement problems. Although more research on the incidence of state and local taxes is clearly needed, in this paper I have argued that the best available evidence suggests that, on average, state and local tax systems are mildly regressive. States differ substantially, however, with some states having highly regressive tax systems and a few having mildly progressive systems.

Predicting whether state tax systems will become more or less progressive over the next couple of decades is particularly difficult, in part because any effort at prediction requires that we understand how tax decisions are made in each of the fifty states. As the federal government struggles to maintain a balanced budget and to cope with its rapidly growing fiscal responsibilities as the baby boom generation begins to retire, states will be under increasing pressure to raise taxes. How states respond to this pressure will largely determine whether the progressivity of state and local taxes increases or decreases in the twenty-first century.

How they respond, however, will depend to a large extent on whether states perceive that competition among states for resources—both highly skilled labor and capital—is becoming more heated. If either the reality or the perception of interstate competition grows, then state legislatures will be under tremendous pressure to take steps to enhance their competitive positions. In the past this has usually translated into reductions in the progressivity of state tax systems. Whether states respond similarly to competitive pressures in the future will depend in part on the patterns of factor demand. In the past few decades the demand for skilled labor has been high, and states have sometimes responded by using their tax systems to try to attract skilled labor. If this trend continues, pressure to reduce the progressivity of state tax systems (and ease tax burdens on higher-income taxpayers) may continue. If, on the other hand, shortages of low-skilled labor arise, states may feel pressure to increase progressivity by reducing tax burdens on low- and moderate-income taxpayers.

Notes

I would like to thank Howard Chernick, Brian Knight, Judy Temple, and Michael Wiseman for very helpful comments.

1. For an excellent summary of this literature see Wasylenko (1997).

2. This total includes the District of Columbia, but excludes two states, New Hampshire and Tennessee, that only tax interest and dividends.

3. The assumption of this kind of mobility is the basis for the well-known Tiebout (1956) hypothesis. Empirical support for fiscally motivated mobility within a single metropolitan area was provided by Reschovsky (1979).

4. Sally Wallace (1993) finds limited evidence that in some cases labor may not bear the full burden of state income taxation because employers will raise gross wages in response to higher tax rates.

5. The use of state fixed effects may be inadequate to control for factors correlated with both gross wages and tax rates.

6. This example somewhat overstates the advantage of deductibility for high-income taxpayers whose total itemized deductions are subject to a partial phaseout.

7. Although in 1994 only 28.5 percent of all federal income tax returns were filed by individuals who itemized deductions, among those individuals with the highest probability of voting, namely those with adjusted gross incomes over $50,000, over 70 percent of returns included itemized deductions (Internal Revenue Service, 1997).

8. Goodspeed (1995) argues that deductibility can provide at least a partial remedy to the inefficiencies caused by interstate migration attributable to progressive state income taxation.

9. Gyourko and Summers (1997) document the fact that large cities (with populations over 300,000) spend much more money from own-source revenue on city services for the poor than do small cities (with populations under 75,000).

10. Although tax progressivity can be measured in many different ways (Kiefer, 1984), it is almost certain that any progressivity measure will indicate substantial differences among states in the progressivity of their tax systems.

11. Both Berch and Chernick and Reschovsky also use data from a 1985 incidence study conducted by the Citizens for Tax Justice.

12. This argument, which is based on Friedman's (1957) permanent income theory of consumption and the companion life-cycle model of saving (Ando and Modigliani 1963), has been made recently by Lyon and Schwab (1995), Caspersen and Metcalf (1994), Poterba (1989, 1991), and Fullerton and Rogers (1991, 1993).

13. This approach has been used by Fullerton and Rogers (1991, 1993), Lyon and Schwab (1995), Caspersen and Metcalf (1994), and Rogers (1995).

14. This approach has also been used by Poterba (1989, 1991) and the U.S. Congressional Budget Office (1990).

15. Some economists have argued that property taxes are benefit taxes, with the amount individuals pay corresponding directly to the benefits they receive from goods and services provided by local governments. If this were the case, property taxes should not be included in a tax incidence analysis. I find the argument unconvincing, in part because proponents rarely provide any evidence to support their argument.

16. The CTJ-ITEP does not display data for the top quintile. They divide taxpayers in the top quintile into the highest (in terms of income) one percent, the next four percent, and the next highest fifteen percent. My figures for the top quintile, come from a weighted average of the burdens faced by these three groups.

17. In a number of case studies of how city governments responded to large cuts in federal aid in the early 1980s, Peterson (1986) and Nathan et al. (1987) concluded that city governments tended not to replace federal funds when the federal funds had been used for redistributive purposes or had been segregated into separate funds used for the provision of noncore services, often targeted for the needy.

18. Hines and Thaler (1995) provide an excellent review of this literature.

19. For example, although money invested in a backloaded IRA comes from after-tax income, after a specified holding period, the original investment plus all earnings can be withdrawn without payment of any income taxes. At any point in the future, the Congress could obviously decide to prohibit new investments in backloaded IRAs, but it would be legally bound to allow for the payment of tax-free distributions from existing IRA accounts.

20. In an attempt to increase the cyclical responsiveness of welfare block grants, Congress allocated $2 billion to a contingency fund to be used over the next five years. The fund, however, is almost certainly not large enough to meet demands during a major recession. Furthermore, because of the nature of the eligibility requirements, some states will remain ineligible even if they suffer from substantial increases in their unemployment rates (Reschovsky, 1996).

21. The fiscal behavior of individual states will be influenced by the presence of either constitutionally or legislatively imposed limitations on the power of legislatures to tax.

These limitations include traditional tax limitations, supermajority requirements, and voter referendum requirements.

22. See Aaron and Gale (1996) for a detailed discussion of various tax reform proposals.

References

Aaron, Henry J., and William G. Gale, eds. 1996. *Economic Effects of Fundamental Tax Reform.* Washington, D.C.: The Brookings Institution.

Advisory Council on Social Security. 1997. *Report of the 1994–1996 Advisory Council on Social Security. Volume 1: Findings and Recommendations.* Washington, D.C.: U.S. Government Printing Office (http://www.ssa.gov/policy/adcouncil/toc.htm).

Ando, Albert, and Franco Modigliani. 1963. "The 'Life Cycle' Hypothesis of Saving: Aggregate Implications and Tests." *American Economic Review* 53 (March): 55–84.

Bahl, Roy, Jorge Martinez-Vazquez, and Sally Wallace. 1996. "State and Local Government Choices in Fiscal Redistribution" Report No. 58. School of Policy Studies, Georgia State University (January).

Berch, Neil. 1995. "Explaining Changes in Tax Incidence in the States." *Political Research Quarterly* 48 (September): 629–641.

Caspersen, Erik, and Gilbert Metcalf. 1994. "Is a Value Added Tax Regressive? Annual Versus Lifetime Incidence Measures." *National Tax Journal* 47 (December): 731–46.

Center on Budget and Policy Priorities. 1997. *What's in the Budget Agreement?.* Washington, D.C.: Center on Budget and Policy Priorities (June 12).

Chapman, Jeffrey I. 1995. "California: The Enduring Crisis." In *The Fiscal Crisis of the States: Lessons for the Future,* edited by Steven D. Gold, pp. 104–40. Washington, D.C.: Georgetown University Press.

Chernick, Howard. 1991. "Distributional Constraints and State Decisions to Tax." Paper presented to the National Bureau of Economics Research Summer Institute on State and Local Public Finance.

―――――. 1992. "A Model of the Distributional Incidence of State and Local Taxes." *Public Finance Quarterly* 20 (October): 572–85.

―――――. 1994. "Tax Incidence, Tax Revenues, and Economic Performance: Is Progressivity Self-Defeating?" Working Paper No. 94-1, Department of Economics, Hunter College (April).

―――――. 1997. "Tax Progressivity and State Economic Performance." *Economic Development Quarterly* 11 (August): 249–67.

Chernick, Howard, and Andrew Reschovsky. 1987. "Comment on 'The Deductibility of State and Local Taxes.'" *National Tax Journal* 40 (March): 95–102.

————. 1990. "The Taxation of the Poor," *Journal of Human Resources* 25 (fall): 712–35.

————. 1993. "Evaluating the Long-Run Burden of the Residential Property Tax and Selected State and Local Consumption Taxes." Paper presented at the Annual Conference on Taxation of the National Tax Institute, St. Paul, Minn. (November).

————. 1996. "The Political Economy of State and Local Tax Structure." In *Developments in Local Government Finance; Theory and Policy,* edited by Giancarlo Pola, George France, and Rosella Levaggi. Cheltenham, U.K.: Edward Elgar.

————. 1997. "Who Pays the Gasoline Tax." *National Tax Journal* 50 (June): 233–59.

Ettlinger, Michael P., et al. 1996. *Who Pays? A Distributional Analysis of the Tax Systems of All Fifty States.* Washington, D.C.: Citizens for Tax Justice and Institute on Taxation and Economic Policy (June).

Feldstein, Martin, and Marian Vaillant. 1994. "Can State Taxes Redistribute Income?" Working Paper No. 4785. Cambridge, Mass.: National Bureau of Economic Research (June).

Friedman, Milton. 1957. *A Theory of the Consumption Function.* National Bureau of Economic Research, Princeton, N.J.: Princeton University Press.

————. 1991. "Lifetime versus Annual Perspective on Tax Incidence." *National Tax Journal* 44 (September): 277–87.

————. 1993. *Who Bears the Lifetime Tax Burden?* Washington, D.C.: Brookings Institution.

Fullerton, Don, and Diane L. Rogers. 1991. "Lifetime Versus Annual Perspective on Tax Incidence." *National Tax Journal* 44 (September): 277–87.

Gamkhar, Shama, and Wallace Oates. 1996. "Asymmetries in the Response to Increases and Decreases in Intergovernmental Grants: Some Empirical Findings." *National Tax Journal* 49 (December): 501–12.

Gold, Steven D. 1995. "State Fiscal Problems and Policies." In *The Fiscal Crisis of the States: Lessons for the Future,* edited by Steven D. Gold, pp. 6–40. Washington, D.C.: Georgetown University Press.

Goodspeed, Timothy J. 1989. "A Reexamination of the Use of Ability to Pay Taxes by Local Governments." *Journal of Public Economics* 38 (April): 319–42.

————. 1995. "Local Income Taxation: An Externality, Pigovian Solutions, and Public Policies." *Regional Science and Urban Economics* 25 (June): 279–96.

————. 1996. "The Relationship Between State Income Taxes and Local Property Taxes: The Case of New Jersey." Unpublished paper. New York: Department of Economics, Hunter College, (October 17).

Gramlich, Edward M. 1985. "The Deductibility of State and Local Taxes." *National Tax Journal* 38 (December): 417–65.

Gyourko, Joseph, and Anita A. Summers. 1997. "A New Strategy for Helping Cities Pay for the Poor." *Brookings Policy Brief Series*, No. 18. Washington, D.C.: Brookings Institution (June).

Hettich, Walter, and Stanley L. Winer. 1978. "Economic and Political Foundations of Tax Structure," *American Economic Review* 78 (September): 701–712.

Hines, James R., and Robert Thaler. 1995. "The Flypaper Effect." *Journal of Economic Perspectives* 9 (fall): 217–26.

Inman, Robert P. 1989. "The Local Decision to Tax: Evidence From Large U.S. Cities." *Regional Science and Urban Economics* 19 (August): 455–92.

Internal Revenue Service. 1997. *Statistics on Income—1994*: Individual Income Tax Returns. Washington, D.C.: Internal Revenue Service.

Kiefer, Donald W. 1984. "Distributional Tax Progressivity Indices." *National Tax Journal* 37 (December): 497–513.

Lav, Iris J. 1997. *The Final Tax Bill: Assessing the Long-Term Costs and the Distribution of Tax Benefits*. Washington, D.C.: Center on Budget and Policy Priorities (August 1).

Liebschutz, David S., and Steven D. Gold. 1995. *State Tax Relief for the Poor*, Albany, N.Y.: Nelson A. Rockefeller Institute of Government, Center for the Study of the States.

Lowery, David. 1987. "The Distribution of Tax Burdens in the American States: The Determinants of Fiscal Incidence," *Western Political Quarterly* 40 (March): 137–58.

Lyon, Andrew B., and Robert M. Schwab. 1995. "Consumption Taxes in a Life-Cycle Framework: Are Sin Taxes Regressive?" *Review of Economics and Statistics* 77 (August): 389–406.

Menchik, Paul L., and Martin David. 1982. "The Incidence of a Lifetime Consumption Tax." *National Tax Journal* 35 (June): 189–203.

Metcalf, Gilbert. 1994. "The Lifetime Incidence of State and Local Taxes: Measuring Changes During the 1980s." In *Tax Progressivity and Income Inequality*, edited by Joel Slemrod, pp. 59–88. New York: Cambridge University Press.

McNichol, Elizabeth C., and Edward Lazere. 1997. "State Income Tax Burdens on Low-Income Families in 1996: Assessing the Burden and Opportunities for Relief." *State Tax Notes* 12 (June 16): 1819–36.

Morgan, David R. 1994. "Tax Equity in the American States: A Multivariate Analysis." *Social Science Quarterly* 75 (September): 510–23.

Musgrave, Richard A. 1959. *The Theory of Public Finance*. New York: McGraw-Hill.

Musgrave, Richard A. 1997. "Reconsidering the Fiscal Role of Government." *American Economic Review* 87 (May): 156–59.

Nathan, Richard P., et al. 1987. *Reagan and the States*. Princeton, N.J.: Princeton University Press.

Oakland, William H. 1992. "How Should Businesses Be Taxed?" In *State Taxation of Business: Issues and Policy Options*, edited by Thomas F. Pogue. New York: Praeger.

Oates, Wallace E. 1972. *Fiscal Federalism*. New York: Harcourt Brace Jovanovich.

Oates, Wallace E., and Robert M. Schwab. 1988. "Economic Competition Among Jurisdictions: Efficiency Enhancing or Distortion Inducing?" *Journal of Public Economics* 35 (April): 333–54.

Oates, Wallace E., and Robert M. Schwab. 1991. "The Allocative and Distributive Implications of Local Fiscal Competition." In *Competition Among States and Local Governments: Efficiency and Equity in American Federalism*, edited by Daphne A. Kenyon and John Kinkaid. Washington, D.C.: Urban Institute Press.

Office of Management and Budget. 1997. *Budget of the United States Government, Fiscal Year 1998: Analytic Perspectives*. Washington, D.C.: U.S. Government Printing Office.

Pauly, Mark V. 1973. "Income Redistribution as a Local Public Good." *Journal of Public Economics* 2 (February): 35–58.

Pechman, Joseph A. 1985. *Who Paid the Taxes, 1966–85?* Washington, D.C.: Brookings Institution.

Pechman, Joseph A., and Benjamin A. Okner. 1974. *Who Bears the Tax Burden?* Washington, D.C.: Brookings Institution.

Peterson, George E. 1986. "Urban Policy and the Cyclical Behavior of Cities." In *Reagan and the Cities*, edited by George E. Peterson and Carol W. Lewis. Washington, D.C.: Urban Institute Press.

Phares, Donald. 1980. *Who Pays State and Local Taxes?* Cambridge, Mass. Oelgeschaler, Gunn, and Hain.

Poterba, James M. 1989. "Lifetime Incidence and the Distributional Burden of Excise Taxes." *American Economic Review* 79 (May): 325–30.

Poterba, James M. 1991. "Is the Gasoline Tax Regressive?" in *Tax Policy and the Economy*, Volume 5, edited by David Bradford. Cambridge, Mass.: National Bureau of Economic Research and MIT Press.

Reschovsky, Andrew. 1979. "Residential Choice and the Local Public Sector: An Alternative Test of the Tiebout Hypothesis." *Journal of Urban Economics* 6 (October): 501–20.

————. 1996. "How Will States Cope With Devolution?" Paper prepared for the Annual Conference of the James A. Baker III Institute for Public Policy, Rice University, (November 12–13).

Reschovsky, Andrew, and Chad Reuter. 1997. "Has Wisconsin's State Tax System Become Less Fair? Changes in the Distribution of Tax Burdens from 1974 to 1995." Milwaukee: Institute for Wisconsin's Future, (June).

Rogers, Diane Lim. 1995. "Distributional Effects of Corrective Taxation: Assessing Lifetime Incidence From Cross-Sectional Data." *Proceedings* of the Eighty-Sixth Annual Conference on Taxation, 880, 192–202. National Tax Association.

Shannon, John. 1991. "Federalism's 'Invisible Regulator'—Interjurisdictional Competition." In Competition Among States and Local Governments, edited by Daphne A. Kenyon and John Kincaid. Washington, D.C.: Efficiency and Equity in American Federation, Urban Instititute Press.

Slemrod, Joel. 1986. "The Optimal Progressivity of the Minnesota Tax System." In Final Report of the Minnesota Tax Study Commission. Volume 2: Staff Papers, edited by Robert D. Ebel and Therese J. McGuire. St. Paul, Minn.: Butterworths Legal Publishers.

Stine, William F. 1974. "Is Local Government Revenue Response to Federal Aid Symmetrical? Evidence From Pennsylvania County Governments in an Era of Retrenchment." National Tax Journal 47 (December): 799–817.

Tiebout, Charles. 1956. "A Pure Theory of Local Expenditures." Journal of Political Economy 64 (February): 416–424.

U.S. Congressional Budget Office. 1990. Federal Taxation of Tobacco, Alcoholic Beverages, and Motor Fuels, A CBO Study. Washington, D.C.: Congressional Budget Office.

Wallace, Sally. 1993. "The Effects of State Personal Income Tax Differentials on Wages." Regional Science and Urban Economics 23 (November): 611–28.

Wasylenko, Michael. 1997. "Taxation and Economic Development: The State of the Economic Literature." New England Economic Review (March/April): 37–52.

Winer, Stanley L., and Walter Hettich. 1992. "Explaining the Use of Related Tax Instruments." Working Paper, Sonderforschungsbereich 178, Serie II, No. 189, Faculty for Economics and Statistics, University of Konstanz, Germany, September.

Wisconsin Department of Revenue. 1980. The Wisconsin Tax Burden Study, Madison: Department of Revenue, Division of Research and Analyis.

Wolff, Edward N. 1994. "Trends in Household Wealth in the United States, 1962–68 and 1983–89." The Review of Income and Wealth 40 (June): 143–74.

Chapter Eleven

STATE PERSONAL INCOME TAXATION IN THE TWENTY-FIRST CENTURY

David Brunori

When contemplating the future of the state income tax, one must consider the vital role the tax plays in state government finance. The enormity of that role is not a startling revelation, for everyone familiar with public finance is aware that the tax has long been a primary source of revenue for state governments. Indeed, in recent times, the tax has consistently accounted for about a third of the tax revenue raised by the states—far exceeding that raised by levies on corporate income as well as taxes levied on tobacco, gasoline, and alcohol. Only the sales tax has provided a comparable source of revenue. The tax is widely used; only seven states have chosen not to impose some form of personal income tax. Simply put, the personal income tax has been a very successful means of collecting revenue.

The income tax, then, is well entrenched in the state government systems of finance—and the reason for that entrenchment is that it satisfies the basic principles of sound tax policy. That is, the income tax has proven to be an efficient, fair, and effective method of collecting revenue. Its adherence to the principles of sound tax policy has met with approval by economists and political theorists and is also the primary reason for its widespread acceptance by the public. Without that public acceptance, the personal income tax could not have evolved into the major source of revenue that it is today.

There are several aspects of the tax that accord particularly well with widely accepted notions of sound tax policy. First, the state personal income tax generally conforms with the federal income tax system. That conformity has resulted in only marginal taxpayer compliance burdens, as state taxpayers experience few burdens independent of those already experienced as part of the federal tax system. Conformity with the federal tax system has also rendered government administration of the tax economical and efficient.

Second, in most states the income tax has been a part—albeit a large part—of an intricate mix of revenue sources. In addition to taxing personal income, most states also tax sales, corporate income, alcohol, tobacco, and fuel. This balance of revenue adds stability to state fiscal systems and allows states to minimize the rate for all types of taxes.

That the tax is the least regressive of all methods of raising revenue has led most commentators to declare it the most equitable of state taxes. More importantly, the personal income tax is generally viewed by the public as fair, or at least as the most fair of all taxes.

These aspects of the tax have led to its widespread public acceptance, which in turn has led to its tremendous growth over the last century. This essay discusses the future of the state income tax in terms of both its compliance with the principles of sound tax policy and its widespread acceptance by the public. Our conclusion is simply that, barring a radical change in the federal income tax structure, the state personal income tax will remain a dominant source of revenue for state governments. Indeed, there is no reason to believe that the continued growth of the tax—a seventy-year trend—will abate. For there are neither technological nor economic developments that will change the structure of the tax or the public's perception of the tax as an acceptable means of raising revenue.

PERSONAL INCOME TAX AND SOUND TAX POLICY

In 1776, Adam Smith enumerated four principles by which to evaluate a revenue system (Papke 1993).

> The subjects of every state ought to contribute towards the support of government, as nearly as possible, in proportion to their respective abilities; that is in proportion to the revenue which they respectively enjoy under the protection of the state.
>
> The tax which each individual is bound to pay ought to be certain and not arbitrary.
>
> Every tax ought to be levied at the time, or in the manner, in which it is most likely to be convenient for the contributor to pay.
>
> Every tax ought to be so contrived as both to take out and to keep out of the pockets of the people as little as possible, over and above what it brings into the public treasury of every state.

These maxims are widely cited principles of sound tax policy, and Smith's views have, over time, been echoed by scholars, policy-makers, and practitioners (Shoup 1937; Reese 1980; Blough 1955). Indeed, those principles represent our "highest aspirations, if not our noblest achievements" in the pursuit of a workable tax system. (Galper and Pollack 1988, p. 108). Over time, four broad concepts of sound tax policy have emerged (National Conference of State Legislatures [NCSL] 1992):

1. Tax systems should provide appropriate revenue;
2. Tax systems should be equitable;
3. Tax systems should be easily and economically administered; and
4. Tax systems should ensure accountability.

As will be discussed below, the state personal income tax generally meets all of these requirements of a sound tax system. There are, of course, areas in which the personal income tax does not neatly fit into those widely accepted concepts; those apparent shortcomings will be discussed as well. Nonetheless, the tax remains the one method of taxation that comes closest to fulfilling the principles that Adam Smith articulated more than two hundred years ago. More importantly, there is no reason to believe that its adherence to those principles will abate.

Billions in Revenue

It is widely accepted that a tax system should provide appropriate revenue to support the costs of government (Blough 1955; Brunori 1997). Indeed, this is the primary goal of tax systems (Ladd 1988). This principle has been discussed in terms of three contexts: sufficiency, stability, and certainty (NCSL 1992). Sufficiency requires that revenue be adequate to meet the needs of government spending. The personal income tax has been one of the primary sources of revenue for state governments for a good part of this century. The tax currently accounts for about 32 percent of state tax revenues (U.S. Department of Commerce 1997). Its importance to the fiscal health of state governments cannot be overstated. In 1996, state governments raised over $134 billion from taxing personal income (Ibid. 1997). Thus, it would be difficult to argue that personal income taxes do not provide an appropriate level of revenue to support state government operations.

In addition to meeting the needs of current spending, a sound tax system requires stability—the ability to raise a consistent amount of revenue over time (NCSL 1992). A stable source of income does not fluctuate greatly with changes in the economy. In this regard, the income tax is less stable than most other sources of tax revenue. Indeed, the income tax tends to be the most elastic of all forms of state revenue (Gold 1991).

Personal income tax revenues increase more rapidly when the economy is growing and fall more precipitously when the economy slows. Personal income tax revenue grows faster than income because 1) marginal rates rise as income increases; and 2) taxable income grows faster than personal income, because exemptions and standard deductions are usually fixed in value (Gold 1991). There is a tension, then, between the desire for stability and the elasticity of the income tax.

What balances the relative instability of the income tax is that it is part of an intricate mix of sources of revenue. The NCSL has noted that a stable tax system requires a mix of taxes with some expanding less sharply to economic change (NCSL 1993). Sales taxes, for instance, tend to be more consistent during economic swings. Balanced or mixed tax systems have proven to be more stable, since the slow growth of sales taxes is offset by the faster growth of income taxes (Ladd 1988).

In any event, the state income tax has, in fact, continued to grow over the years, and there is no indication that in the future the state personal income tax will not remain a major source of income for state governments. Between 1980 and 1993 alone, revenue from individual income tax grew by an astonishing 204 percent (Megna 1997). And this is not a recent phenomenon; over the last fifty years, the share of income taxes as a percentage of total state taxes has continuously risen. In 1950, the income tax accounted for 9.13 percent of state tax revenue; by 1993, that percentage had risen to 31.86 (Holcombe and Sobel 1997). While concerns about the stability of the tax in the short run (during a recession) are legitimate, the income tax has proven to be not only a consistent, but a consistently growing, source of revenue over the long term.

Finally, successful tax systems provide certainty (NCSL 1992). That is, the number and type of tax changes should be kept to a minimum, and taxpayers should be neither burdened nor surprised by changes in the tax code. Over the years, state income tax regimes have been remarkably consistent. Certainly changes to the income tax laws occur in many states in most years. But the changes tend to be relatively minor; they amount to tinkering with the system. Exclusions, deductions, and credits have been added, or less frequently, taken away. Rates have been increased, and, more frequently of late, decreased. But the nominal effect of these changes has had a negligible impact on the average individual. For example, small changes in income tax rates or in the amount of standard deductions—and that is what state income tax changes generally amount to—will not affect an individual's life in a significant way. In the end, because of the certainty of state income tax systems, the average individual is not "caught off guard" by revisions in the personal income tax system. And that is the hallmark of consistency.

A Fair Tax

Every commentator since Adam Smith has asserted that tax systems must be fair (Brunori 1997). Fairness, of course, is often in the eye of the beholder. Yet, the personal income tax is generally viewed by experts and the public alike as the most fair of all state tax levies. Fairness has historically been broken down into two aspects: vertical and horizontal equity (NCSL 1992). The state personal income tax meets both tests of fairness, although it has proven more successful in satisfying the former than the latter.

Vertical equity is the concept that a tax system should be based on one's ability to pay. A tax system based on ability to pay, according to most tax experts, promotes the most fairness (Utz 1993; Warren 1980). One might argue whether vertical equity requires a progressive or a proportional form of taxation. But most would agree that a sound tax system minimizes regressivity (Brunori 1997). The most pervasive argument against sales and use taxes is the fact that such taxes are inherently regressive. The same can be said of excise taxes. The state personal income tax, however, is generally viewed as the least regressive of all taxes levied by state governments (NCSL 1993).

A recurring problem with progressive income tax rates is that they inevitably lead to political debate over the proper distribution of tax burdens among taxpayers with different levels of income (Cline 1986). Such normative debates are legitimate, indeed healthy, in a democratic society. They have not, however, shaken the public's acceptance of the income tax. It should be noted that, in any event, there is evidence that the state personal income tax has become less progressive over the years (Lav and Gold 1993). Widespread tax cuts over the last ten years in the form of rate reductions and the expansion or creation of deductions, credits, and exclusions have narrowed the tax base, and reduced the tax burden on the wealthiest taxpayers. In 1996 alone, eight states lowered their tax rates, while six states increased standard deductions (Mackey 1996). But the desire for lower taxes should not be confused with dissatisfaction with any particular type of tax.

Despite the trend toward more regressive systems, the state income tax complies with the requirement of vertical equity far more than other types of state taxes. Even in those states that impose a flat rate of taxation—i.e., those with the most regressive income tax systems—the system exempts enough income so that lower-income persons are removed from the tax rolls. Thus, even in states with flat rates of income tax, the tax is levied on a proportional basis.

Current state personal income tax systems do less well in satisfying the concept of horizontal equity. Horizontal equity is based on the notion that similarly situated taxpayers should be treated the same. That is achieved optimally with a broad tax base and minimal use of exclusions, deductions, and credits. While the personal income tax is generally applied to most income sources, the proliferation of personal loopholes cuts against the horizontal equity of the tax. States have been steadily increasing the number of deductions over the years. For example, virtually every state has enacted extensive personal exemptions and credits and increased standard deductions that benefit senior citizens (Mackey and Carter 1994). In many states, pension income and social security benefits are excluded from taxable income. While it is neither politically feasible nor necessarily desirable to repeal these preferences for senior citizens, they are a stark indication of the horizontal inequities of the tax. Individuals with the same income often experience vastly different tax obligations on the basis of age.

The foregoing highlights one of the most serious problems with overreliance on the income tax. For overreliance on the personal income tax leads to greater pressure to provide more exclusions, deductions, and credits, further narrowing the tax base (Cline 1986). Despite calls from scholars and theorists to curtail use of tax preferences, states cannot seem to resist the temptation to riddle the tax system with loopholes.

Efficient Administration

The administrative requirements of sound tax policy revolve around minimizing the costs of compliance for taxpayers and of collection for the government (NCSL 1992). First and foremost, conformity with the federal income tax system greatly reduces the administrative burdens and costs of state income tax compliance for taxpayers and government alike. Taxpayers generally do not incur substantial compliance costs or burdens independent of those created by the federal income tax system (Pomp 1986). In most states, the starting point for determining income tax liability is taxable income as reported on the federal income tax return. The taxpayer takes his or her federal taxable income, adds or subtracts state items to calculate state taxable income, then applies state tax rates to determine liability. This system allows the taxpayer to maintain one set of records for income tax purposes.

That is not to say that taxpayers face no burdens in complying with state income tax laws. Virtually all states allow for additional deductions from federal taxable income. Those deductions must be reported, and records in support of those deductions must be retained. States also generally tax some forms of income not accounted for in federal taxable income. And, of course, returns must be filed, and in some states those returns are complicated. Thus, for filing purposes, taxpayers do incur more burdens than incurred when complying with state sales and excise taxes. But despite filing and record-keeping requirements, conformity with the federal tax system lessens the burdens of compliance with state income taxes.

The government, too, has found the state income tax an efficient and economical means of collecting revenue, again largely because of conformity with the federal income tax. Federal-state conformity greatly reduces the number of issues, whether factual or legal, involved in the administration of the tax. Again, because most states start with federal adjusted income to calculate state taxable income, many of these issues have been or will be resolved at the federal level (Ibid. 1986). That is perhaps why states face minimal controversies with taxpayers over the personal income tax, especially when compared with sales and corporate taxes.

Moreover, all states have entered into information-sharing agreements with the federal government. These agreements greatly assist state revenue departments in administering their income tax laws. There is a perception, at least, that because of their ability to obtain information from the federal government, states generally leave the enforcement of personal income tax laws to the IRS. That is, except for questions of domicile, states generally do not audit income tax returns. Rather, the states patiently await news from the IRS of adjustments to federal taxable income, then proceed to readjust income for state tax purposes. While the personal income tax is in many ways more difficult to administer than sales taxes, the relationship between the state and federal systems decreases the costs of administration.

Accountability

That tax systems ensure accountability is essential in a democratic society (NCSL 1992). Accountability is generally discussed in several contexts. Some discussions center on whether the system holds taxpayers responsible for complying with the law (Brunori 1997). While the income tax is more difficult to enforce than most other state taxes—thereby making it more difficult to hold taxpayers account-able—the system does not lead to widespread evasion. This is pri-marily because most state income taxes are collected through with-holding, a system that at least minimizes evasion.

Another aspect of accountability is that tax burdens should be vis-ible (NCSL 1992), and one of the virtues of the state personal income tax is that it is highly visible. Whether through withholding or via estimated payments, citizens routinely witness the amount they are paying to support their government. The tax is neither hidden nor passed on through transactions. If they wish, most citizens can weigh the costs and benefits of government services simply by looking at their paychecks.

Accountability also demands that tax changes, especially those that increase tax burdens, be arrived at openly and explicitly. The people who make decisions regarding tax policy should be respon-sible for their actions. Most income tax changes are made by elected officials through the legislative process and thus meet this impor-tant requirement.

For many years, the failure of many states to index their income tax systems to inflation has resulted in substantial tax increases without legislative action. As two prominent commentators noted, "elected officials should not be allowed to hide in the inflationary weeds and watch taxpayers be bumped up gradually into higher tax brackets" (Kleine and Shannon 1986, p. 35). While this has been and remains a serious problem for tax policy, there is evidence that more states are adopting indexing as part of their income tax systems (Gold 1986; ACIR 1995).

PUBLIC ACCEPTANCE

That the personal income tax has generally met the requirements of sound tax policy would satisfy most scholars and political theorists. But scholars and political theorists neither make policy nor have par-ticular influence with those who elect policy-makers. It is the public that must be satisfied that a tax system is sound. How do we know that the public supports (or at least tolerates) the personal income tax? Before its untimely demise, the Advisory Commission on

Intergovernmental Affairs (ACIR) commissioned a series of public opinion polls examining the public's views on a variety of tax and budget issues. In each of the twenty-two years the ACIR conducted its poll, the state income tax was judged to be the most fair (Dearborn 1993). Every year the state income tax was preferred over the sales tax, as well as over the federal income tax and the local property tax. While the inaccuracies and inconsistencies of such surveys have been discussed at length (Hansen 1983), the ACIR data do provide some indication of the public's acceptance of the tax.

There is more, although less scientific, evidence of the public's perception of the tax. Over the years, the personal income tax has been one of the least controversial sources of revenue. This is certainly true when measured against other state taxes, such as sales and use and corporate income taxes. It is especially true when measured against the federal income tax or local property taxes. The public is rarely involved in serious disputes with state governments over the collection of personal income taxes. With a few exceptions, namely those dealing with issues of domicile, state personal income taxation rarely leads to precedent-setting court decisions and, unlike sales and corporate taxes, virtually never generates issues that come before the United States Supreme Court. Only a handful of the hundreds of state tax cases before the Supreme Court have involved personal income taxes (Nagel and Dyk 1995). And a survey of the most important state tax developments of 1996 compiled by a leading New York law firm lists no personal income tax cases (Rosen and Smith 1997). Corporate and sales and use taxes are far more likely to result in court litigation.

Moreover, during the course of its history, the personal income tax has generated few political upheavals. Certainly, the property tax is more likely to raise the ire of the public; the widespread public dissatisfaction with that tax led to the tax revolts of the 1970s. There have been no similar popular uprisings in the personal income tax arena. There certainly have been no major attempts to fundamentally change the income tax system. To be sure, the tax has led to political controversy at times. Many believe that Christine Todd Whitman's victory over New Jersey Governor James Florio in 1993 was the result of Florio's large tax increases and Whitman's promise to slash the income tax. When Connecticut Governor Lowell Weicker spearheaded the introduction of a state income tax in 1991, he encountered fierce opposition; over 40,000 Connecticut residents marched on the capitol calling for his impeachment (Ritchie 1995), and Weicker did not seek reelection. Similarly, Michigan's income tax increases in the early

1980s led to the recall of two senators and a change in party control in the state senate (Ibid. 1995). But these examples exhaust the incidences of political controversy in the last quarter-century.

Part of the political drama stems from the simple fact that the public does not care for taxes, period (Hansen 1983). To the extent possible, that general dislike of taxes will be exploited by those seeking elected office. But as the late Steven Gold noted, supporting income taxes and even income tax increases is not invariably fatal to politicians (Gold 1992). While Lowell Weicker chose not to seek reelection, the state legislators who supported the adoption of an income tax in Connecticut were not drummed out of office. Similarly, Pennsylvania lawmakers who supported large income tax increases did not suffer electoral harm as a result (Ibid. 1992). Perhaps the public, while not liking taxes much, is savvy enough to decide when taxes, and even tax increases, are necessary. Political leaders who can successfully convey that message stand a better chance at the polls.

That the personal income tax generates relatively little significant litigation, has not sparked widespread demands for reform (such as Proposition 13), and is not the subject of widespread political debate is not proof of public acceptance of the tax. It is, however, an indication that the tax is at least tolerated by the public.

Aside from its fairness and administrative ease, the personal income tax is tolerated by the public because the rates have been low. In 1997, most state income tax rates hovered around 6 percent, and only four states (California, Hawaii, Montana, and Oregon) set their top marginal rates above 9 percent (State Tax OneDisc 1997). Compared with federal income tax rates, also highly visible to the public, state income tax rates are low. The state income tax burden is further reduced when one considers that state and local income taxes are deductible for federal income tax purposes. While this adds to the regressivity of the tax (wealthier households claim greater amounts), it also lessens the burden on all state taxpayers who itemize their federal tax returns. Moreover, since the majority of taxpayers pay their state income taxes through withholding, each payment is never as pronounced as a lump-sum, end-of-the-year payment would be. Certainly, the tax liability is visible on every paycheck, but when compared with federal withholding, the state tax withholding burden seems less onerous.

There are two factors that keep personal income tax rates at acceptable levels. First, the personal income tax is part of a mix of taxes (sales, excise, and corporate). Because a majority of states impose a combination of these taxes, they are able to minimize the rates for all taxes. Indeed, there is evidence that overreliance on particular taxes leads to above-average tax rates (Ladd 1988).

Second, interstate competition keeps income tax rates in check. While there is some disparity in rates among the states, the disparity cannot become too great. Competition leads to a reduction in top marginal rates in states with relatively high tax rates (Gold 1991). While there is ample scholarly evidence that taxes do not influence locational decisions of households (Ladd 1988), there is an undeniable perception among political leaders that taxes matter a great deal (Brunori 1997). Thus, increased interstate competition for business and for middle- and upper-income individuals has focused attention on the potential negative effect of relatively high tax rates on the locational decisions of households (Cline 1986).

Another reason for the acceptance of the income tax is that state taxpayers rarely are confronted by state tax collection authorities. As noted above, there is a perception that state revenue departments generally do not audit personal income tax returns. Rather, states generally leave enforcement of the tax to the IRS. If so, it is much more likely that a taxpayer will have an encounter with the IRS than with a state revenue department. While the public may not be fond of tax collectors in general, one cannot find many instances of public vilification of state revenue officers similar to the IRS bashing that so frequently occurs.

THE FUTURE OF THE TAX

For many of the same reasons that the tax has endured for better than half a century, it will, I believe, remain a mainstay of state revenue in the future. There is simply nothing likely to occur that will change the public's perception that the income tax is an acceptable method of collecting revenue. The tax has consistently grown in importance. It is viewed favorably, at least relative to other taxes. And it has avoided political controversy. The public is not overly concerned with the tax, and that bodes well for its future.

Furthermore, changes in the economy and in technology do not greatly affect the administration of the personal income tax as they do that of the corporate income tax and the sales tax. The age of electronic commerce, for example, will have relatively few side effects with respect to the state personal income tax—for one thing, because the personal income tax liability is more susceptible to geographical determination than either the corporate tax or the sales tax. Electronic commerce creates numerous difficulties for both sales and corporate income taxes (Hellerstein 1997). Taxing sales in the age of electronic commerce is replete with problems, such as determining jurisdiction, defining the tax base, and the situs of sales; taxing corporate income when electronic commerce is involved requires solving immensely complicated questions of jurisdiction and division of the tax base. Since where a taxpayer lives and works, on the other hand, is relatively easy to determine, advances in technology and changes in commerce have less of an impact on the individual's income tax liability.

Nor are other fundamental economic changes likely to affect the tax. The American economy has in the last half-century become much more dependent on international trade. America has also moved dramatically from a manufacturing-based economy to a service-based economy. But these economic changes occurred during the same time period that the personal income tax was growing in importance.

That is not to say that the future of the state income tax will be without problems. The growth of fringe benefits not subject to federal income tax will slow the growth of the state personal income tax. Over the last thirty-five years, fringe benefits—such as pre-tax contributions to pension plans; health insurance; and flexible spending accounts—have grown from 8 percent to 17 percent of total compensation (NCSL 1993). An aging population will also slow the growth of the state personal income tax. By 2030, one in five U.S. residents will be over 65 years of age, up from about 12 percent in 1990 (NCSL 1993). As Americans grow older they will earn less taxable income and benefit from more income tax preferences.

While the increase in fringe benefits and the aging population may slow the growth of the personal income tax, however, neither development is likely to undermine popular satisfaction with the tax. After all, both fringe benefits and the elderly receive beneficial treatment under most state income tax systems.

Moreover, even if there were a serious challenge to state income taxes, proponents of such changes would have a difficult task developing viable alternatives to the billions of dollars raised by the states through the tax. Those who might call for elimination of the income tax would have to propose either significant increases in other taxes—always a politically risky maneuver—or the elimination of billions of dollars of government services. Neither option is likely.

To be sure, there will be problems with the personal income tax. It is not a perfect system. Whether a taxpayer is domiciled in a particular state for the requisite statutory period, and the sourcing of income earned in multiple jurisdictions, will challenge both planners and administrators. Those who spend time in or receive income from more than one state can logically be expected to argue that they reside or are taxable in the state with lower (or no) income tax. In the same vein, there will be the inevitable complaints of high tax burdens, and political pledges of "no new taxes." But those problems have persisted for years. There is no indication that they will increase.

A Potential Achilles Heel

The only development that would significantly affect the personal income tax is a fundamental shift away from the income tax on the federal level. During the past years, there have been several proposals to radically change or eliminate the federal income tax. These proposals include adoption of a national sales tax, a value-added tax, a flat tax on wages, or an income tax allowing for substantial deductions for savings (Strauss 1996). All of these proposals would produce a consumption-based federal tax system.

Because state administration of the personal income tax is so closely tied to the federal system, changes in federal income taxation will have tremendous consequences for administration of the tax on the state level. Take, for example, the possibility of adoption of a national sales tax, coupled with the elimination of the federal income tax. On the state level, everything from record-keeping to return filing, and even calculating tax liability, would become more complicated and costly. Because compliance with state income taxation has largely been the same as compliance with the federal system, such a change would focus public attention on compliance to their state returns. Similarly, elimination of the federal income tax would lead taxpayers to more closely examine their state tax liability. The state income tax would, assuming the states could overcome legal hurdles, become the only major tax withheld from taxpayers' paychecks. Elimination of the federal income tax would certainly change the public's perception of the state income tax—and that change could be for the worse.

For state *governments*, an end to the federal income tax would have a similar negative effect. An end to the federal personal income tax would place tremendous administrative costs on the states (Sheffrin 1996). Indeed, several state officials have opined that elimination of the federal income tax would effectively force states to repeal their personal income taxes (Megna 1997; Bucks 1995).

CONCLUSIONS

The personal income tax has remained a major component of state revenue collection. Its dominance is a result of adherence to the accepted principles of sound tax policy, which in turn has led to widespread public acceptance of the tax. Much of its success, though, has been the result of its general conformity with the federal income tax system. Elimination of the federal income tax would have devastating repercussions for the state personal income tax. State governments can be expected, therefore, to resist fundamental changes in the federal tax system. Assuming the federal income tax system remains intact, the personal income tax will continue its pivotal role in state government finance.

References

Advisory Commission on Intergovernmental Affairs (ACIR). 1995. *Significant Features of Fiscal Federalism*. Washington, D.C.: ACIR.

Blough, Roy. 1955. *The History and Philosophy of Taxation*. Williamsburg, Va.: College of William and Mary.

Brunori, David. 1997. "Principles of Tax Policy and Targeted Tax Incentives." *State and Local Government Review* 29, No. 1 (winter): 50–61.

Bucks, Dan R. 1995. "Federal Tax Restructuring: Perils and Possibilities for States." *State Tax Notes* (August 7): 415.

Cline, Robert. 1986. "Personal Income Tax." In *Reforming State Tax Systems*, edited by Steven Gold. Washington, D.C.: National Conference of State Legislatures.

Dearborn, Philip M. 1993. "ACIR 1993 Poll Takes the Public Pulse on Taxes." *State Tax Notes* (October 4): 981.

Galper, Harvey, and Stephen H. Pollack. 1988. "Models of State Income Tax." In *The Unfinished Agenda for State Tax Reform*, edited by Steven Gold. Washington, D.C.: National Conference of State Legislatures.

Gold, Steven. 1986. "State Tax Policy." In *Reforming State Tax Systems*, edited by Steven Gold. Washington, D.C.: National Conference of State Legislatures.

———. 1991. "Interstate Competition and State Personal Income Tax Policy." In *Competition Among State and Local Governments*, edited by Daphne Kenyon and John Kincaid. Washington, D.C.: Urban Institute Press.

Gold, Steven. 1992. "What do the 1992 Elections Results Say About State Fiscal Policy?" *State Tax Notes* (December 14): 897.

Hansen, Susan. 1983. *The Politics of Taxation: Revenue Without Representation.* New York: Praeger.

Hellerstein, Walter. 1997. "Telecommunications and Electronic Commerce." *State Tax Notes* (February 17): 519.

Holcombe, Randall G., and Russell S. Sobel. 1997. *Growth and Variability in State Tax Revenue.* Westport, Conn.: Greenwood.

Kleine, Robert, and John Shannon. 1986. "Characteristics of a Balanced and Moderate State-Local Revenue System." In *Reforming State Tax Systems*, edited by Steven Gold. Washington, D.C.: National Conference of State Legislatures.

Ladd, Helen. 1988. "The Meaning of Balance for State and Local Tax Systems." In *The Unfinished Agenda for State Tax Reform*, edited by Steven Gold. Washington, D.C.: National Conference of State Legislatures.

Lav, Iris, and Steven Gold. 1993. *The States and the Poor.* Washington, D.C.: Center on Budget and Policy Priorities.

Mackey, Scott. 1996. "State Tax Actions 1996." *State Tax Notes* (November 18): 1461.

Mackey, Scott, and Karen Carter. 1994. *State Tax Policy and Senior Citizens.* Denver: National Conference of State Legislatures.

Megna, Robert. 1997. "Potential Impact of a National Sales Tax on State Fiscal Policy. *State Tax Notes* (June 2): 1168.

Nagel, Walter, and Timothy Dyk. 1995. *Leading United States Supreme Court State Tax Cases.* Washington, D.C.: Tax Management, Inc.

National Conference of State Legislatures. 1992. *Principles of a High-Quality State Revenue System.* 2nd ed. Washington, D.C.

National Conference of State Legislatures. 1993. *Financing State Revenue Government in the 1990s.* Washington, D.C.

Papke, James. 1993. "A Reexamination of the Indiana Tax Structure." *State Tax Notes* (February 22): 386–404.

Pomp, Richard. 1986. "Simplicity and Complexity in the Content of a State Tax System." In *Reforming State Tax Systems*, edited by Steven Gold. Washington, D.C.: National Conference of State Legislatures.

Reese, Thomas. 1980. *The Politics of Taxation.* Westport, Conn.: Quorom Books.

Ritchie, Sara. 1995. "The Political Environment." In *The Fiscal Crisis of the States*, edited by Steven Gold. Washington, D.C.: Georgetown University Press.

Rosen, Arthur, and Diann Smith. 1997. "1996 Developments in State and Local Taxation." *State Tax Notes* (March 3): 677.

Shannon, John. 1995. "Can New Federalism Tax Reformers Clear the High Middle-Class Hurdles?" *State Tax Notes* (October 16): 1995.

Sheffrin, Steven. 1996. "Should the Federal Income Tax Be Replaced With a National Sales Tax?" *State Tax Notes* (October 21): 1147.

206 The Future of State Taxation

Shoup, Carl. 1937. *Facing the Tax Problem*. New York: Twentieth Century Fund.
State Tax OneDisc. 1997. Arlington, Va.: Tax Analysts.
Strauss, Robert P. 1996. "Further Implications of a Federal Consumption Tax for State and Local Tax Administration." *State Tax Notes* (October 14): 1085.
United States Department of Commerce, Bureau of the Census. 1997. State tax data. Washington, D.C.: Government Printing Office.
Utz, Stephen. 1993. *Tax Policy*. St. Paul, Minn.: West Publishing Co.
Warren, Alvin. 1980. "Would a Consumption Tax be Fairer Than an Income Tax?" 89 *Yale L. J.* 1081.

Chapter Twelve

ELECTRONIC COMMERCE AND THE FUTURE OF STATE TAXATION

Walter Hellerstein

The coming of the information age has profound implications for state taxation, as it does for just about everything else. The exponential growth and increasing commercialization of the Internet,[1] along with the sweeping technological and regulatory changes that have reconfigured the telecommunications industry, pose a daunting challenge to the states' traditional approaches to taxing business activity and the telecommunications system that facilitates it. State tax administrators and policy-makers, alarmed at the prospect that their tax bases will disappear into cyberspace, are seeking means to accommodate their taxing regimes to the new technological environment (Fuchs 1997, p. 281). The business community, on the other hand, has voiced fears that state legislative or administrative action in this domain could lead to extensive—and potentially destructive—taxation of electronic commerce.[2] These concerns have already led to the introduction in Congress of the Internet Tax Freedom Act "[t]o establish a national policy against state and local government interference with interstate commerce on the Internet or interactive computer services, and to exercise congressional jurisdiction over interstate commerce by establishing a moratorium on the imposition of exactions that would interfere with the flow of commerce via the Internet."[3]

In this paper, I take a step back from the technical questions raised by state taxation of electronic commerce and focus more broadly on the challenges that the advent of electronic commerce raises to our conventional modes of thinking about state taxation. Specifically, I consider whether the current statutory and constitutional framework that governs the taxation of sales and income today is adequate to deal with the electronic commerce that is likely to play a substantial (if not dominant) role in our economy tomorrow—and, if it is not, how that framework might be altered to deal with electronic commerce effectively.

TECHNOLOGICAL BACKGROUND

Any serious effort to come to grips with the legal and policy issues raised by state taxation of electronic commerce must begin with an understanding of the technological background in which they arise. Accordingly, this section briefly describes the Information Superhighway, the Internet, the World Wide Web, and electronic commerce.[4]

The Information Superhighway

The Information Superhighway is a descriptive umbrella referring to the next generation of communications systems (Grierson 1996, pp. 603–4). It embraces telephone systems, cable and satellite communications, and computer networks. Eventually, the Information Superhighway will likely be capable of transmitting a wide spectrum of information (including audio and video programs) into every business and household. One of the signal features of the Information Superhighway is the convergence of technologies that traditionally have been viewed as separate. Two major technological changes have provided the impetus for this convergence: the replacement of copper wire by fiber optic cable and the "digitization" of information.

The telecommunications industry has traditionally employed copper wire to transmit voice and data from one point to another. Copper wire has a relatively limited transmission capacity. Fiber optic cable, on the other hand, has virtually unlimited transmission capacity. The replacement of copper wire by fiber optic cable has substantially increased the telecommunications industry's ability to transmit large amounts of information, including videos and x-rays.

Digitization is the conversion of text, sound, images, video, and other content into a common digital format, comprising a series of ones and zeros. Any type of information that can be digitized can be transmitted electronically.

The Internet

The best-known lane of the Information Superhighway is the Internet. It is typically described as a "network of networks." Originally designed as a system of computers connecting governmental and academic institutions, the Internet has expanded into a worldwide communications network accessible through commercial access providers, with user estimates ranging from thirty to sixty million and growing exponentially.

The Internet has no central computer or organizational structure. Computers communicate with one another through the Transmission Control Protocol/Internet Protocol ("TCP/IP"), which specifies how data are subdivided into "packets" and assigned to different addresses, to be transferred over the Internet.

The Internet employs hundreds of thousands of computers called "routers" to direct packets of data to their destinations. Individual packets constituting a single message may take different routes and then be recombined when they reach their (common) destination. The packets are transmitted over existing telephone networks. Since the Internet is not dependent upon any particular communications technology, however, Internet traffic may also travel over cable TV systems, satellite links, and fiber optic cables not linked to the telecommunications network. Computers generally called "servers" store large amounts of information that may be accessed by users of the Internet (and of other networks).

The World Wide Web

The World Wide Web ("WWW" or "Web") is a component of the Internet that includes graphics, video, and audio in addition to standard text. "Hypertext" Web documents contain links to other Web documents that one can access simply by "clicking" a computer mouse at a designated spot on the Web document. To access the Web, one needs a browser program, which is software that reads information accessed from the Web and presents it to the user in a readable format. Individuals, institutions, and commercial enterprises often establish "Web sites," which are composed of collections of documents relating to the individual, institution, or enterprise that are accessible to any Web user who knows the Web site address. Web documents are stored on servers, which may be located anywhere in the world.

Electronic Commerce

"Electronic commerce" has been defined as "the ability to perform transactions involving the exchange of goods or services between two or more parties using electronic tools and techniques" (Dept. of the Treasury 1996, p. 8). Electronic commerce already exists in a number of forms and contexts, and such commerce is likely to expand dramatically in the future, assuming both an increase in the speed at which communications networks can transfer data and the development of improved payment systems. Examples of electronic commerce include:

- on-line catalogs, displaying images of goods, which permit Web users around the world to select and order books, clothing, wine, and other products;
- computer software, which can be transferred electronically to the user's computer;
- photographs, which can be transferred digitally, and where price varies according to the customer's intended use of the photograph;
- on-line information, such as Lexis, Nexis, and other electronic databases, which is available to users through the Internet and through standard telecommunications networks;
- services, such as legal, accounting, medical, and other consulting services, which subscribers can access for a fee using an electronic password to obtain access to the service provider's Web site;
- videoconferencing, which is currently used principally by large businesses and institutions that possess the expensive dedicated equipment necessary to participate in a videoconference, but which ultimately may be accessible to many more users with the introduction of inexpensive desktop video cameras that can be connected to a personal computer;
- securities trading, which is currently offered by some stock brokerage firms through Web sites that permit customers to trade bonds, mutual funds, options, futures, and commodities; and
- offshore banking, now being offered at some Web sites, including incorporation, banking services, and credit card payments.

JURISDICTION TO TAX

Location in Electronic Commerce

Perhaps the most fundamental question raised by state taxation of electronic commerce is jurisdiction to tax. If massive amounts of economic activity will soon be conducted through electronic commerce on the part of remote service providers engaged in nontraceable transactions from unidentifiable locations, the question naturally arises as to which states, if any, will have jurisdiction to impose (or require collection of) taxes on the sales or income generated by such economic activity.

Historically we have looked for the answer to that question by investigating the connections between the taxpayer and the taxing state. It is, after all, a "fundamental requirement of both the Due Process and Commerce Clauses that there be 'some definite link, some minimum connection between a state and the person, property, or transaction its seeks to tax.' "[5] This so-called "nexus" requirement derives from the virtually axiomatic proposition that the exercise of a state's tax power over a taxpayer or its activities is justified by the "protection, opportunities, and benefits" that the state confers upon the taxpayer or its activities. If the state lacks a "definite link" or "minimum connection" with the taxpayer or its activities, it has not "given anything for which it can ask return."[6]

But are traditional nexus criteria well suited to the creation of sensible and administrable rules for determining the taxability of taxpayers or transactions in electronic commerce? Traditional nexus principles, after all, are rooted in concepts of territoriality, and the physical presence of the taxpayer in the state.[7] Indeed, although the U.S. Supreme Court has abandoned physical presence as the touchstone of due process clause nexus,[8] it has retained the physical presence standard, however grudgingly (Hellerstein 1996, p. 120), as a litmus test of commerce clause nexus,[9] at least in the context of sales and use taxes.[10] In any event, whether we are talking about traditional concepts of jurisdiction based on physical presence or more "modern" concepts of jurisdiction based on "economic" presence, the fact remains that we are still, in the end, counting contacts—be they tangible or intangible.

But such an approach makes little sense in cyberspace. The signal characteristic of cyberspace is the irrelevance of geographical borders. As the codirectors of the Cyberspace Law Institute have declared, "[g]lobal computer-based communications cut across territorial borders, creating a new realm of human activity and undermining the feasibility—and legitimacy—of laws based on geographic boundaries" (Johnson and Post 1996, p. 1367). This thought has not been lost on those seeking a solution to the problems raised by state taxation of electronic commerce. Indeed, to ask about the "location" of electronic commerce—whether that location is defined in terms of physical contacts (e.g., the presence of computer servers or leased telecommunications lines) or nonphysical contacts (e.g., the deemed presence of intangibles or electromagnetic impulses)—is to ask a question that is not worth answering. The reason is twofold.

First, the location of those tangible or intangible contacts will often bear little relationship to the location of the essential economic activity that electronic commerce comprises—the production and consumption of information. Second, even if the location of those tangible and intangible contacts was thought to be relevant to the location of the electronic commerce itself, that location can be changed so easily (without affecting the underlying electronic transaction) that efforts to prevent creative tax avoidance are likely to be futile. If the server's presence is relevant, Oregon (a state with no sales tax) will soon become the server capital of the world; if the presence of an electronic impulse is relevant, those impulses will be routed through nontaxable paths, assuming one can even trace the paths through which they are routed.

A Fresh Approach

What we need instead is a fresh approach that essentially "reverse engineers" the nexus issue. In other words, the first question ought to be what kind of taxing regime will allow participants in electronic commerce to pay taxes in an administratively feasible fashion to those states with a legitimate claim to the tax revenues—and will allow states with legitimate claims to collect such taxes. Once we answer that question, we can build our nexus rules (and, also, our tax sourcing or situsing rules) around such a regime.

With regard to sales and use taxes imposed on transactions in electronic commerce, we need a regime in which vendors can be certain about their tax collection obligations and can comply with them at reasonable administrative cost. One possible means of achieving these objectives would be the establishment of nexus over the out-of-state vendor in the state of the purchaser, defined by reference to the purchaser's billing address or other locational information furnished to the vendor by the purchaser (e.g., the area code and local exchange from which the purchaser accessed the seller's Web site). The vendor who obtained such information in good faith would be able to rely on it in remitting tax to the purchaser's state. To deal with cases in which the vendor is unable to determine the purchaser's billing address, such a taxing regime might include a sales tax version of the familiar income tax "throwback" rule.[11]

Similar considerations ought to inform the ideal nexus rule in the context of income taxation of electronic commerce. We need a nexus rule that will allow participants in electronic commerce to ascertain with certainty the jurisdictions where they have income tax liability and to comply with their tax obligations in an administratively feasible manner.

One cannot sensibly evaluate the suitability of a nexus rule for taxpayers deriving income from electronic commerce, however, without thinking about the sourcing principles that will apply to such income. For example, it makes little sense to have a bright-line nexus rule of substantial physical presence in order for a state to tax income from electronic commerce if income from such commerce is going to be assigned to states in which the taxpayer has no physical presence. To be sure, a throwback rule can assure that income will be "resourced" from a state in which the taxpayer is not subject to tax to a state in which it is taxable. But from a normative perspective, which is the perspective of this paper, it makes more sense to create nexus rules that generally are in harmony with sourcing rules than to have nexus and sourcing rules that lean in opposite directions and thus have to rely heavily on a second-best default principle (such as the throwback rule) for sourcing substantial amounts of income.

With these design features in mind, one can posit two alternative nexus/sourcing regimes. One could construct a taxing regime that adopts a bright-line, physical presence rule for nexus over income taxpayers engaged in transactions in electronic commerce coupled with sourcing rules that attribute income only to jurisdictions in which the taxpayer has such physical presence. Indeed, because the physical location of tangible property used in the conduct of electronic commerce often bears little relationship to the underlying economic activity involved, and because such location (of e.g., computer servers) can easily be shifted to states that do not tax income, it may well be that a residence-based sourcing principle would be the most satisfactory in this context.

Alternatively, one might construct an income tax regime for electronic commerce that is more analogous to the sales and use tax regime suggested above. In such a regime, nexus over those engaged in transactions in electronic commerce would exist in the states of their customers' billing addresses, when these addresses could be ascertained at reasonable administrative cost. Income would likewise be assigned to those states. If the billing address could not be ascertained at reasonable administrative cost (so that nexus based on billing address would not exist), a throwback rule "re-sourcing" the income to a state where the taxpayer *was* taxable (e.g., its principal place of business) would apply.

The choice between these two regimes obviously involves fundamental policy choices about where income should be taxed. The first regime favors the states in which electronic commerce is "produced" (assuming it is produced either where the seller's physical facilities are located or at its principal place of business) over those states in which it is "consumed" (assuming it is consumed at the billing address of the purchaser). The roughness of these assumptions, however, may undermine any principled arguments favoring the attribution of income to "production" states rather than to "consumption" states or vice versa. Moreover, in the context of electronic commerce, it may well be that a bias in sourcing income to "production" states rather than "consumption" states would have a less pronounced distributive effect than it would, say, in the context of an income tax on heavy industry, where the dichotomy between "production" states and "market" states is more perceptible.[12] Under these circumstances, perhaps one ought to opt for the simpler regime (and the first regime is plainly simpler than the second).

OTHER ISSUES

Although the question of nexus has attracted the greatest attention in discussions of taxation of electronic commerce, there are a number of other important issues raised by state taxation of electronic commerce that we will also have to confront in the future.

Sales and Use Tax Issues

DEFINITIONAL ISSUES

The most basic question raised by state sales taxation of electronic commerce is whether such commerce is taxable at all. The answer to the question would be relatively straightforward if the states had made deliberate legislative decisions in this regard. That they have failed to do so is due not to any Hamlet-like ambivalence over the question "To tax or not to tax?" but rather to the simple fact that, in many instances, states have not specifically addressed the question at all. Moreover, since much of electronic commerce involves the sale of services rather than the sale of goods, transactions in electronic commerce are likely to be characterized as nontaxable unless they fall within one of the selective categories of services that states, to varying extents, have decided to tax. As a consequence, taxpayers and tax administrators are forced to struggle with the question of whether transactions in electronic commerce fall within the definition of taxable "telecommunications services," "data processing services," "information services," etc.—terms that were not designed with the Internet in mind but that may well embrace various aspects of electronic commerce.

One of the principal challenges facing the states in the future will be to clarify the definitional morass that currently characterizes state taxation of electronic commerce. There is not only the basic political question of what to tax, but also the "level playing field" concern of assuring that economically equivalent goods or services are taxed (or not taxed) in the same way. Moreover, the states' efforts in this regard may well be confined by federal legislation, should efforts in Congress to curtail state taxation of the Internet result in restrictive legislation.[13]

SALE-FOR-RESALE ISSUES

One of the essential features of a retail sales tax structure is the sale-for-resale exemption, which is designed to remove from the tax base intermediate transactions in the economic process—at least when the goods or services involved will be subject to tax at some later stage in the economic process. This principle, however, is not fully implemented in practice, if implementation is to be judged in economic terms, because a substantial amount of business consumption is included in the sales tax base, even though the cost of such business consumption will find its way into the subsequent sale of a good or service (Ring, Jr. 1989, pp. 167, 175).

The problem of pyramiding is particularly acute in the context of electronic commerce for two reasons. First, the states' separate taxation of related services (e.g., telecommunications, data processing, and information services) creates the risk that each separately identified service will be separately taxed even if they are all part of a single economic process. Second, the sale-for-resale exemption is not as clearly refined with respect to the sale of services as it is with respect to the sale of tangible personal property, both because states generally have less experience in dealing with taxation of services and because services, by their very nature, are often more difficult to trace in space and time than are items of tangible personal property. Consequently, while it is easy enough to follow the steel used to manufacture a car from the foundry to the retail showroom (and thus to exempt it under a sale-for-resale exemption until the final sale of the car), it is more difficult to follow the telecommunications services used to provide an information service purchased through an on-line service provider.

Courts are therefore more likely to find the latter "consumed" rather than "resold" by the information or on-line service provider.

One of the key tasks for the states in the future is to sharpen and rationalize their sale-for-resale exemption so as to avoid excessive pyramiding of the tax in the context of electronic commerce. By embracing a concept of resale tied more to economic than to physical flows, the states could go a long way toward resolving this issue not only for electronic commerce but with respect to other forms of commerce as well. The problem, of course, is that broadening the resale concept shrinks the tax base. Unless states are willing to expand the tax base in other areas (e.g., to household services that are not currently taxed) or to raise their rates, it may be difficult politically to address the resale issue.

Situsing Issues

The question of where a taxable sale of electronic products or services occurs is difficult because the transactions frequently have meaningful contacts with more than one jurisdiction. For example, an information provider in State A employing a server in State B can sell access to its database through an Internet service provider in State C to a customer in State D who is billed by a financial intermediary in State E. Which state can and should tax the sale?

One of the key choices states will confront in the future is whether to situs a sale involving sale of electronically transmitted services on a destination basis or a performance basis. Suppose, for example, that an oil company in Ohio uses the Internet to access the database of an oil industry consulting firm in Texas. Assume further that both Ohio and Texas have decided, as a matter of principle, that information services are taxable. Will (or should) a Texas sales tax—or, alternatively, an Ohio sales or use tax—be added to the consulting firm's bill to the oil company?

Texas's claim to tax the transaction is based on the position that a sale of services should be deemed to occur where the services are performed rather than where they are consumed. The position is consistent with the rule applied to taxation of services by some states— namely, that the sale of services is taxed by the state in which the services are performed, even though the services are in effect "delivered" and consumed outside the state.[14] This position may also recommend itself from an administrative perspective, because the taxing authorities of the state in which services are performed will always have jurisdiction over the service provider and will thus be in a position to enforce collection of the sales tax.

On the other hand, it must be recognized that a performance-based rule for taxing the sale of services is inconsistent with the general rule that the sale of tangible personal property is taxed by the state in which the goods are delivered to the purchaser. This rule reflects the view that goods are consumed in the state of the purchaser rather than in the state of the seller. A performance-based rule cannot be squared with the premise that a sales tax is a tax on consumption. Consistently with this view, many states adopt the rule that services should be taxed in the state in which they are delivered or enjoyed, and they exempt services "if the beneficial use of the service occurs entirely outside the state."[15]

If, however, one adopts the view that a consumption-based rather than performance-based approach to taxing services is appropriate, the question may be raised whether it is possible to implement such a rule, since the "sale" of the service in the contractual sense will typically occur in the state in which it is performed, and the state in which the service is consumed will have no power to tax the "sale" of the service. The answer, of course, is the adoption of a "use" tax on services.

The theory underlying a use tax on services is identical to that underlying a use tax on the sale of tangible personal property. The tax is designed to counteract the potential loss of business and revenue that states might incur if in-state consumers of services sought to avoid taxes by purchasing services from out-of-state service providers. By imposing a use tax equal in amount to the sales tax that would have been imposed on the sale of the service if the sale had occurred within the state's taxing jurisdiction, the state removes the incentive for local consumers of services to purchase services outside the state.

The legal basis for imposing a use tax on services is the same as that for imposing a use tax on tangible personal property. Just as a state has ample authority to impose a tax on the use or consumption of tangible personal property within the state, so it has the power to impose a tax on the use or consumption of services in the state. Although the notion of taxing the use of services purchased in other states may seem strange to the casual observer, it is no stranger in theory than the notion of taxing the use of tangible personal property purchased in other states. Moreover, as a decision of the Ohio Supreme Court reveals, the theory has been sustained in its application to the use of electronically delivered information services.[16]

In the end, the question remains as to which sourcing rule makes the best sense (and, therefore, the best law) in the context of electronic commerce. The answer is essentially the same as that suggested above in the context of nexus: a rule that is workable and that allows the states to collect their fair share of sales tax revenues. This would call for the adoption of situsing rules that follow (or are consistent with) the nexus rules for sales taxation of electronic commerce.[17]

Income Tax Issues

Aside from jurisdictional questions, which have been considered above, the critical income tax issues raised by state taxation of electronic commerce relate to division of the tax base. The division-of-income issues raised by taxation of electronic commerce are no different in principle from those raised by taxation of other industries. Under the regimes in force in almost all of the forty-six states with income taxes,[18] income from electronic commerce, as well as from other activities, is apportioned among the various states in which the taxpayer is taxable by a three-factor formula consisting of property, payroll, and sales.[19]

In practice, there is relatively little controversy surrounding the first two factors. Most state statutes define the property factor as a fraction with a numerator as the average value of the taxpayer's real and tangible personal property owned or rented and used in the state, and a denominator as the average value of all such property.[20] The payroll factor is typically defined as a fraction with a numerator that is generally the total compensation paid by the taxpayer in the state and a denominator that is the total compensation paid everywhere.[21]

In the context of electronic commerce, one could object to the property factor on the ground that it fails to reflect the taxpayer's intangible property, which no doubt contributes substantially to the income of many enterprises engaged in electronic commerce. If such property were included, however, it would raise the question as to where such property should be assigned for tax purposes. As I have discussed at length elsewhere, the locus of intangible property is often as geographically indeterminate as the income it produces, and the exclusion of such intangibles from the property factor may therefore amount to a pragmatic solution to an intractable problem (Hellerstein 1993, pp. 840–46). More refined rules might be developed, however, for assigning particular types of receipts from intangibles used in electronic commerce, such as royalties and license fees (Hellerstein).

The most controversial apportionment issue in the context of electronic commerce is the delineation of the sales or receipts factor. The standard sales factor employed in many state apportionment formulas assigns receipts from sales of tangible personal property to states on a destination basis;[22] "[s]ales, other than sales of tangible personal property" are assigned to the state in which "a greater portion of the income-producing activity is performed . . . based on costs of performance."[23]

The application of the traditional sales factor to electronic commerce raises a number of difficult questions. First, there is the question of whether the transaction involves tangible property, on the one hand, or intangible property or services, on the other. The answer to this question will determine which sales attribution rule is applicable. While most transactions in electronic commerce will presumably be viewed as involving transfers of intangible property or services, some electronic transfers of information or software may also involve related transfers of tangible personal property (e.g., diskettes). In such cases, taxpayers and tax administrators will confront the question of how to treat the overall transaction. There are scores of sales tax cases—many of them hopelessly inconsistent with one another—that seek to draw the line between taxable sales of tangible personal property and non-taxable sales of services or intangibles (Hellerstein and Hellerstein 1993, pp. 12.07, 13.02–13.05). These cases provide what little guidance there is for resolving analogous issues for sales factor purposes.

Second, assuming the transaction is not one involving tangible personal property, the question generally becomes where the income-producing activity is performed. Under the standard cost-of-performance rule[24] embodied in the Uniform Division of Income for Tax Purposes Act (UDITPA)[25] and similar statutes in other states, the receipts would be assigned to the state in which the taxpayer incurred the greatest costs of performance. To analyze the costs of performing a complex electronic transaction on a geographical basis, however, can be quite daunting.

Beyond the technical question of where receipts from electronic commerce should be sourced under traditional sales factor rules, there is the more fundamental question of whether the traditional rules are consistent with the purposes of the sales factor. The sales factor was designed to recognize the contribution of the states in which a firm's products are marketed to the generation of a firm's income. With the nearly universal use of a destination test to assign sales of tangible personal property, the sales factor attributes income to states in which goods are consumed and serves as a counterbalance to the property and payroll factors, which tend to attribute income to states where goods are produced.

In the context of sales in electronic commerce, however, the sales factor fails to serve its intended function. By looking to costs of performance as the governing attribution principle, it tends to assign receipts to the state where services are produced rather than where they are consumed. It thus tends to duplicate the property and payroll factors, which already attribute income to the production states. And it fails to give the consuming states their due.

The challenge for the future is how to modify the sales factor to enable it to perform its intended function, but in a manner that assigns the tax base to a state in which the taxpayer is taxable—and that is administratively workable, besides. In my view, the sales factor rules should track the nexus rules that one adopts for income tax purposes. Accordingly, if one were to embrace the first regime described above— one in which there is a bright-line, physical presence rule of nexus and a sourcing principle that assigns income only to states in which there is nexus—the sales factor would continue the consumption state-oriented sales destination rule that UDITPA employs for sales of personal property, in cases where the taxpayer can determine the purchaser's billing address at reasonable administrative cost and where the taxpayer has the requisite physical presence in the state. In other cases, the sale (and, hence, a portion of the taxpayer's income) would be assigned to the taxpayer's principal place of business.

If one were to embrace the second regime described above, in which nexus exists over an out-of-state vendor of electronic services when the purchaser's billing address is in the state and the vendor can determine that address at reasonable administrative cost, the corresponding sales factor rule would assign income only to states in which there is nexus. The sales factor would continue the consumption state-oriented sales destination rule that UDITPA adopts for sales of personal property, in cases when the taxpayer is subject to tax in the state of the purchaser's billing address. In other circumstances, the sale (and thus a portion of the taxpayer's income) is thrown back to the state of the taxpayer's principal place of business.

CONCLUSIONS

The problems raised by state taxation of electronic commerce are profound. Efforts to resolve them through traditional state tax structures are unlikely to meet with much success. The challenge for the future is to find a means of modifying our existing state tax regimes to deal with these problems in an administratively sensible and fiscally responsible manner.

Notes

This article draws freely from my earlier work in this area, including "Taxation of Telecommunications and Electronic Commerce: Overview and Appraisal," *State Tax Notes*, Feb. 17, 1997; "State Taxation of Electronic Commerce: Preliminary Thoughts on Model Uniform Legislation," *State Tax Notes*, April 28, 1997, p. 1315; and "State Taxation of Electronic Commerce," *Tax L. Rev.* (1997) (forthcoming).

1. Though electronic commerce is still minuscule by comparison with commerce conducted offline, one estimate places the volume of sales generated by the World Wide Web in 1995 at $436 million, with a prediction that this figure will rise to $46 *billion* in 1998.

2. See Houghton 1997 p. 8, and Grierson 1997, pp. 363, 373 (observing that the imposition of taxes on those engaged in Internet-related activity "could very well sound the death knell for many businesses trying to make their way into this young industry").

3. S. 442, 105th Cong., 1st Sess. (1997); H.R. 1054, 105th Cong., 1st Sess. (1997).

4. The discussion in this section is based primarily on the description set forth in a U.S. Treasury Department paper discussing the tax policy implications of electronic commerce from an international perspective. Department of the Treasury (November 1996).

5. *Allied-Signal, Inc. v. Director, Division of Taxation*, 504 U.S. 768, 777 (1992) (quoting *Miller Bros. v. Maryland*, 347 U.S. 340, 344–45 (1954)).

6. *Wisconsin v. J. C. Penney Co.*, 311 U.S. 435, 444 (1940).

7. Cf. *Pennoyer v. Neff*, 95 U.S. 714 (1877).

8. *Quill Corp. v. North Dakota*, 504 U.S. 298 (1992).

9. *Quill*, 504 U.S. at 309–19.

10. But see *Geoffrey, Inc. v. South Carolina State Tax Comm'n* 437 S.E.2d 13 (S.C.), cert. denied, 510 U.S. 992 (1993). (A state has jurisdiction to tax an out-of-state taxpayer with no physical presence in the state on income earned from licensing trademarks to in-state licensee.)

11. Under the "throwback" rule embodied in the Uniform Division of Income for Tax Purposes Act, 7A U.L.A. 331 (1985) (hereinafter cited without cross-reference as "UDITPA"), sales of tangible personal property, which are normally assigned to the destination state in the sales factor of the state's tax apportionment formula, are "thrown back" to the state of origin when the taxpayer is not taxable in the destination state (UDITPA § 16). The sales could just as easily be thrown back, proportionately, to all of the other states in which the taxpayer collects sales and use taxes. The latter form of throwback might be more equitable than one that assigned all of the "unsourceable" sales to a single state.

12. We are assuming that firms engaged in electronic commerce would not systematically relocate their principal places of business to states with no income taxes or with low income tax rates. To the extent that they did, of course, a bias toward "production" states could have distributive effects. I am unaware, however, of any noticeable migration from Silicon Valley—the heart of the electronic commerce industry—despite California's relatively high corporate income tax rates.

13. See note 3 above and the accompanying text.

14. See, e.g., *Airwork Service Division v. Director, Division of Taxation*, 2 N.J. Tax 329 (1981), aff'd, 4 N.J. Tax 532 (Super Ct., App. Div. 1982), aff'd, 478 A.2d 729 (N.J. 1984), cert. denied, 471 U.S. 1127 (1985) (sustaining a tax on repair services performed in state on airplane engines delivered to a customer outside the state); *Matter of Airlift*

International, Inc. v. State Tax Commission, 382 N.Y.S.2d 572 (App. Div., 3d Dep't 1976) (sustaining a use tax on repairs of airplanes used in interstate and international commerce). See, generally, Hellerstein and Hellerstein, 2nd ed. 1993.

15. In re *State and Municipal Sales and Use Tax Liability of K.O. Lee Co.,* 489 N.W.2d 606 (S.D. 1992).

16. *Quotron Systems, Inc. v. Limbach,* 588 N.E.2d 658 (Ohio 1992).

17. See note 11 above and accompanying text.

18. Only Nevada, Texas, Washington, and Wyoming have no corporate income tax, although Texas's franchise tax now resembles a net income tax in many respects. See Tex. Tax Code Ann. § 171.001 et seq. (Vernon's 1994).

19. *Multistate Corporate Income Tax Guide* 1997. Roughly half the states weight the three factors equally, with the other half giving greater weight to the sales factor.

20. See, e.g., UDITPA § 10. Of the forty-six states with corporate income taxes, twenty-one have adopted UDITPA. 7A U.L.A. at 45 (West Supp. 1994).

21. See, e.g., UDITPA § 13.

22. UDITPA § 16.

23. UDITPA § 17.

24. See supra note 23 and accompanying text.

25. 7A U.L.A. 331 (1985).

References

Ashraf, Sabra. 1997. "States' Net Fails to Ensnare Internet Vendors," *State Tax Notes* (March 31): p. 999, n. 1.

Department of the Treasury, Office of Tax Policy. 1996. *Selected Tax Policy Implications of Global Electronic Commerce* (November).

Fuchs, Larry H. 1997. "Telecommunications Taxes in Florida," *State Tax Notes* (Jan. 17): p. 281.

Grierson, R. Scot. 1997. "Telecommunications Taxation in the Information Age," *State Tax Notes* (Feb. 3): 363, 373.

————. 1996. "State Taxation of the Information Superhighway: A Proposal for Taxation of Information Services," Loyola Entertainment L. J. 16: 603–4.

Hellerstein, Jerome, and Walter Hellerstein. 1993. *State Taxation,* 2nd ed. Boston, Mass.: Warren, Gorham, and Lamont.)

Hellerstein, Walter. 1997. "Taxation of Telecommunications and Electronic Commerce: Overview and Appraisal," *State Tax Notes* (Feb. 17).

————. 1997. "State Taxation of Electronic Commerce: Preliminary Thoughts on Model Uniform Legislation," *State Tax Notes* (April 28): p. 1315.

————. 1997. "State Taxation of Electronic Commerce," *Tax L. Rev.* (forthcoming).

————. 1993. "State Taxation of Income From Intangibles: *Allied-Signal* and Beyond," *Tax L. Rev.* 48: 739: 840–46, 865–69.

————. 1992. "Supreme Court Says No State Use Tax Imposed on Mail-Order Sellers . . . for Now," *J. Tax'n* 77:120.

Houghton, Kendall. 1997. "Where Electronic Commerce is Concerned, Caveat Emptor (Let the Buyer Beware): An Analysis of Ongoing Efforts to Define State and Local Taxation Policy," *State Tax Report* 97 no. 2: 8.

Johnson, David R., and David Post. 1996. "Law and Borders—The Rise of Law in Cyberspace," *Stan. L. Rev.* 48: 1367.

Multistate Corporate Income Tax Guide (CCH). 1997. 1: 146, 148.

Ring, Jr., Raymond J. 1989. "The Proportion of Consumers' and Producers' Goods in the General Sales Tax." *Nat'l Tax J.* 42: 167, 175.

INDEX

ABOUT THE EDITOR

David Brunori is a contributing editor of *State Tax Notes* magazine. He teaches state and local tax law at the George Washington University School of Law. Previously, he practiced with a Washington, D.C. law firm specializing in tax litigation, and served as an appellate trial attorney with the Tax Division of the United State Department of Justice. He is the author of "Principles of Tax Policy and Targeted Tax Incentives" in the *State and Local Government Review*.

ABOUT THE CONTRIBUTORS

Peter D. Enrich is a professor at Northeastern University School of Law in Boston, where he specializes in state and local tax policy and state and local government law. Earlier, he served as counsel for revenue policy and as general counsel to the Massachusetts Executive Office for Administration and Finance, and was a clerk for Judge (now Justice) Stephen Breyer on the U.S. Court of Appeals.

William F. Fox is professor of economics and director of the Center for Business and Economic Research at the University of Tennessee. He is also president of the National Tax Association. He is the editor of *Sales Taxation: Critical Issues in Policy and Administration* (Praeger, 1992) and co-editor of *The Sales Tax in the 21st Century* (Praeger, 1997). His research interests include taxation and economic development.

Walter Hellerstein is professor of law at the University of Georgia Law School and a partner in the law firm of Sutherlan, Asbill & Brennan. Mr. Hellerstein has written and practiced extensively in the state tax field, and he has been involved in numerous state tax cases before the United States Supreme Court. He is also deeply involved in issues relating to state taxation of electronic commerce, and is currently chairman of the drafting committee of the National Tax Association's Electronic Commerce Project.

John L. Mikesell is professor of public and environmental affairs at Indiana University and specializes in government finance and budgeting. He is the editor of *Public Budgeting and Finance*, the journal published by the American Association for Budget and Program Analysis and the Association for Budgeting and Financial Management, and his column on sales taxation is a regular feature of *State Tax Notes*. He is author of *Fiscal Administration*, the standard budgeting text in many graduate public administration programs, and co-author with John F. Due of *Sales Taxation: State and Local Structure and Administration* (Urban Institute Press, 1995, 2nd edition).

Thomas F. Pogue is professor of economics at the University of Iowa. His research, specializing in state and local government tax and expenditure policy, is widely published in academic and professional journals and books. He has prepared research reports for studies of taxation in Arizona, Minnesota, and Iowa, and has also directed Iowa-based studies of economic development policy, labor supply, and school finance.

Richard D. Pomp is the Alva P. Loiselle Professor of Law at the University of Connecticut Law School. From 1981 to 1987, Professor Pomp was director of the New York Tax Study Commission, a period during which New York restructured its personal and corporate income tax. In addition to having published over 60 articles, he is the co-author of *State and Local Taxation* (West/Wadsworth, 1998, 3rd edition).

Andrew Reschovsky is a professor in the Robert M. La Follette Institute of Public Affairs and the Department of Agricultural and Applied Economics at the University of Wisconsin–Madison, where he teaches public finance, microeconomic analysis, and urban economics. Most of his research focuses on issues related to state and local public finance. In addition to his work on the distributional patterns of state and local taxes, he is conducting research on the design of school finance formulas, land taxation, and state government responses to block grants for welfare.

Steven M. Sheffrin is professor of economics at the University of California, Davis, and also serves as director of its Center for State and Local Taxation. In addition, he is an adjunct fellow of the Public Policy Institute of California. He has worked as an economist in the Office of Tax Analysis of the U.S. Department of the Treasury. He is a co-author of *Property Taxes and Tax Revolts: The Legacy of Proposition 13* (Cambridge University Press, 1995). His work in macroeconomics and tax policy has been widely published.

William L. Waugh, Jr., is professor of public administration, urban studies, and political science at Georgia State University. He has written extensively on disaster management, economic development, administrative theory, state and local government capacities, and tax policies. He has been a consultant to federal, state, and local governments; private firms; nonprofit agencies; and international organizations. He worked with the Atlanta city charter commission on education issues and on a study of the financing of the Atlanta public school system, both projects for Research Atlanta, Inc.

Joan M. Youngman is a senior fellow at the Lincoln Institute of Land Policy and director of its programs on the taxation of land and buildings. She is an attorney specializing in state and local taxation, especially in property valuation and taxation. She is also a research fellow with the Harvard Law School International Tax Program and has served as chair of the National Tax Association Committee on Property Taxation. She is the author of *Legal Issues in Property Valuation and Taxation* (Lincoln Institute of Land Policy, 1994) and co-author with Jane H. Malme of *An International Survey of Taxes on Land and Buildings* (Kluwer Law International, 1994).